Sandbox Capitalism:

Creating Shareholder Value - At The Point Of A Gun

by Paul F. Buse

ISBN: 978-1-7344967-1-0

For more information contact:
plkrstnjn@gmail.com

Dedication

This book is dedicated to my two daughters
Kristen and Jessica

—∞—

And Chris Bailey

Contents

CHAPTER 1
The Darkest Hour is Just Before Dawn

—𝔪—

"EARTH TO FRANK...COME in, Frank. Frank, are you OK?"

"Not really," Frank muttered to Larry, looking at him with a stare that would melt ice. Larry knew that what was to come was severe. Frank handed Larry the letter.

Three weeks before Christmas of 2004, Frank wondered when it would all stop. Like AM radio in the sixties, the hits just kept on coming. The letter introduced the real message in the thick envelope. The legalese in the court documents was like a punch to the stomach. His wife was filing for divorce.

"She's going through with it," Larry said sadly.

"Why is she doing this?" Frank stammered, his voice at sentence's end reduced to little more than a whimper. "I just need a freaking job."

"I am so sorry," Larry said, clamping Frank's shoulder. "Could you use a beer? I could." Frank saw Larry's lips move, but he never heard the sound. Larry turned and went inside the house.

Frank Davenport had entered the land of the un-dead; not clinically deceased, but feeling numb in an almost surreal dimension of sight and sound. Vehicles passed on the street, birds chirped, and children played in the park, but to Frank it was if he was outside of his body looking at himself.

This is what it feels like to die, Frank thought.

But he wasn't dead he was going to live but he knew that deep down inside, something had, in fact, died that day.

His former life and sense of self-worth was washing away in those court documents. He had life wrapped up in a high-profile job and a marriage to someone it now seemed he hardly knew, a woman who cared more about her status than their marriage or the divorce's effect on their two young children.

Frank had been desperately seeking work, but the business climate in the Cleveland/Akron area had been anything but forgiving. Amidst all of the manufacturing moving offshore, he'd been sacked at work for something over which he had no control. The divorce documents brought all of that bitterly home.

Get used to it, he told himself. *Life as you know it is over.*

LOOKING BACK, IT was only six months ago, in mid-2004, that it happened. At six foot three, tall and rangy, with an engaging smile and a tennis player's body, Frank Davenport was a high-powered marketing manager at ImageSinc, a manufacturer of medical devices in Akron, Ohio. With a toothy grin and still dark, wavy hair, Frank made friends effortlessly. Women liked him, men wanted to be around him, and the guys in the corner office liked his style.

Marketing was a bit like the Holy Grail in corporate America, the epicenter of American business, a place where you really ran the company. If you were both competent and a bit lucky, it was a place where young Turks like Frank could make his mark. At forty-six, he was no longer young, and at his level, you are only as good as the last deal. It was all about what have you done for me lately, and Frank knew it.

Frank was a steel town guy from Pittsburgh. With an MBA from Case Western University in Cleveland, Frank had come from a background in corporate supply chain management. It was an unusual career transition after his MBA, but then Frank was a unique guy.

The marketing folks, with their flashy smiles, expensive suits, and always-ready PowerPoint presentations were like a corporate version of a wild west gunslinger. They made their living by selling tomorrow.

By comparison, the supply chain types were typically nameless, faceless creatures draped in ill-fitting polyester, stuck in the back office either sweating over systems that did not work correctly, or talking down some internal customer with a lousy attitude who wanted it cheaper, faster, yesterday. As a result, most supply chain folks were crisis managers who tended to focus on today. Frank was different. Frank was the rare breed who could manage for both today and tomorrow.

Frank had sold senior management on a plan to create Business Partners in ImageSinc's service division. Like most manufacturing companies, ImageSinc sold equipment with the express intent to sell service. Follow-along service for their medical products was usually very profitable. Frank often chuckled that it was not unlike the old adage of selling razors to sell razor blades.

The problem was that independent service organizations were aggressively pursuing ImageSinc's business, taking the very profitable service contract business from ImageSinc's lower end, lower-tech products. Unlike ImageSinc's high-end software-intensive products, the low-end mostly mechanical product lines had few barriers to entry. The independent service organizations had gladly driven a truck through this opening, seizing forty percent of the total service market in the U.S.

As bad as this was in the States, it was worse in Europe where ImageSinc's installed base was insignificant. ImageSinc International was international in name only, and so for them, it was either grow or die. The Business Partner labeling concept was Frank's gunslinger plan to expand, domestically and internationally, and fast.

The concept was to link up with strategic independent service organizations. It was to be a win for the small guys who got more service business along with the prestige of a link to a major though second-tier domestic player. Business Partners allowed ImageSinc to remain a player in the low-end local business through equipment and parts sales and service consulting. More importantly, it allowed ImageSinc to shift existing capital to where its business would be growing, which was Europe and Asia.

Putting the plan together was a dogfight. The product line manufacturing vice president's bonuses were based mainly on equipment sales. It was up to somebody else to sell the service. If Frank's service division could not sell the service, then somebody else's head was on the block.

Frank had spent much of his political capital on the Business Partner concept. Late nights, weekends, and some holidays were spent lashed to an office desk for a year, fighting in the trenches to gain traction with his plan; negotiating Business Partner agreements, battling for scarce internal funding and resources, and all at the expense of his family. That was how it worked in corporate America. He just needed a break, and things would be better.

The break came, or so he thought, in a call from the CEO of a Dutch electric utility. The CEO had a small independent medical equipment service organization on his books. Recently hired as CEO and not knowing how it got there, his interest was in quickly dispatching something that had little to do with an electric utility.

The Dutch CEO disclosed in confidence to ImageSinc's international service division folks over dinner that the Dutch electric utility had also been approached on this matter by GLSDV, a large aggressive American conglomerate with whom Frank and ImageSinc International competed, and who more importantly had seats on the Dutch electric utility's board of directors. The CEO did not want to sell to GLSDV, with whom he did not get along, so if ImageSinc could put together a reasonable offer, the business was theirs.

That phone call and dinner resulted in three feverish weeks of analysis as the Frank and his cross-functional band of marketers rushed their international service management across the pond to the U.S. for consultations. Huddling day and night, Frank and his group cobbled together a plan for the purchase of six additional related businesses that he and the international team felt would sell to ImageSinc and, along with the Dutch electric utility acquisition, form the basis for its European entity.

Installed base extrapolations begot income projections. Those projections became the basis for a financial plan which required $200 million in equity from the parent company; itself British, and very much interested. Frank and his team celebrated. For once, they had a head start on a behemoth for GLSDV, although a significant player in the U.S., was small potatoes in Europe. Frank had what he thought was the right plan at the right time.

It did not take long to get the green light from ImageSinc's British masters. The GLSDV CEO was an American business icon and a sometimes golf partner of the Brits, who were equally competitive and about to delight in the Dutch serving up the GLSDV CEO's head. British approval in hand, the ImageSinc CEO, Frank's boss and an engineer by training, calmly picked up the phone and committed a cardinal sin.

Many engineers, although technically competent, lack the basic skills required to negotiate themselves out of a wet paper bag. Those that could master deals tended to rise up in the organization, but they were the exception to the rule. Frank's boss was the exception that proved the rule. And so, deal in hand, Frank's boss proceeded to snatch defeat from the jaws of victory. In a transatlantic conference call, with representatives of both senior management's teams on the line, Frank's boss proceeded to lecture the Dutch CEO, someone that he had never met before and with whom he had no relationship, like a seventh-grade schoolboy on just how ImageSinc was going to do the deal.

Recognizing an ugly American when he heard one, the Dutch CEO calmly ended the conference call and promptly sold the company to GLSDV. It did not take long for the news to reach the Street. ImageSinc and its multi-billion-dollar parent needed even relatively small but significant deals like this. The Brits were not happy campers. But in the axiomatic world of corporate America, for better or worse, when the CEO gets a rhetorical cold, others get the flu.

For Frank, it was even worse. GLSDV used Frank's business model as a beachhead in Europe and was in the process of establishing a one billion dollar plus sales and service juggernaut on the Continent. One of his senior executive marketing counterparts at GLSDV - and yeah, everybody knew each other in this incestuous high-tech market niche - even stopped Frank in the Frankfurt airport and thanked him for the gift. Frank, on the other hand, was now unemployed and, in his small netherworld of medical products - radioactive. Nobody wanted to touch him. Not even his soon-to-be ex-wife, judging from the court papers in his hand.

Six months later, without a job and in need of some free mental health counseling from his good buddy Larry, Frank agreed to construct a deck in Larry's backyard near his pool, preferring the relative warmth of December in Pensacola, Florida to the biting cold of northeast Ohio at that time of year. Larry was great with people, less so with tools.

Frank felt the small Nokia cell phone in his pocket buzz, calling him back to the land of the living. He peered at the screen, noticing that in his short-term psychotic break with reality, some three individuals had cared enough to try to reach him. OK, so care might not have been precisely the right word, although one call was from his daughter Kate telling him she appreciated her birthday gift, and she did care. Listening to her message, he smiled and made a mental note to call back.

The second call caused his face to darken, and the ends of his mouth twisted upward at the silent rage boiling from within. It was Jeff Michael, VP of Center View Savings and Loan, who wanted to discuss foreclosing on all nine apartment buildings for which Frank was now almost sixty days past due.

The third call was from a DC area code. A monotone, impersonal, business-as-usual female voice had left a message informing Frank that she was from Cork and Hammer and wanted to discuss a job offer. Frank turned down the volume on the portable radio. He preferred not to focus on some talking head's righteously indignant blathering over Vice President Cheney's deliberate and politically-motivated decision to select Halliburton. Cheney, who had been CEO of Halliburton, had apparently given his former company a $7 billion sole-source contract in Iraq. Frank dialed the DC area code number that glowed a fluorescent blue on his phone. A job! He could put off Jeff Michael and the genuine prospect of losing his life savings for at least a phone call.

Frank unsnapped his tool belt and perched on the edge of Larry's unfinished deck.

"Thanks for returning my call, Mr. Davenport," the recruiter announced. "We have your file complete, and are now prepared to make you an offer."

Frank had been in discussions with Cork and Hammer for approximately six weeks, but before an offer could be made, there had to be preliminary background checks, along with a medical check-up that Frank had to get done with his own doctor and his own money, cash that was now becoming scarce. He checked out fine physically but wondered how Cork and Hammer had reconciled his now tarnished credit score. Frank surmised that, if they were going to ask you to not only walk unarmed into an active war zone but also work twelve hours per day, seven days a week with people you had never met and actually accomplish something, they were not going to ask many questions about being late on a credit card bill or a mortgage payment. Or check with the CEO at his last job as to exactly why he had been unemployed.

A remnant from the time he was happily married and working in a real job that now seemed a lifetime ago, Frank's credit score had been a source of immense pride. It had led in part to being able to purchase and develop the income-producing real estate that now hung in the balance. But that was then; life had a sense of urgency now. Credit scores paled in comparison to a lack of a job and meaningful job-related income, not to mention the sleepless nights.

"We are prepared to offer you a subcontract administrator position in Iraq," the recruiter said, in a manner that indicated she had done this more than once. "You will be offered a one-year at-will agreement, a performance period that can be continued, but is subject to termination by either party with thirty days written notice."

Dazed, but not confused, Frank listened intently to the recruiter.

While he had negotiated much larger deals than this before, none were more critical, or urgent.

"I can email you the balance of the offer, which will include a base salary and an uplift schedule," she continued, "but the total yearly compensation with uplift should be approximately one hundred and fifty thousand dollars. You need to review those documents, sign them, and return them to me as soon as possible. And you do understand that you are going to work in a war zone. Is that OK?"

It was an understatement to say that this was a step or two down from what he had done. He had all manner of supply chain personnel working for him in the past, prior to transitioning into marketing and business development. But beggars could not be choosers right now. For a hundred and fifty grand, Frank would walk into a war zone, unarmed.

"What is uplift?" Frank asked the recruiter.

"Uplift is an additional amount, on top of your base salary. It is to compensate you for working in a hazardous environment." The recruiter answered in a manner that indicated she had been asked that question more than once.

"Thanks, but just how much is this uplift, anyway?"

This was Frank's first lesson in how government contracts worked.

"Well, your base salary is five grand a month or about sixty thousand dollars in twelve months," the recruiter quickly responded. "With uplifts, your compensation, including salary, comes to about one hundred and fifty grand, assuming that you work eighty-four hours per week, which is the current work schedule. That said, you are eligible for three R&R's, which are vacation time totaling ten days each, but you only get paid for base pay during that time. Understand?"

Frank was beginning to understand better the financial implications of "unarmed" in a war zone. Meals were paid for, as was a full benefits package, including transportation and accommodations - to the extent that you survived. Uncle Sam chipped in generously with a nice tax shelter on the first one hundred grand or so of income, assuming that you remained outside of the U.S. for more than three hundred and thirty days per year.

And assuming you survived.

War could be a very profitable business, Frank thought, impressed with how casually recruiters like this tossed around salaries that, in the real world, only senior executives could hope to realize. Frank at this point had no idea just how extraordinarily profitable war could be. That would change.

"Sounds great, when do I start?" The phone felt slightly warm on his ear, there in the cold, crisp December twilight in Pensacola.

"Just as soon as we get your papers back, we will book your flight and send you an itinerary. One other thing, sweetie," she said.

Sweetie? he thought. She truly was practiced at this.

"You will do the bulk of your in-processing in Dubai, including code of business conduct training, psychological profiling, and the like. That in-processing will include a complete medical by our folks on staff, but they will have the medical records that you provided. Read through what we send you. If you have questions, call me."

And just like that she was off the phone and, in all likelihood, onto another recruit.

Frank turned and saw Larry standing in the open door, holding two beers. He shared what had happened on the call.

"Do we party?" Larry said hopefully, handing Frank a Bud.

Frank's mind was working overtime.

"Yeah, but I am short of cash." He smiled. "For now, anyway," he added, forcing a weak grin. "Tomorrow, I deal with the bank, but tonight it is party time."

"That contract is a negotiable instrument, Frank. I am not the contracts guy; you are, but from where I stand that contract gets you more time; at least to Dubai for processing into theater, correct?"

Frank nodded and took a sip of the beer.

"And the medical should be a no-brainer." A stack of papers on

Larry's nightstand comprised the results of Frank's medical work done up by a physician in Pensacola who was one of Larry's buddies.

"Nothing in my life is simple now, Larry." Frank sighed. "But then, is it ever?"

CHAPTER 2
When You Need a Shoulder to Cry On

—⁓—

FRANK AND LARRY went back a long way. They became roommates at the end of their freshmen year at University Park on the Penn State campus in the mid-1970's. Frank found common cause with Larry over a shared affinity for beautiful blondes with, as the saying went, a body by Fisher and a brain by Mattel. (Fisher being the body design division of General Motors until 1984.) Unfortunately, Penn State was on the quarter system, which meant that school did not end until June, which was much too late to get that prized Jersey shore waiter job that guys counted on getting to bank some cash and also burnish their reputation with the opposite sex.

Fortune, in the form of Frank's grandmother, smiled on both Frank and Larry and their social life. A sweet, adorable, smooth southern drawl waif of a woman, she charmed a Holiday Inn hotel manager into getting the boys jobs as waiters on the beach in Gulf Shores, Alabama. This was at a time when the white sand quartz that spilled out from the mouth of the Apalachicola Bay onto Gulf beaches contended mostly with footprints, not high-rise hotels and condos. East to Destin and west to Mobile; endless stretches of beautiful beach, with sand every bit as white as that found on Maui. This was the setting where Frank and Larry's lifelong friendship developed.

Larry initially drifted into psychology because it was a great way to get laid in school by girls who were looking for analysis. Jobs were hard to come by in a weak economy without hard skills, so he kicked around doing odd jobs on the Gulf Coast until he landed a position at a mental health facility in Pensacola, Florida. In doing so, Larry Wilson found his calling. Now with both a Ph.D. and a two-decade marriage to a devoted wife who had been unable to conceive, Larry shepherded a small private practice. On weekends, he counseled dying AIDS patients, of which there were plenty in northwest Florida. He dealt with a side of life that most business guys would never know.

Larry Wilson was the perfect father-confessor figure, possessed with the ability to be genial, non-judgmental, and yet direct. Not a religious type, he was a liberal in a sea of hardcore Florida panhandle Christian conservatives, although you would never know it because he did not wear either his politics or his religion on his sleeve. Small in stature, wearing horn-rimmed glasses between his receding hairline and a beard, Larry had been a mini-marathon runner until a motorcycle accident put an end to that pastime. Now he not only acted like the clinician he was, he looked the part.

When you spoke to Larry, you knew he was listening, actively and aggressively but without an attitude. Larry could tell you what you needed to know, not what you wanted to hear. He accomplished it with smiles and a great sense of humor. People paid for his time in this economic backwater of Florida, and Frank knew why. You wanted Larry listening to you, and Larry had heard a lot over the years from his buddy. Right now, Frank badly needed a caring friend to listen.

"So, what happened, Frank?" When Larry asked a question like that, he just really wanted to know.

"Life happened, Larry. I had a high-pressure job in marketing and bet the ranch on a business plan. Maybe I should have never put all of my eggs in that basket, but I did. It's complicated."

Larry had no experience working in a Fortune 500 corporation; or any corporation, for that matter. He didn't bother to find out about that; he just got to the point.

"So, un-complicate it."

For the next six hours, long past dinner and into the night, Frank revisited the corporate machinations that led to the CEO hanging him out to dry to camouflage from his British masters why a good deal went south.

The talk then turned to his wife, the kids, and the future.

His ex-wife would take care of the kids while he was away, should this job pan out. She was moving on; he was still struggling with it all. The kids were taking the divorce about as well as could be expected.

Larry listened intently, just trying to keep it together. The approach worked. Frank felt the tension draining away, if for only a moment.

Larry knew that Frank was going through a tough transition, the kind that could break some people. Depending on how things turned out with the banks, a friend might be all that Frank would have left, and they would know the outcome very soon.

"Hang on. I will put you through to Mr. Michael in just a minute," the secretary said.

Frank glanced down at his watch. It was just past ten in the morning, Tuesday, the seventh of December 2004, the sixty-third anniversary of Pearl Harbor. America had been brutally ambushed back then in a surprise attack that led the nation to war. That attack on Pearl Harbor transformed a nation in mourning into a force bound by a mutual desire to right an obvious wrong.

America of the 1930s had been struggling with its role in the world. The country was gripped in the throes of an economic depression. It had returned to isolationism after its reluctant involvement in the "war to end all wars" known as World War I. America, initially neutral, entered that fray in 1917 only after the Germans targeted American shipping in the Atlantic. And then only after an intercepted telegram, later infamously called the Zimmermann Telegram, reached American newspapers.

That telegram, named after the German ambassador to the U.S.

who launched the ill-conceived missive, contained shocking details of Germany's convoluted attempt to lure Mexico into invading the U.S. in return for a set of border states to call their own. Those were states like Texas, New Mexico, and Arizona, territory Mexico had lost in the 1848 Mexican-American War. Mexico at that point, however, was realistically little more than Poncho Villa and some armed thugs. Following the First World War, America would remain isolationist until the Japanese sunk its ships that momentous Sunday morning in Hawaii almost a quarter of a century later.

Now, six decades after Pearl Harbor, Frank was planning to join in the response to yet another surprise attack. This time, the target was the World Trade Center in New York City. Frank was about to present a binding employment agreement to a bank in Ohio that would affirm his role in helping to avenge one of the worst disasters ever to hit the U.S. mainland.

Although only a prospective contractor, Frank confessed to a certain amount of pride in helping the nation, if what was said about Saddam Hussein and his links to terrorists were to be believed. That said:

You have to be slightly crazy to enter a war zone unarmed just for money, he thought.

Frank would soon learn how many people had done exactly that, with the same mentality.

It wasn't often that a civilian was able to take an active part in a war. Major conflicts were thought generally to be fought by soldiers, a model that seemed in flux now. While Frank's prospective role would be limited to a support function, he would be closer to a war than most civilian Americans would ever get. This would also probably be the last time in his life that he would get such an opportunity.

And yet, Frank could not help feeling a certain amount of ambivalence about the transition from what had transpired at the World Trade Center and what was now happening in Iraq. Frank was just a guy from the business world looking for a job. He had no political science background, not even a subscription to *Foreign Policy* magazine. On the other hand, he did like to keep up with current affairs, and with politics when his busy corporate life afforded him the time. Like most Americans, the vast majority of which did not own a passport, his knowledge of foreign affairs was limited to what he saw on television or read in newspapers.

Frank voted more often than not as an independent. He understood the Democratic Party's humanist tendencies against entering wars. He also understood the limits of that humanist tendency, like when it went off the rails in Vietnam, where we confused nationalism with communism.

Frank also understood the Republicans and the right-wing neocons that never seemed to meet a war they did not like. The hateful rhetoric directed at an Iraqi dictator worried him. Like most dictators, Saddam was probably as nasty as advertised, but Frank suspected that the ruler's only crime wasn't possessing nuclear weapons or terrorism. His biggest mistake was probably limited to being at the wrong place at the wrong time.

Now, both political parties would align, if only in a marriage of convenience to decry the terrorist attack on the World Trade Center. The Democrats were cowed into appearing unpatriotic if they spoke up against going to war. The Republicans in power were looking for any ass to kick, and hoping to profit by it along the way.

Frank would not reconcile the moral conundrum of which political party was right, or wrong. He recalled F. Scott Fitzgerald's observation that the test of a first-rate intelligence is the ability to hold two opposing ideas in mind at the same time and still retain the ability to function. Frank simply believed in America, right or wrong. He also needed a job. And so, even if this latest engagement turned into a Vietnam quagmire, he would support his country, if not always what his country did in the world.

The phone finally transferred through to Jeff Michael, the vice president.

"Hi Frank, I received your email with the attachments."

The tone in Michael's voice communicated a total lack of feeling. His job was to manage risk and convert that into reward, and he saw a lot of risk with little upside now. Northeast Ohio real estate was going through a retrenching after the expansion of the nineties under Clinton as globalization hit. Once thriving office parks and small manufacturing facilities in the towns and villages near Lake Erie were turning into ghost towns, and Michael's performing loan customer base was vanishing along with it.

"We've gone about as far into forbearance as we can go," he told Frank. "If nothing happens, you will be ninety days past soon. I would like to discuss with you coming in to sign over the buildings."

Frank had put thirteen years into developing the nine apartment buildings that he owned, all of which were mortgaged to Michael's S&L. Between jobs for six months now, Frank had been living off the rent stream, but the recently purchased and rehabilitated buildings offered little in the way of positive cash flow. The lousy economic environment meant that sales of real estate were slow, temporarily depressing the value of the properties to a negative equity situation. Not surprisingly, Jeff had earlier refused to entertain a refinance without either a job or more equity for collateral. Frank's wife had a good job, but was never a fan of the rehabilitated properties. She refused to entertain a refinance thus making the issue mostly moot. Time was running out.

"Look, Jeff, I have always made the payments to you," Frank almost snarled into the phone.

"Until now, and it is now that matters," Michael droned in reply.

"Take a look at the papers, Jeff. I have a job lined up which will allow me to get back on track. You can fight this in court, or you can allow me to take this contract and work out the repayment plan through the revenue stream from the contract. Court proceedings can be expensive, and from the looks of the market, there isn't much opportunity for you on the other side, either. Is there?" Frank was trying hard not to scream.

He knew he had a point. Banks did not like to foreclose, particularly when there was a good chance that the bank would take a loss by selling the assets into a depressed economy. Banks were in the business of loaning money, not managing real estate. Frank knew it. This game was hardball, with his whole sense of being on the line, and so that was how he would play the game.

"Okay, Frank, what is the plan?" Michaels shot back, sounds of frustration starting to build. He had a growing sense that what Frank was going to offer was what they were going to do, at least in the short term.

"I am on a plane next week to Dubai. In Dubai, I process through medical and some other stuff. Once that happens, we sign the contract. I will email you that signed contract. Once signed, I deploy to Iraq and should be getting paid thirty days later. I need your assurance that we are at a standstill until that time - no foreclosure."

"What happens if you do not pass the physical?" Michaels asked, not familiar with how wartime contracting worked.

Frank was only slightly more familiar with that part of his soon-to-be new life. "Well, I guess no physical, no contract. No contract, no job. In that case, you get the buildings, so this game should end rather soon," Frank wearily explained.

"I have always had a good relationship with the bank, Jeff. Let's play this one out," Frank continued, trying to close the deal. He knew this was one of those turning points in life where, almost no matter how things turned out, it was going to be a relief, with a sense of finality.

Silence. "Okay, Frank. I will need to bring this up to the loan committee, but I think we will go with this. They will see it your way, but I am warning you, if we do not see that contract, we will do things my way," Jeff warned.

The answer felt almost surreal. "Okay, Jeff. No problem, and happy holidays if we do not speak before."

Frank hung up and sunk down into the chair in Larry's den, sobbing uncontrollably. He had lost his job, his wife and family. Frank was now desperately trying to fight off losing his real estate, in the process fouling off a high, hard heater of a fastball up and in tight; a sure strike three. Frank would get up close and personal with that knockout pitch again in Dubai.

CHAPTER 3
In the Beginning...Cork and Hammer

—ɱ—

It had been one of those long mid-December days for Case Hammer. Work started early, in the dark, and frequently ended late when it was both dark and cold. He hurriedly entered his office and tossed his briefcase onto the desk then picked up the phone and called out to his secretary in the outer office.

"Julie, please have Dr. Marsh see me before he leaves tonight."

Julie Tuck appeared around the corner, seemingly from nowhere. "Will do, sir. And good night, sir," she said on the way out the door.

Hammer's eyes raised to acknowledge his secretary's departure for the evening. A moment later, Marsh appeared, pad in hand.

"Yes, sir?"

"C'mon in and shut the door, Bill," Hammer muttered quietly, almost with an air of resignation.

Marsh had seen that look before in the two decades he had known Hammer. He could not put his finger on it, but somehow this was different.

Hammer came right to the point.

"Look, I need to tell you something, but you need to keep this confidential for now, okay? I have another meeting on the Hill. We can talk further in the morning."

“S-s-sure,” Marsh stammered, uncertain as to what was to come.

“I’ve decided to sell the business,” Hammer uttered, staring at the floor as he spoke. Telling Marsh was a calculated decision because the sale was not finalized, not by a long shot. But Washington was a sieve; the useful life of secrets there was measured in nanoseconds, not days, or even hours.

To close this deal, he needed Marsh, especially during the due diligence phase when both the buyer and the government would have involvement. Marsh probably couldn’t derail the deal, but he was essential. He knew the operations better than anybody except Case Hammer.

Marsh was speechless for a moment, trying but failing to get his head around what he had just heard. Looking straight into the old man’s eyes, he grasped for words. “Why...and why now... of all times?”

Hammer returned the stare.

“Because now is a great time. That Iraq contract revenue stream anchors the valuation for the company. The board sees a valuation of at least five bucks a share and possibly more; a nice 40% premium over where we are today, and they want out. Now.” Hammer locked his briefcase.

“Let’s you and I talk about some compensation for you when we get a little closer to finalizing the deal,” he told Marsh. “But you have to keep this confidential.”

Left unsaid was that if Marsh did disclose, and Hammer found out, he stood to get nothing.

And with that, Hammer ushered Marsh out the door and was gone for the night.

Marsh was floored.

—ɱ—

Charley Cork and Carl Hammer had been a couple of enterprising GIs' when the Second World War ended in 1945. Trained as aviators during the war, they started Cork and Hammer as a transport company working the Pacific Rim on a shoestring, a prayer, and the wings of a couple of Lockheed Model 12 Electra's, planes kept together by duct tape and baling wire. But if you wanted someone or something delivered on time in places few people knew about or ventured into, no questions asked, you called Charley and Carl. They delivered.

When the Office of Strategic Services - the forerunner of the Central Intelligence Agency - came calling, Charley and Carl became converts to the cause. Neither Charley nor Carl were deep political thinkers. Their business was more about doing than pontificating. But it did not take a degree in political science to see that the end of the war meant the fight merely shifted from the nazis to the communists, and Cork and Hammer despised both. It was not a fight they sought, but once engaged, they were all-in.

Charley and Carl found out they could do their part to save the world, and at the same time make a lot of money. What could be better? Flying was in their bones. They loved serving their country, but unlike being in uniform, the life of a contractor afforded them fast cars, nice digs, and faster women; an ample supply of mostly young, nubile Asian beauties who could suck the chrome off of a '57 Chevy bumper. Life was good.

Thailand, central to Southeast Asia, had become one of the first countries in Southeast Asia to side with the United States against communism in the late '40s. The Thais resisted communism because it sought a total transformation of Thai institutions like Buddhism and the Thai monarchy. This was no small feat, given its proximity to China, which would itself fall to the communists.

Even so, the war against communism in the Pacific and anywhere else was going to be a long slog, as the case for capitalism and democracy was still very much an open question. This was a battle for more than hearts and minds, one that argued for a presence on the ground.

In the Eisenhower era in foreign policy, America had war debts to pay down, a civilian infrastructure to build that had been neglected by economic depression and a world war, and kids to send to college. The U.S. elected Ike twice, each time with landslide majorities, to deliver to the world the message that America could walk and chew gum at the same time. America could make great, market-based products that gave people a better life, keep the world nominally at peace with the threat of nukes, and fight communism across the planet.

For the Eisenhower Administration, the struggle meant underwriting the French in Indochina in the 1950s, rather than sending in troops. As for Charley and Carl, that translated into what marketers would call a product line extension of the transport business. Their CIA customers wanted logistics hubs, short term depots, and base support arrangements throughout Southeast Asia.

It was all about moving men and material in and out. Bases, mostly small out of the way encampments, got erected and torn down as the need arose. There was a lot of contingency work with short time-lines and demanding customers for which they were very well paid - no questions asked. There were no rules then, few if any acquisition regulations or competitive bidding. Just get 'er done. Cork and Hammer had become a CIA front in the Cold War.

CHRISTMAS WAS IN the air this Monday evening, the 13th day of December 2004. Donaldson Wickes entered a small upscale restaurant off of Chain Bridge Road in McLean, in the Northern Virginia suburbs. It would be a private affair; just a meal, a couple of drinks, and some conversation with an old friend. He liked the food here. The prices were high, but that is what you got when you sought out both upscale and private in McLean, Virginia, one of the more expensive parts of the world.

Wickes was the senior senator from South Carolina, a conservative sixty-five-year-old Republican and a member of the Senate Armed Services Committee. His was a formidable position, with legislative oversight of the nation's military. Wickes came from a powerful, southern aristocratic family. His father was a prominent member of the bar, as was his grandfather. Like most of the men in his family, he had served in the military; in Wickes' case, in Vietnam as a Marine lieutenant.

The senator settled into his chair in a private room with a private bar reserved for he and Case Hammer. He reflected back to those days more than thirty years prior when he had met Case, a fellow young Marine officer, in a rice paddy where they were calling in air cover while dodging incoming rounds from the Vietcong. Leaving the Marines after the war, Wickes had been at a crossroads in his life so, when offered a job by his friend Case at Cork and Hammer, Wickes jumped at the opportunity. For three years, they kicked around Southeast Asia doing odd jobs for Case's father's business and - by implication - the CIA, Cork and Hammer's biggest client.

At a certain level, it was an exciting, carefree single life, always on the run to new destinations at a moment's notice. He had moved on from there to law school, state politics, and ultimately a run for the United States Senate during the waning days of the Clinton administration, but he always retained a unique understanding of how contractors work with the government. That knowledge would come in handy in the run-up to Iraq, a war in which civilian contractor logistics would be necessary. Wickes knew that you were only as good on the battlefield as your support logistics allowed.

Increasingly, during the Reagan defense buildup, that meant reaching out to civilian contractors to do the work that GI's once did. Knowing this, Wickes cultivated relationships early on in his career with then-Senator Dan Quayle, whose office had a hand in drafting some of the legislation critical to subcontracting out services that had previously been done in-house. Those relationships would come in handy for Wickes's old friends like Cork and Hammer, who would demonstrate their friendship during election season.

If politics is about the art of gaining and holding power, something that politicians spend a lifetime learning how to master, then friendships are essential. Relationships were the grease in the cogs of state that allowed the political machine to run. This was one reason that

Wickes made time on a busy Monday to schedule a quiet dinner with his old Marine Corps buddy. But, as with any politician, it was not the only reason.

Wickes knew that Hammer was entertaining a sale of his company. He knew it because he was quietly, behind the scenes, trying to orchestrate it. The CEO of BLTVDef, a large high-tech defense firm, had come to him informally, knowing of his relationship with Hammer. Seeking the inside track to such a sale, the CEO had queried Wickes about BLTVDef possibly buying Cork and Hammer. Wickes's official reply to the BLTVDef CEO was unequivocal. He knew Case, but he stayed out of those type of business deals.

Wickes could not officially be seen as meddling with the DOD or CIA supplier base. Not only was it out of his lane, but he was a hard right-wing, free-market Republican. The last thing he wanted to get accused of by liberals was using his perch in government to push around suppliers on a global chessboard, the way that the Chinese and their state-owned enterprises operated. The reality, however, was that the American government often did just that. Wickes also knew that BLTVDef was a significant campaign contributor, and money talked.

And so, maybe this was the right time. Senator Wickes did not know the financial ratios in terms of valuing the company, but he did know its history. He also knew that the timing could not be better. Cork and Hammer had always been one of those little companies operating in the background. It was one of those nameless, faceless companies that the United States had all over the world, doing odd jobs both for Democratic and Republican administrations, with little accountability.

As he surveyed the world from his position on the Armed Services Committee, he knew that the cloak and dagger days had mostly passed. The United States defense budget had exploded in terms of size and was now larger than the next eight countries' defense budgets put together.

A little less noticed, but even more significant trend was that it had gone ultra-high-tech but increasingly low-touch. The spy business had become technology-heavy, but without that human touch and feel that gives it both context and subtle nuance. It was allowing high technology to do the work that was formerly relegated to the personal touch world of spies.

Cork and Hammer was mostly small, low-tech and high-touch, a yesterday business. There was still a niche for low-tech and high-touch. You still needed to press the flesh on a personal level, but timing was everything in life, and that niche in the spy business was increasingly narrow. As he sat down for dinner, Wickes hoped his friend saw it the same way.

CHAPTER 4
Dinner and Politics

CASE HAMMER SMILED when he saw his old friend Senator Wickes enter the private room of the restaurant in McLean. Now sitting at the apex of money and politics, the two had done well. Case had gone on to become the CEO of a billion-dollar corporation, while his old friend from Vietnam had gained entrance to one of the most exclusive clubs in the world: the United States Senate.

Case had been carefully groomed to take over his father's business. But those years between Vietnam and Reagan had been hard on the company, and so his father prevailed upon him in the late '70s to take an MBA at Harvard. A lucrative career in consulting beckoned, but both his father and his father's partner had become ill at about that time, each ultimately passing from the scene in the late eighties. For Case, this began a multi-decade run at the helm of the only business he really knew, chasing government contracts during the Reagan build-up, and behind it, the ramp down under Clinton. And now it was yet another ramp-up; this time in Iraq, under Bush and Cheney.

Managing a business in such an environment - riding the tiger - had been a drain on Case. As he sat in front of his friend, the strain on his face showed.

"How's Liz?" Wickes asked, getting immediately and without any formalities to a personal question, something that only good friends could do properly. The senator had been at Case's wedding to his wife

Liz, and had managed to stay in touch as good friends do, although less than both would have liked.

"Looking forward to relaxing and doing some traveling," Case replied. "But with what we have going on right now, that's just a dream." Case was referring to the work in Iraq. "And how is Charlene?" he continued, referring to Wickes' wife of thirty years.

The wives had been good friends, both stay-at-home moms of an earlier generation who lived a type of sisterly kinship that had formed over years at home without globe-trotting spouses.

"Just doting on the grandkids, you know," Wickes replied, while ordering some fine wine, knowing that this meal was going to be paid for by the taxpayers. "But do tell me how that contract is going. How is life in a war zone?" He chuckled, knowing full well from having toured Iraq himself that things there were in a controlled state of chaos.

"Well, as you know, the original statement of work envisioned twenty-five forward operating bases. They now want twenty-five more at a minimum and, as usual, want them yesterday." Case smiled, not wanting to convey a sense of concern. What was going on behind the scenes was a full-blown panic over having to recruit, transport, train, and manage civilian personnel in a very fluid situation in a war-torn foreign country.

In the initial ramp up to Iraq, Cork and Hammer had been turned on to mobilize two hundred and fifty mostly American workers - ex-pats - for each of the initial twenty-five bases. Time was of the essence. The client wanted them on the ground as soon as possible in order to support base operations while the military did the fighting. That total did not count an equal number of third-country nationals. And now those extra twenty-five bases would necessitate a similar, equally urgent demand.

Case was used to the lack of planning. He had realized a long time ago that the United States government does not plan; it reacts to events. Most defense contractors counted on Uncle Sam not being able to plan. A cynic would say that it was the contractor's reason for existence, not to mention the economic profit to be had - but you had to deliver - and the military was dead serious about those additional twenty-five bases. Now. No bullshit. Case knew that Marsh, his senior vice-president, was struggling with the logistics, even though Marsh was good at logistics.

Sensing Case's unease, Wickes was quick to reassure him.

"You will handle it, Case. Just business as usual. This may not be what they taught you at Harvard Business School... but your government is counting on you. I have faith in you." Wickes smiled, jabbing in jest at his friend as he dug into his taxpayer-funded, New York Strip sirloin steak, medium rare. "Not to mention the revenue side, which should be looking up. Huh? Merry Christmas."

Wickes laughed, then hoisted his wine glass up to where Case instinctively raised his own. It was then that he first realized the depth of the worried look in Case's eyes that his friend had been struggling to avoid showing. It had been years of holding things together on a shoestring, and now he felt like things were moving faster than he could handle, like a runaway freight train. Maybe it was time.

Wickes lowered his glass, and then he lowered his voice, sensing the concern on his friend's face. He had known Case for a long time, but had never seen him like this. "What is it, my friend?"

"Well, the revenue side projections are nice. Our sales essentially doubled on a year-to-year basis, which is good." Case was not breaking any news here: both the DOD and the CIA had the company's financial statements. Wickes knew exactly how good those numbers were.

"Yeah, Case, and both Defense and the Company are only looking to do much more in Iraq, and Afghanistan, Pakistan, and possibly Iran. Bush is an ideologue; he wants more of this stuff, just like the crusades a thousand years ago. Hell, he was stupid enough actually to call it a crusade after the 911 attacks. But politics aside, let's just stick to the business piece of this for a minute. If I am not mistaken, your stuff is all cost reimbursable, right? So... what am I missing here?"

Most businessmen would ejaculate in their jeans for a cost-reimbursable contract that would double their sales. It had taken Case Hammer more than fifty years to reach a billion in sales. Now, he had done that again almost overnight, and with relatively little upfront investment. This was Cork and Hammer's first cost reimbursable contract ever. It could get Case "fuck you" rich in a New York minute, and he knew it.

Case knew well that most government contracts were both small and fixed price. But Case also knew that most of the money was spent on a relatively few cost-reimbursable items, things like high-tech weapon systems. Low-tech base support agreements in the States would probably be let on some form of a fixed price arrangement, but because this particular base support agreement was located in a war zone and entailed a lot more risk, it was being let on a cost-reimbursable basis.

Wickes's face hardened as he leaned into Case across the table. "And don't forget, we both know that you got this agreement even after some serious questions were raised about Cork and Hammer's financial and logistical ability to keep up with what is going on over there. I hate to tell you, Case, but a company with a billion in sales, with comparatively little hard assets on the balance sheet and no direct experience at this level, isn't anything special. Other companies had much deeper pockets, like BLTVDef."

"Shit, Case," Wickes continued, "all the compliance boys need to do is start questioning your paperwork. Next thing you know, they are withholding payments, and you have serious cash flow problems. We can't have that, where we are going." Case's eyes lit up at the mention of BLTVDef, although he could not disagree with the assertions.

Wickes wasn't done. Only now, his voice lowered almost to a conspiratorial whisper in a room that except for Hammer and Wickes, was empty. "The argument was made; quietly, of course, on the Hill and in the Pentagon." Senator Wickes smiled knowingly; he knew much more than he was saying, of course. "Time-to-market was critical. The DOD boys had to get boots on the ground, and quickly. We could have been negotiating with some of the other, bigger guys and their legal departments until the cows came home, and missed the window. The decision was made to go with Cork and Hammer given your track record of agility and responsiveness."

And with no questions asked. Wickes left out that part.

—⁂—

Wickes was preaching to the choir. Case Hammer knew the numbers; he also understood the marketing piece. Hell, Case even knew the politics like few folks in the world did. A confluence of education and experience had taken him to where he was today, but there comes a time in life when you wake up one day and say that it's over. Case Hammer had climbed the mountain, but having reached the top, he was prepared to declare victory and walk away. His get up and go had got up and left.

But there was more to it. Case thought that the people who were running this war were more than a little crazy. Senators like Wickes, whom he liked, were nothing but glorified staffers. The Senate was set up to be the cooling saucer of democracy, as Washington had put it to Jefferson more than two hundred years ago, but lately it had mostly abrogated its responsibility for oversight after the atrocity at the Twin Towers in New York City. Now the Senate seemed relegated to little more than cheerleaders out of fear of being called non-patriotic.

Most senators had never planned or implemented a military operation. Senators didn't invade countries; they wrote letters, raised money, and made speeches. The operations guys in the Executive Branch were in charge after 911, in a part of the world that they knew little about and cared for even less, except that they just wanted to kick some ass. Any ass, it almost did not matter whose ass.

Case had severe reservations as to whether or not the government was right. But he did know government project guys well. Few, if any of them, in his opinion could manage financial risk in a commercial sense. In fairness, that was not their job, but hell, even if they were wrong, they could just print more money and go on to the next fiasco.

As CEO, Case could not manage that way. He had a responsibility to his shareholders. Not necessarily to maximize the shareholder price - nothing in corporate law required either a CEO or his board of directors to focus exclusively on optimizing the share price of a stock

- but certainly to minimize risk. And there was a ton of risk in a war, even with a cost-reimbursable contract.

Case knew that many of the agreements let for goods and services, especially at the subcontract level, were done by folks just hired with little or no understanding either of how government contracts worked or appreciation of the concept of risk, particularly in a war. Under severe pressure to expand forward operating bases from both his civilian and military counterparts, Marsh was hiring people that had never worked with Cork and Hammer; or, for that matter, any defense contractor.

They were literally taking people off of the street who had little or no experience and placing them into positions of authority because they had to fill positions. HR told Case that one of his so-called senior managers in the field had been pulled from a homeless shelter in Houston. Case was having nightmares about that, knowing that he had put decades of effort into building a business. Now he was hiring people that had quite possibly been living on the street and eating out of dumpsters before deployment?

To be sure, Case was going to hire somebody to fill those positions. His company was mission-oriented, and time was of the essence here. The weekly meetings with the client were getting more intense; his staff continually briefing the client on how they were progressing. Tempers, already short, were getting frayed.

Everything else aside, this game was all about getting reimbursed, and Cork and Hammer was motivated. Case knew how the game was played. In the upside-down world of government cost reimbursable-type contracting, expenses were actually revenue, because costs incurred got turned in, along with a bill to the USG for profit, and thirty days or so later, a check arrived.

Uncle Sam did pay on time, assuming that the invoicing was correct. And those checks were the mother's milk of his business. Case needed them to stay one step ahead of the creditors as the work in Iraq exploded and the bills rolled in each month.

The more the expenses, the more the revenue. Tack on your profit to the additional revenue and life was getting good, fast. Cutting costs to save the client money? Are you kidding? Case Hammer wasn't about to reduce any costs.

In fact, there was every motivation to do the exact opposite and incur costs. Cutting expenses was something any household in America would think to do naturally, and something that Marsh would only half-kiddingly joke about in his senior staff meetings. Cutting costs was something for which you got fired at Cork and Hammer, ladies and gentlemen, because you just reduced your cost basis on which your profit was calculated.

When, as likely as not, the war started to go badly, when the relationship between the client and C&H became adversarial, rather than collegial, after the love was gone, then what? What happened when the government found out that formerly homeless, knuckle-dragging thugs were paid exorbitantly for pretending to manage whatever they were supposed to manage? Who paid for that?

The USG could be incompetent at times, but they were not stupid. Uncle Sam only reimbursed on allowable, allocable, and reasonable costs. They had an endless sea of nameless, faceless bureaucrats that raised both children and grandchildren in jobs by picking over complex pieces of paper in an audit, looking for mistakes.

Once that happened, once questions were raised, these people were no longer nameless or faceless. They would pounce with glee on their unwitting prey. That is, after all how government audit careers were made. They had the ability to yank your next receivables payment, not only blowing up your internal cash flow forecast, but forcing you to defend the alleged gaffe in microscopic, excruciating detail. To Case, those were claims waiting to happen which could take years, perhaps even decades, to resolve.

Big profits could quickly turn into significant losses as cash flow dried up. Credit lines would be eviscerated. The company's stock price would tank as the claims were disclosed in his mandatory disclosures to the Securities and Exchange Commission, and then drilled endlessly into people's consciousness via the mindless talking heads on cable TV.

In that scenario, Case would be forced to spend all of his time in a rearguard action with lawyers defending what happened long ago in the fog of war, instead of moving on to the next big project. That was how you went belly up, and the client could give a shit. They ate contractors for lunch.

There was also a little jealousy mixed in. Case Hammer and his defense contractor brethren were perceived to be getting rich, while the lowly government bureaucrats were up to their asses in alligators. Case knew all about the jealousy thing, and it could be dangerous.

Case Hammer swirled the wine in his glass and gazed across the table at his senator friend. "Got a call from Jim Witt at BLTVDef. Asking me again if I want to sell the company." He wanted to quietly but effectively change the subject. He had his own war going on, inside.

—ꟽ—

"REALLY?" WICKES FEIGNED surprise. "You serious?" He knew the answer before he asked the question.

"Well, I need to do right by the board here, which means that the numbers have to work, but I just get the feeling that you guys are on to something a little bigger than what we can provide. We have always supported you guys, all over the world." Case looked directly at Wickes. "In good times and bad..."

"And you know that we appreciate it, Case," Wickes replied evenly, a sense of resignation in the air as if he sensed what was to come.

"I know you do, my friend," Case said, looking down at his wine and suddenly feeling much older.

"Witt and I have been talking for some time now, batting around some numbers and some scenarios. I know that this is not a secret. Hell, we would have to come to you for your blessing, anyway."

Case was correct, of course. You did not just sell out to anybody. Uncle Sam had an abiding interest in making sure that services were delivered, and that meant a supplier base that could make it happen. Corporate profits were essential to maintaining a viable supplier base, but in a war zone, the United States government's chief concern was in producing a good or service when needed.

Case continued to explain. "Up until now, I... and I have to confess the board... have been on the fence about whether or not to sell out. After all, it took us decades to get to this place. We are fighters, Don. You don't just throw away a lifetime's work doing good work in the service of the country in which we live, and in which we believe..." Case's words trailed off softly as bits of his life flashed before him. There were moments in life when you took stock of what you had done and accomplished, and this was one of them.

"Understood, Case." Wickes did understand. There was a part of him that knew that Case may just be negotiating with him for more money. Not that he was the guy to consult with, but he knew Case would haggle over the opening of an envelope if need be. Still, neither man was young anymore. And a lifetime of work, much of it in service to the country that they both loved, transcended profits. Wickes flashed back to the lean years when he had worked with Case's father's small company, jumping from one shithole to another. You did it for more than money.

He had to level with Case. "Look, as a friend here - not as an official of the United States government, but as a friend - I am officially going to stay out of this because if I start stepping on some bureaucrat's toes, then I never hear the end of it. But see where it goes with BLTVDef. Nobody wants a train wreck here. And yeah, this thing could get big; no telling how this is going to end up." Wickes studied Case, who had long since stopped eating and was now staring blankly to the side.

"Any compliance issues to deal with?" Wickes said in an off-handed sort of way, again knowing more than he was letting on.

"Uh, no. Nothing that we can't handle. Nothing that should get in the way of a deal." Case continued to stare into space, but the question had not gotten by him, not by a long shot.

"Great. There was one other issue that some of the boys at Langley were working on that we thought you might like to help with while you were still with us..." Wickes' voice trailed off again and he remained silent until Case turned his gaze back to the table. "We can help you, if you can help us."

Case blinked before answering. "Sure. What is it?"

CHAPTER 5
Derya Ali

—ꟽ—

"I NEED YOU THERE," he said.

Derya Ali stared out of the back-seat window of her white, chauffeur-driven Infiniti as it approached the first border station at the end of the King Fahd Causeway. As usual, the view of the Gulf of Bahrain from this twenty-six-kilometer marvel was stunning. But this was not a time for sightseeing.

Derya reached for her overnight bag while considering her brother's request. Until now, the conversation had been the usual chit-chat between two siblings. But suddenly, the conversation turned to business, which meant that it became deadly serious.

"How soon, and for how long?" she asked. It wasn't a question of if she would accede to Jamal's request; she would. She would do anything for her brother, whom she loved, including working in a war zone, which is what he was asking her to do.

It was a busy day, the tenth of December, 2004. The tenth was a Friday which meant that it was the start of a weekend. For those who worked in Saudi Arabia's Khobar Province, the hour and a half drive to Bahrain along the causeway started early.

To the expats working in the oil and gas industry, it was a chance to relax with a drink and chase whores in Manama, the capital of Bahrain.

For the Saudi nationals; especially the women, it was a place to relax without either the hijab or the abaya.

"There is so much to tell you," her brother Jamal said. "As you know, our organization is doing some financing with Khan, who is working with the Americans at Camp Bradley in Baghdad."

Derya's smile turned quickly into a frown as she began to remove her hijab and abaya in the car. This first border station, officially used to check passports, signified that you were leaving Saudi Arabia. But it also served another, informal and more personal purpose. That first border station was the first place to disrobe, revealing more conventional western jeans, form-fitting T-shirts, along with a fair amount of ostentatiously displayed bling-bling. By the time that most Saudi's arrived at that third border station, where one officially entered Bahrain, the evolution to western garb was complete. Derya would be no exception to that unwritten rule.

"You mean Jabil Khan, the lowlife Paki?", she asked, reaching for a mirror to apply some lipstick.

"Yes," her brother replied. "Khan is not providing the numbers that we need. He is also not providing the intelligence that we want. At some point soon, I have to decide as to whether or not to cut my losses. My patience with Mr. Khan is running thin." Jamal Ali grew quiet, obviously considering his next move with Khan.

"I do know of the financing to Khan, my brother," Derya said, again smiling sweetly. "But tell me more. I have been busy wrapping up our financial affairs in Khobar, as you know, so I confess not knowing all of the details of the Khan financing in Baghdad."

Derya had been busy. She was referring to the Khobar Towers bombing and massacre which occurred earlier on the twenty-ninth of May 2004 and took place in the hub of the Saudi oil industry. Twenty-two people died as a result of that terror strike. An additional twenty-five people were injured. And her brother Jamal knew precisely what she meant because he had been a party to it.

—∞—

Jamal Ali finished his wine and looked out over the Gulf of Bahrain. His multi-million-dollar condo took up the entire top floor. The meal with Derya had been quiet, but enjoyable. He relished his time with his sister. He had looked forward to this weekend for a long time. These moments were precious in a war, and they both knew it. Time passed this particular Friday evening in no particular hurry, sometimes wordlessly, as often happened with two people who knew each other intimately.

With the dinner done and the Filipino servants gone for the evening, their casual conversation turned back to the business at hand. To Jamal, it seemed that he needed to be everywhere at once, with projects in a constant state of flux. His sister was the one constant in his life; he trusted her implicitly. And yet as good as she was, he worried that this assignment would task her in new ways.

Until now, Jamal had intentionally confined Derya to the wholesale end of the business. Immersing herself in the internal affairs of their boutique private equity operation, Derya spent her days raising capital from wealthy stakeholders throughout the Middle East. In the States, she would be something akin to an investment banker, but this was the Middle East, and the types of investments for which they raised capital never made it to the stock or bond market.

This role would no longer be a back-office role. Jamal was going to ask her to raise capital at the retail end of the business. That meant working in a war zone without back-office support. She would be truly alone, and that worried him.

"Khan contacted us not long after the Americans went into Iraq in 2003," he said. "As you know, we get requests for money all of the time, but this was a little different."

"Really? How so?" She had been silently watching her brother throughout the meal and could tell that he was carrying the weight of the world on his shoulders. He was relatively young, but his job was starting to age him.

"Khan was approached early on by the American contractor Cork and Hammer," Jamal replied slowly. "Cork and Hammer runs the base support at Camp Bradley. Their project manager, a man named Buck, is taking money from the operation and putting it in an account in Kuwait. He is funneling it through Khan."

"Okay, so what is our interest in that operation?" Derya asked the question as though this was just another financial transaction.

"Khan did not have any money to finance that operation, or much of anything else leading up to the war, but he did have access to the American managers on base he'd worked with. He wanted some seed capital quickly. He approached us through intermediaries."

"Doesn't Khan live on a yacht?" she asked.

"That is all show."

"What are our terms with Khan?" Derya was utterly unfazed by the fact that most people she dealt with in business were liars, thugs, criminals, or worse.

"We were seeking some sort of access to the base in order to gain useful intelligence," Jamal responded. "Not only on the existing camps, but also near the Iraq border with Iran. The Iranians are concerned that the camps are being built near the border for an invasion. When Khan came to us for financing, we imposed several conditions. We wanted seventy-five percent off of everything that he made, and we wanted base access so that we could get to the intel. Khan said that he could arrange it without raising suspicions with Buck."

Jamal Ali's face darkened.

"But now, he is more than a year into the operation and he is crying to us that his numbers are low because the colonel on base inhibits his activity. We ask about the intelligence at the border, and we are told the same thing: the colonel is preventing us from gaining either the work at the border, or the intelligence associated with that work."

"Why do we care about the Iranians?" Derya asked. She and her brother were Sunni. The Iranians were Shiites.

"Because we both hate the Americans, and the Iranians will pay nicely for good intelligence."

"What do you want me to do, my dear brother?"

"I need you to find out why Khan is not delivering his numbers. If he is lying to us, I will have him killed. He is stupid, but I do not think that he is that stupid."

"Officially, you will be working for Khan. We also need to know what is going on, both on the camps, and at the border. But there is a third reason, as well," Jamal Ali looked directly at his sister. "Khan says there are whispers that Cork and Hammer is going to sell the company. If so, we need to know so that we can adjust."

"When do you want to do this?" Derya asked, her head spinning.

"Now, or as soon as possible. We will have to arrange base access for you. But before you say that you will do this, think it through. You will be alone on that base, with little or no support. You cannot call me from there unless it is absolutely necessary because they will be bugging everything that you own. Even calling from Kuwait should be avoided. You don't know how they are listening. Think about it and let's talk in the car on the way back to Khobar on Sunday."

The return drive back over the King Fahd Causeway came with a strange sense of foreboding. Jamal knew that Derya would agree to the assignment. He knew that she would do anything for him. But that was always the problem, and he knew it.

Jamal came to grips with the downside of his business a long time ago. Accordingly, he kept her confined to the margins. It was safer that way.

Sending her to Camp Bradley was asking her to engage in the business outside of the confines of the office, away from the margins. She was organized, tough in negotiations, resilient in adjusting where obstacles cropped up, and yet possessed a calm air of determination that made her wise beyond her years.

But Camp Bradley was not a back-office job. It was closer to the retail end of the business, and at that end, people got hurt. The pressure on him to deliver both the revenue stream and the intelligence was intense. He had been casting about, looking for other alternatives. Finding none, he turned to his sister out of a sense of desperation, rather than any sense of planning.

Situations like that always tended to end badly and he knew it which is why during the return drive, he found himself with her hand in his, as if to say that he did not want to do this. He was losing control of something special.

He would be in Afghanistan soon, far away from her. Only this time, there would be no spontaneous chats via cell phone or cryptic emails regarding some minor financial detail. He hoped that this time would be the last time they would be apart. But as the Infiniti pulled into the driveway at the Khobar offices, the little voice inside told him to prepare for that eventuality.

What he didn't know was that his sister was quietly thinking the same thing.

CHAPTER 6
Marsh, and Plan B

—ɯ—

DR. WILLIAM MARSH was in a rage. As a senior vice president at Cork and Hammer and program manager for the Iraq project, he saw everything he had worked for since the early '80s begin to unravel. In the beginning, he was a rising young star with a Ph.D. in management science from American University in Washington D.C. The Reagan defense buildup, which began in earnest as Reagan took office after the Carter years of malaise post-Vietnam, provided Marsh the opportunity to work on many of the weapons systems from the government side as a procurement contracting officer, or PCO.

A middle to an upper-level government bureaucrat with a decent salary, Marsh was authorized to enter into legal and binding agreements for the government. His job, among other responsibilities, was to ensure that all of the legal requirements were satisfied. That meant making sure that funds were available, assuring that contractors received fair and equitable treatment, and at the end of the day, making sure that what was contained in those sets of agreements was in the best interests of his client, Uncle Sam.

His guide was the Federal Acquisition Regulations, or FAR. The FAR, essentially a straitjacket of government rules and regulations, was designed to provide a uniform set of policies and procedures for acquisition. Unlike the private sector, procurement officers at the federal level were prohibited from doing anything except that which was authorized by law, statute, or administrative regulation. For their counterparts in the private sector, it was the opposite: everything was fair game, except that which was prohibited by law, statute, or administrative regulation.

The problem for Marsh was that he knew the rules of the game. He knew how it was played; what to do, and what not to do. The paperwork was stifling, the personalities dysfunctional, and the tension between wealthy contractors trying to game the system and the contracting offices with too much work and too little pay was interminable. On the other hand, Marsh saw a lot of money getting made, and he wanted a part of it.

The opportunity came during the Reagan years, and it all revolved around cost. It did not take a financial genius to figure out that the rise in military expenditures was unsustainable. Things like health, personnel, and pension benefits were fixed costs, and they were forecasted to skyrocket.

Like others, he felt that the only way to control costs with a massive Pentagon overhead in an era of small, in-and-out global conflicts as the Cold War made its way towards the exits was to begin to contract out functions that formerly were performed by the United States government. Contracting out these functions would introduce competition where it did not exist. It would also make fixed costs not only more variable but also more just in time and nature. For instance, paying for a dining hall only when and where you needed it.

Contracts were to be let to a competitively bid contractor who paid his own (though most likely, lesser) benefits than if they worked for Uncle Sam. The marginal costs were higher because you paid the contractor a profit. Those costs were incurred, however, only during the duration of what was assumed to be short-run conflicts, after which the obligation to that contractor for that dining hall ended precisely when a shortened conflict finished.

For the next six years, Marsh worked in various staff positions on the Hill, mostly for conservative Republican senators whose mission it was to disassemble the government bureaucracy. It gave him a chance to work on the legislation vital to the contracting-out process. Even better, it allowed him to rub elbows with those who stood to gain from that process, for that was where the action was, and so where he wanted to be.

Still, Marsh wanted more. He knew where the real money was made, on the revenue side, not the cost of goods side in a boring government contracts job. This was the inside baseball, game-within-the-game that went on all of the time in DC. You worked for the government to learn the rules, then jumped to a contractor to make some money, then back to the government at an elevated level, and finally went out to the right contractor at a senior level position.

Only Marsh did not want a mere senior level position; he wanted ownership. You got old but not wealthy in high-level positions. He wanted to be old and obscenely rich.

The press coined a term for the mostly DC-area located contractors who got rich off of government contracts. They were known as Beltway bandits, originally a pejorative term for a set of criminals who jumped on the I-495 Beltway, a sixty-four mile of interstate highway that encircles the nation's capital, after holding up a bank or breaking into a home in an attempt to elude the police.

Now, in an era where "greed is good" they were America's sweethearts. Marsh wanted to be a Beltway bandit, and so when Case Hammer called him one day in the early nineties after the Democrats had assumed the presidency, he listened.

Marsh had known Hammer for at least a decade before, but mostly from afar as an aide on the Hill. He knew that Hammer ran a small logistics and site support business catering primarily to the CIA secret squirrels, but he knew little else about the actual operation or how it worked.

Then, over dinner one night, Hammer pitched Marsh on the idea of leaving government service. DOD budgets were declining in real terms under Clinton. Things were tightening up; contracts were harder to get, and profit margins were thin. Hammer needed somebody to come onboard to help both land and run deals. Defense contracts tended to run in twenty-year cycles, more or less, and this was a low point in that cycle. Hammer needed help from the program management perspective; there was a title and, if things went well, some equity.

Those words now rang bitterly in Marsh's ears a little more than a decade later. He had come on and provided both the program management and the contracts expertise to a company that in his mind had been run on a wing and a prayer. Hammer was good with the government customers at DOD, State, the CIA, and up on the Hill, but Case was not a contracts guy. That had been Charley Cork's acquired expertise, and he had been dead for fourteen years.

After that night at dinner before joining the company, Marsh had never been offered an actual equity stake in the company. That was a problem. In spite of constant requests, he had always been gently but firmly rebuffed - invariably with some song and dance - and now the train was leaving the station. The company he had helped build to almost a billion in sales before the war in 2003 was being sold out from under him.

At sixty-two years of age, you do not get many second chances. Fortunately for Dr. Marsh, he had Plan B already in the works. He wanted an equity stake, and he was going to collect; if not one way, then another.

THE PHONE RANG in Kenny Buck's office in Iraq. The brown, sandstone-colored multi-story air-conditioned building made from stone housed the contractor program management facilities on site. The building was shaded by desert palms that afforded some small degree of relief from the intense heat. The minions, which meant most of the management staff and the underlings that served them, slaved away in cramped quarters on all six floors, staring at computer screens for twelve hours a day. The personnel occasionally mixed in some work between bouts with computer games (or porn when they could get around the filters).

Buck's digs were better. His office, housed on the top floor, afforded a spacious view of the facilities. The space might better be described as a basketball arena-sized testament to his ego. It could easily have accommodated an L.A. Laker full court game within its palatial confines.

In an earlier life before the invasion, this well-built, more than half-century old fortress of a structure had housed the executive offices of an Iraqi oil company. Buck held court here meeting daily both with his support staff and with Colonel Harper, who was himself ensconced in a nearby facility in offices just as ornate. Buck enjoyed a close relationship with the colonel.

If you wanted to see Buck, you scheduled an appointment with his nubile young Turkish administrative assistant. Today's big meeting was with Marsh. The agenda item for which Buck had blocked off two hours was Plan B, but Marsh did not need an appointment; he set them.

Simply put, Plan B was to get rich – quickly - and get out. Most people did it with other people's money. You could do that if you had a rich father who would just give it to you. Marsh would do it the old-fashioned way: he would steal it. Marsh no longer had a father, but he did have an uncle: Uncle Sam, who had a war to prosecute and was not watching the store.

As plans go, Plan B was a good one. Marsh's plan contained two differentiators, and both were crucial to its success. Timing, and chaos.

Timing was everything: no heroics, no bleeding it for the last nickel, just snatch and grab, only on a large scale.

As for the element of chaos, both Marsh and Buck knew that government oversight early on took a back seat to constructing roads, bridges, building camps to house both soldiers and civilian support personnel, hauling water, and a thousand other details from morning to night. The government oversight would come, but later, and much too late - if they managed Plan B correctly. By that time, both Marsh and Buck knew that they had to be long gone.

Things had started slowly during the first six months of the war as they put processes and people into place to execute the plan, but the goal had been to siphon off approximately 15% of the total, or about

$350 million. And now, as Christmas of 2004 was near, they were getting close.

They had just short of $200 million stashed in a small, private Kuwaiti bank. Buck had set up the account with a small Kuwaiti contractor, Jabil Khan, who both he and Marsh knew from earlier contracts. They had a track record with him on smaller jobs and knew what he could do.

That said, as Reagan would say, it was trust but verify. Not trusting Khan as far as he could throw him, Marsh had Buck traveling to Kuwait regularly to monitor the money. For his part, Khan would wind up with thirty percent of the total proceeds, payable at the end. That was a cool $105 million, leaving Marsh and Buck with almost a quarter of a billion dollars.

Not including their salaries and bonuses, of course.

Marsh was on the phone to discuss revision A to Plan B, for Hammer had just thrown a wrench into the plan. Neither thought that Hammer would sell the company at this point. Why sell when the government gave you the mother lode of all cost-reimbursable contracts? You milked it for all it was worth. Nobody was stupid enough to walk away from a gold mine. Were they? Well, to Marsh and Buck, Hammer was doing just that.

The phone call was to discuss just that possibility and the fallout that would come. An acquisition would trigger a reconciliation of accounts. With that reconciliation would come the inevitable oversight - both operational and financial audits, not only between companies but with the government bookkeepers poring over everything.

This prospect was something neither Marsh or Buck had anticipated in their "time to market" scenario. Their snatch and grab plan had just become much more complicated.

—~—

LIKE MOST PLANS in life, simpler is better. Marsh and Buck found that to be especially true since many of their support staff were merely going through the motions, just trying to collect a check. Marsh and Buck wanted very little thinking for twelve hours a day. They wanted *just do what I say.*

As soon as they entered Iraq in March of 2003, Marsh and Buck contacted Khan in Kuwait. They needed a ready source of supply, and Khan was it. The plan was to provide Khan with at least sixty-five percent all of the supply business in the form of single-sourced materials.

They instructed Khan to set up dummy corporations, both in Iraq and Kuwait, to provide the appearance of a supply base for the rest. Those suppliers would participate in what would, by all appearances, be competitive bidding to satisfy the government's requirement for competition. In reality, much of that business went to one of the suppliers that Khan had set up.

Subcontract agreements were straightforward. Buck made sure that most of the original contracts went to Khan. Marsh and Buck skimmed off of the top, as was the case for materials purchases. Once those materials were received, Buck or his subordinates would create dummy demand for auto parts, electrical equipment, plumbing supplies, and the like, essentially raping the materials warehouses.

On hand materials were promptly issued out but, instead of being installed on a vehicle, they were stored in containers awaiting the next step in the process. That process required the materials to leave the base. Some of those goods did find their way either to one of the six fixed bases or to one of the nineteen still under construction. Other material - although billed to one of the bases as a cost of goods - was diverted back to Kuwait in the constant churn that was daily life in what could sometimes be described as a madhouse of a war zone/construction site.

In Kuwait, the materials received back from Iraq were stored in Khan's containers - awaiting the next purchase order from Buck's supply chain people to Khan or his dummy corporations - with Khan stashing the proceeds into the private Kuwait bank account. In concept, the assets were kept in a constant state of float, with Marsh and Buck skimming off their share as materials came and went. It was a game as old as civilization itself; an irony not lost on Marsh and Buck, who were running this scam in an area of the globe where the world was purported to have begun.

There were structural weaknesses to the plan. One fundamental problem: nothing left the base without Base Commander Colonel Rick Harper's authorization. It was one reason that the early implementation of their criminal enterprise had been delayed. Fortunately, Khan, after some negotiation, had recently provided the answer to that in the form of a gorgeous female Turkish-Jordanian project manager named Derya Ali, who had been brought to the base ostensibly to coordinate the logistical functions of his business-related activities.

It did not take long for Buck to introduce Derya to Colonel Harper nor, for that matter, for nature to take over. Buck's IT thugs had provided Derya a small camera, attached to her blouse right next to her ample cleavage, to be taken inside of the commander's forty-foot double-wide living container called a hooch. The hide-in-plain-sight aspect of this had been Buck's idea. The colonel never had a chance.

Buck then met informally with the colonel following his initial tryst with Derya. After some fruitful discussions, along with a promised one percent share of the profits - budgeted to be between $3 million and $3.5 million - which would kick back to the colonel, Buck solved the base access issue. Ever the negotiator who was now negotiating from a position of strength, Buck also took that opportunity to settle in to the mausoleum-sized digs that the colonel graciously provided.

Allowing himself to be seduced was a classically stupid move by the colonel, who was someone trained to know better. Colonel Harper would later find out just how stupid he was. However, faced with the photos of Derya with the commander in all sorts of compromising positions, and possible disciplinary action up to and including a court-martial, the one percent kicker not only upped the ante but also eased the pain of a career gone bad.

There was another structural weakness. Running a supply chain with a lot of moving parts in this dynamic desert environment meant keeping track of who was doing what, and when. Individually, each of the components, from purchasing items to moving materials was not difficult, but it was mind-numbing work that required lots of different people with their fingers in the pie. Those "fingers" could get nosy, particularly fingers with lots of time, like twelve hours per day, seven days a week.

Both Marsh and Buck identified that problem early on. To manage around this structural weakness, Buck employed the usual strategy of divide and conquer, set in an environment of fear and intimidation. It was Management 101 from an autocrat's playbook, keeping them pitted against each other to distract them from Buck's real agenda. Keeping them afraid for their job kept them quiet, but the moment they made waves they were terminated. Those that protested further were quietly and confidentially settled out in binding arbitration.

To make this strategy work, even short-term, you needed a micro-manager. It helped if the micro-manager was a psychopath. Buck fit the bill perfectly. Besides being a competent project manager, Marsh knew that Buck could shoot his own grandmother and send out for pizza in the same breath. He had no problem getting rid of people who were of no use to him.

The current supply chain manager, Jim Coleman, was an example of this strategy in action. In his late fifties, Coleman was chosen because he had been laid off as a clerk in a logistics company before the war. Marsh interviewed him in D.C. and found him to be ideal for the position.

Marsh came away from the interview convinced that Coleman was semi-literate but would do as he was told. Buck agreed with Marsh's assessment. After Coleman finally arrived in theater, Buck observed that the man had the IQ of a fence post.

Coleman had never managed anything, but that was okay. A superficially friendly sort who could prattle on endlessly about nothing, he was in way over his head, which was precisely the point. Bush and Marsh were recruiting for someone who could not manage because there were no costs for not executing. They would show him how to fill out some forms. They did not want him looking into their business.

Having never made more than worker-bee wages in his life,

Coleman was now presented with an opportunity to earn more in one year than he did in the previous decade. "Just do as you are told," Marsh instructed Coleman, "and you will be okay." The implicit assumption was that if he did not do what he was told, the pot of gold at the end of the rainbow would evaporate.

Provided with a lofty-sounding title, Coleman asked only who would be his direct reports, and how many people would report to him. Marsh told him that project management managed the people; he only controlled the process. Buck and Marsh did not want anybody leading; they would do the managing, thank you very much. Never having either relevant experience, or knowing enough to question the logic, Coleman was set up to fail.

Coleman smiled his vacant smile and never thought about it again. That is, until things went wrong and his people hung him out to dry. On paper they worked for him, but never reported to him because they sensed that he was an idiot and it was Buck who had the power. This was the game within the game.

The divide-and-conquer/fear-and-intimidation strategy generally did not work well long-term in commercial organizations. Beating on people to get things done while you were pitting them against each other not only sapped morale but also tended to limit the quality of people who were attracted to that work environment. That type of organizational theory also presumed not only options for those abused, as in other opportunities to go elsewhere, but also economic and possibly legal consequences for bad behavior.

Little of that existed here. Cork and Hammer were virtually the only game in town in a foreign country. U.S. law applied, but nobody in the trenches really knew how that worked. Other contractors existed, but most tended to be mirror images of Cork and Hammer's management style. The other contractors were just as bad; they just paid less than Cork and Hammer.

Marsh and Buck both knew that in the cost reimbursable contract world the United States government took the financial risk. The game was to use more stuff, order more stuff, pay for more stuff, and more importantly, get reimbursed for that extra stuff along with a nice profit, even if real demand for that stuff did not actually exist. Their incompetence, in a surreal way, was being rewarded, at least in the short run. Long term, there was a demanding client to whom Marsh and Buck needed to account.

But Marsh and Buck did not care about the long-term because, as the legendary economist John Maynard Keynes would say when discussing economic theory, we are all dead in the long run. Short-term was all that counted; just snatch and grab and run like hell, baby.

Definitions do matter, of course. What with a now pending acquisition of Cork and Hammer, merely defining short-term was changing. It was what they needed to discuss.

CHAPTER 7
Shakedown

—∞—

A WEEK AFTER ACCEPTING his job offer, Frank Davenport touched down in Dubai to a welcoming breeze and warm afternoon temperatures. The drive to where Cork and Hammer had its offices was a short one, about thirty-five minutes on a desert freeway lined with palm trees, but something more impressive stood out against the skyline. As Frank peered out of the window of the van, he was struck by how many building cranes reached towards the sky in this desert oasis.

Dubai was a place where east met west; a meeting place for the ancient trade routes stretching eastward to India, Pakistan, and China, and over to Europe in the west. A rather sleepy place until oil was discovered in 1966, Dubai was now on its way to becoming a Middle East financial hub. In late 2004, perched on the southeastern side of the Persian Gulf and growing almost organically out of an endless sea of brown sand, it was home to some 30,000 industrial cranes, or approximately 25% of the total worldwide.

Dubai struck Frank as a Middle East version of cosmopolitan, but with a sense of impermanence. It was alive with activity, but always with the look and smell of transience. Tourists flew in and flew out. Workers came from disparate parts of the globe to build buildings and work in offices. People traded in oil or entertained, but few seemed to be from there. Maybe that came from the region's roots as a trading hub, but it seemed that most people came to Dubai to get something done; to do something rather than to be something, and once that deed was accomplished, they were gone. Frank Davenport was one of those; one week in Dubai, then onward to Iraq if all went well.

Roll call was at eight the next morning directly after breakfast. Cork and Hammer had chosen a generously described three-star hotel in a rundown section of Dubai as its temporary headquarters. The food, like the drab, worn look of the place, was anything but enticing. The hotel had evidently seen better days, like fifty years ago when its furnishings were new. The halls were dark, the rooms were small, made even more cramped by placing two, sometimes three ex-pats along with their luggage in one room during their week in Dubai.

Frank was getting a crash course in life on a government contract. A scruffy expat with a three-day growth of beard, who looked to have had way too much to drink the night before, began the cattle call. Names were barked out in alphabetical order. The motley crew, assembled from all over the world and dressed in everything from ex-military attire to the ghetto-stylish gang banger bling-bling, was expected to confirm their presence. They all came with different skills; carpenters, plumbers, low-level clerks, and administrators - mostly blue collar. At first blush, Frank appeared to be the white-collar exception in the room.

You did not want to miss roll call. Bleary-eyed, many had used the previous night to become acquainted with some of the local bars in which some had their first, but most likely not their last, encounter with female talent eager to transact "some business". Not surprisingly, a small percentage of the men missed roll call because of a dalliance between the sheets. For them, the price of that seduction was not just sex. It was a ticket home, combined with the lost opportunity of a six-figure income.

With roll call mercifully ending for those who managed to show up on time, the three hundred or so assembled in Dubai for processing were broken into groups. Some disassembled into a conference room for a psychological profile, while others were given a general company orientation. Employment, credit, and more background checks were conducted in another, separate office.

Some of this looked to be make-work, marking time while others of the group were transported to a local Dubai hospital for the all-important physical, a process that would take the better part of the day. Once the medical was completed, they would return, and others would break out and depart for the hospital. This sort of round-robin activity was to consume the entire group for the week until all groups had dotted the eyes and crossed the tees.

Frank's group was scheduled to complete the psychological profile that Monday. The questions were of the standard multiple-choice variety and chosen apparently to separate out the proverbial wheat from the chaff. Semi-normal, or as average as any group who volunteered to wander into an active war zone unarmed would allow for was on one side, with the psychopaths and trained killers on the other. Given that most of the answers were obvious, Frank wondered what it took to fail the test, then he got another look around at those applying pen to paper, and received his response.

"Hey man." Frank looked up to find a well-worn, fat sixty-plus-year-old apparent ex-biker dude with a southern-fried drawl muttering at the muscled mountain of a man next to him who appeared to be intent on deciphering the contents of the psychological test in front of him.

"What do you do, man?" the biker whispered.

"Truck driver," came the answer.

"You got a lot of tattoos, man," the biker dude whispered loudly.

"Yeah, and so what the fuck is your problem with that?" The muscle-bound, close to three-hundred-pound gorilla never took his eyes off of the test.

The biker dude stared at the man's fists which were engraved with some sort of flame-themed artwork. "I hear 'dem Iraqis don't like dose tattoos, man," the biker dude slowly drawled in his confederate states accented English.

"Well, they're just going to have to get used to them, shithead!" The clearly agitated, large primate's low voice resembled a Clint Eastwood character. He was now glaring downward and to his right, making direct eye contact with the much shorter, smaller, and comparatively frail-looking biker.

"Took me seventeen years in prison to get 'em, motherfucker," he snapped, never breaking eye contact with the now thoroughly intimidated biker punk.

Frank made a mental note to check to see if either or both got on the plane to Iraq.

AT ROLL CALL the next morning, the clerk running the medical part of the in-processing called Frank's group for the medical check. An hour later Frank and his group, three-quarters of which seemed to be either from Bosnia or Kenya, were being shuttled to various stations within the hospital, in the process being examined head to toe. A routine exam, or so it seemed.

The next morning at breakfast was a tense time. Both the Bosnians and the Kenyans had gotten word that everybody over the age of forty was going back to the hospital for an additional electrocardiogram test, or EKG. An EKG was a well-validated stress test designed to diagnose coronary heart disease. Rumor was that the exam was not free, although this financial aspect of the physical had never apparently been mentioned to any of the more than two hundred in attendance.

Frank began searching for the Bosnians and the Kenyans and found them together in groups. He grabbed a Kenyan with whom he had dinner the night before and asked what was going on.

"All of us but one is over the age of forty, which means that we need to retake the EKG test," the Kenyan replied.

"Who said that?" Frank asked.

"The Romanian. He will tell you. Are you over the age of forty?"

Frank nodded, in shock.

"He will tell you, for sure. I have to go back to my friends. We do not have $600 each to spend on a test, and we have no insurance, so that means that we have to choose who stays and who goes back home," the Kenyan said sadly, his eyes moist with tears.

"I think I am one of the ones who will need to go back home, and my family now has no money," the Kenyan whispered, almost in shame. "My family spent all of our money on a broker to get me here... and now this. I do not know what I am going to do."

Frank's next stop was the Romanian clerk's office.

"Mr. Davenport, I need to see you," the Romanian uttered, hardly looking up from a pile of papers. "You need to go back to the hospital for a second EKG."

"There is nothing wrong with my EKG," Frank countered evenly, recalling that his EKG done by Larry's buddy in Pensacola was fine.

"Well, the doctors say you need to get it done. You will have to provide your own transportation and pay for it yourself," the Romanian continued, unemotionally.

"Not before I get a second opinion," Frank stated. I want a copy of that EKG, so I can send it to my physician in Pensacola."

Two hours later, he was on the phone to Larry who, dragged out of bed in the middle of the night due to the time difference, confirmed that his EKG seemed normal, just like the other EKG that he had done in Pensacola.

"What do you recommend Larry?!" Frank almost screamed into the phone, more out of frustration than anything. He knew he was losing a sense of his sanity, which was why he valued Larry even more at times like these.

"Everything looks fine, although I am not a doctor. I can ask Darren, my physician buddy, for a formal opinion, but what option do you have even if Darren gives you a clean bill of health? Sounds like that is what they want to do over there, and you are over forty. Do you have the $600 for the test? If not, I can send you some money," Larry said reassuringly, suspecting that Frank's stateside insurance would not cover routine tests in a foreign country.

Frank did not object to an EKG; what he had severe doubts about was *why*. If this was usual, customary and reasonable for every person over the age of forty, why was this set of extra tests not included in the base scope of agreement along with access to a second opinion? It sounded odd. Frank hadn't seen the contract covering the additional medical screenings, of course; neither had the Bosnians nor the Kenyans, so he gave Cork and Hammer the benefit of the doubt. For now.

Five hours and six hundred dollars later, Frank had undergone a second EKG, a running test on a treadmill, and got the same results. This time his paperwork was stamped by the Iraqi doctor "Clear to Fly" meaning that he had passed the medical portion of the induction, and was prepared for departure. Frank's head cleared and he began to relax. That is, until the Romanian grabbed him just after dinner.

"We're not done. I got a call from the hospital and they want you back for some more tests in the morning," the Romanian informed Frank.

"I am clear to fly," Frank explained, his anger rising. He threw a copy of his paperwork onto the Romanian's desk.

"Sorry, you are going back to the hospital. Bring your credit card," the Romanian said, laughing.

Frank glared back at the little Euro prick, steamed at the casual way the Romanian was going about parting him from his money. "So, this is just like the Kenyans and the Bosnians?!"

"Happens every day," the Romanian shot back. "Not sure why Cork and Hammer keeps this hospital around - probably because they kick back. There was another U.S. contractor here that was using these guys at this hospital for medical screenings, but the other contractor terminated this hospital six months into the agreement for shaking down the patients a lot worse than this. They wanted extra blood tests which I am not sure they needed. But the hospital bid in low and now they make it up on the back end by sucking these guys dry."

"It is sad, really, because the Bosnians and Kenyans get shaken down by the labor brokers just to get here, and then they have no clue that they will have to pay these medical tests out of pocket. One or two have insurance that covers this; the rest do not. They are kind of fucked, when you think about it." The Romanian had an air of resignation about him.

"But the system is set up for this. Cork and Hammer get paid a mobilization fee for every mother fucker they bring to Dubai. If they fail the physical, Cork and Hammer just gets paid to mobilize somebody else. You know, if they really cared about these guys, Cork and Hammer would have required that a physical be completed before arrival in Dubai. But this - this is a license to print money, eh?" And with that, the Romanian gave a give-a-shit look that communicated to Frank that the next move was his.

Frank was struck by the irony. In one room, the Romanian was casually discussing what was quite possibly a felony - on a US government contract – in a tone like someone ordering lunch. In another room not ten feet away, men were getting briefed on the Foreign Corrupt Practices Act, a law explicitly forbidding criminal acts overseas.

It's all a bit surreal, he thought. It would be downright humorous if it wasn't happening to him.

"Yeah, I know," he told the Romanian. "I spoke to a Kenyan here today, and he told me the same thing."

And for that brief moment, his life flashed before him. He'd had more than his share of those moments lately. Without the medical clearance, there was no contract, and without a deal he was probably going to lose his real estate to foreclosure, rendering him homeless and jobless, given what the bank had told him in no uncertain terms.

He probably had just enough money to pay for more tests, although if push came to shove, he could borrow from Larry. *But when would it end,* he thought. It was one thing to shake down some destitute Kenyan migrant worker, but the Iraqi doctors in this Dubai hospital had surely assumed they could get more out of a clean-cut American.

"Okay, dude. Here is how this is going to work," Frank leaned into the Romanian, voice low and measured. Frank had been in a few negotiations and felt that the paperwork gave him at least some leverage to elevate this situation. As to exactly where he was going to get justice in this second-rate company in a third world sand dune of a nation-state, he was not sure.

"You tell your boss that I am good to fly. I have the fucking paperwork. I am cleared to fucking fly - signed by your Iraqi fucking doctor - so I am not going to undertake any more fucking tests."

Frank rarely swore this profusely. Growing up, he never in his life heard his father swear. The man could look right through you when he spoke, and get a point across without four-letter words. His dad had his own way of making a point. Frank had long ago concluded that he would never measure up to his father in that way.

"And so, you have a decision to make. You can send me into theater right fucking now, or you can send my ass right back to the States on the next flight out. The fucking shakedowns are over. And, by the way, I do not stop until I get to the U.S. Attorney's office in Pensacola. Got it, dude?" Frank did not know if or where there was a U.S. Attorney's office in Pensacola, and at this point, he didn't care.

Two days later he was wheels up, leaving the desert of Dubai for a similar desert in Iraq. Contract in hand, and with a new lease on life, he had faxed over a copy to the bank. Frank was thinking he was beginning to see the light at the end of the tunnel. But given what he had just been through in the medical shakedown, Frank hoped the bright light was not an oncoming locomotive. Unfortunately for Frank, there was a locomotive, and his name was Kenny Buck.

CHAPTER 8
'Ole Kinney-boy

—∞—

"How's 'ole Kinney-boy?" It was Marsh on the speaker phone to Kenny Buck. Marsh had taken to calling Buck "'ole Kinney-boy" after George W. Bush, then Governor of Texas, began referring to Enron CEO Ken Lay that way. This was at a time in the nineties when Enron was riding high, at one time the seventh largest U.S. corporation before it imploded in an accounting and corporate corruption scandal, resulting in bankruptcy in late 2001. Now Buck would own that moniker, fake Texas accent and all, for Marsh was a D.C. liberal who loved to mock Bush by deliberately butchering his Texan twang.

"Just another day in paradise, Bill," Buck responded.

Having just ended a meeting with his direct reports, Kenny Buck settled his six-foot-five-inch frame into the chair behind his desk. Alone in his basketball court-sized office, his voice reverberated on the sixteen-foot high stone walls as if he was in some sort of canyon which, in a sense, he was.

At fifty-one, born in a small town in south Louisiana to itinerant, sharecropping folks that always had to move to get work and stay one step ahead of the law, Kenny never knew any stability in his life growing up. Always on the run, Buck had never gained any real respect. He felt like he came out of the womb hustling. It was the only way he knew how to live.

Now he had made it, or so he thought, and he had the office to prove it, not to mention an entire camp kissing his ass every day for twelve hours each day, seven days a week. Buck didn't just like it, he got off on it.

This was Marsh's first official chance to brief Buck on what he knew about the proposed sale of Cork and Hammer. He and Buck had been exchanging emails, but they had been careful not to transmit in a way that could be intercepted at IT and fed back to Case Hammer. Marsh set up a secure line at the beginning of the war so that he and Buck could chat, but nothing was foolproof, and so they usually kept communication to a bare minimum.

Marsh compensated for the lack of instant communication with frequent trips to Iraq. It was there that both he and Buck would stand out in the open courtyard, outside of Buck's office in the quiet, after dinner when the temperature was more comfortable and the minions had gone back to their individual hooches. In their private place, they could discuss issues like money transfers with less of a chance of being overheard. Marsh was booking a plane to Iraq, needing just such a meeting with Buck. He urgently wanted to convey not only what he knew, more importantly things Marsh did not know, but also how he wanted Buck to adjust in light of the proposed acquisition.

The difference between a leader and a manager, it is often said, is that managers do things right while leaders do the right things. Marsh had no illusions about Buck being a leader, but he knew the micro-manager in the man. What worried him most was that under pressure from a curveball like this, Buck would start doing the wrong things. Doing the wrong things could raise oversight questions. Unforced errors were something that neither could afford.

Marsh had correctly sensed that Buck's life was flashing before him as things appeared to spiral out of control. They were not; at least not yet. Buck feared that while they had been cautious in constructing their little criminal enterprise, if things went wrong, and they always seemed to go bad in the blink of an eye, then Buck wanted to begin planning for the phase-out immediately, ready to cut and run.

Marsh took a more sanguine, big picture view from his vantage point at corporate headquarters in the States. As Marsh saw it, both Cork and Hammer and the client's attention was elsewhere; it was focused not only on the existing sites but also on the additional twenty-five sites. Marsh wanted to leverage all of the barely contained chaos of the war zone to hit their financial targets, even if it meant making some small adjustments - like regularly firing people to create a diversion. And so, despite their mutual qualms about discussing an issue like this on the phone, they agreed to a short meeting.

—∞—

MARSH AND BUCK had a history. They met when Buck worked at another contractor, before Cork and Hammer. Marsh found much to be impressed with in Buck. Unlike many project managers, Buck had actually both read and understood the contract, an impressive feat given that agreements like these could run to twenty-one hundred pages. Many of his peers, unlike Buck who had obtained some education at LSU before dropping out to get a job on a shrimp boat, were at best marginally educated, and at worst functionally illiterate, not unlike Jim Coleman.

More importantly, Buck could "manage the white spaces" in an agreement, which usually was not all that tough to do in this environment. The specifications within contracts like these tended to be poorly written by dull-witted bureaucrats who just wanted to get the work off of their desk. Many times, they were people that, in the rush to war, failed to understand either the project or the war-zone environment.

The resultant ambiguous specifications - those "white spaces" - were a bit like venereal disease; they were the gift that keeps giving to a contractor - as in opportunities for change orders. It was an old game; bid low, and get well on changes. Buck was good at converting those opportunities into additional revenue streams for the company.

But there was more to Buck, much more; the other side of Buck that Marsh had kept hidden from Case Hammer. For while Buck was good at what he did, he had come to Marsh as damaged goods. Growing up on the run, and now, living life on projects in the middle of nowhere could be hard. It aged you fast. There were long hours, clients that frequently gave conflicting instructions, and the unrelenting pressure to perform. As a contractor, you ultimately had to produce. Decades of this life had taken its toll; first on his marriage at a very young age, then on his health in the form of drug addiction, and finally on his job.

Kenny Buck had become addicted to cocaine as a young adult while shrimping on the Gulf Coast. Now, thirty years later, despite a substantial six-figure income which was common on projects like these, abusing coke drained him financially. Buck had been terminated from his last job by somebody that did not take kindly to his cocaine-fueled psychopathic personality. It was then that they discovered Buck running a somewhat smaller skimming operation to feed the drug beast. He was officially allowed to quietly resign "to spend more quality time with his family" so as not to raise the government's suspicions. Issues like this could have opened the company up to back charges for the skimming operation, at a minimum, were their client to discover what had happened.

Now broke and unemployed, Buck had been living in a drug rehabilitation facility when Marsh called. Despite that, Marsh called because he knew that Buck was that rare combination of both manager and career criminal. Most criminals wound up either dead or warehoused in prison because they could not manage eight ducks across the road, let alone mastermind a criminal enterprise. Most managers made poor criminals either because they did not think - their crime being a crime of passion - or they were never bred to think criminally. The exceptions to that rule wound up in places like Wall Street or in the defense industry, where both the incentives and support structure for fraud were built into the system.

Kenny Buck had no remorse for what he had done; predators never do. He was back in the game, and that was all that mattered. Marsh, his protector, had given him the opportunity, and so Buck would do anything that Marsh asked. He was looking to get well on this project, and if he had to step on a few people along the way, like Colonel Harper, well, the rules were somebody else's problem.

Buck absolutely should have gone to prison for what he had done. But he had the memory of an NFL cornerback who gave up the winning score. As in, no memory at all. Like the cornerback, Buck had just gotten burned at his previous job. Now with Cork and Hammer, his sole focus was on the next play. He was determined more than ever not to screw this one up.

—∞—

"Let me brief you on what I just learned," Marsh stated. "I do not want to be on this call long, for obvious reasons. We can talk more when I get into theater. Hammer has told me in no uncertain terms that he is going to sell. In fact, he is in negotiations now with BLTVDef."

"For sure?" Kenny had been in a sort of denial, but this was huge. Like everyone else, he had heard the rumors, but this was for real. Marsh would not call just to kid around on an issue so central to their plans.

"Oh, no bullshit for sure," Marsh said. "And by way, that is confidential, so do not put it out to your staff. A lot could go wrong between then and now."

"Yeah, sure. But how do we want to handle our own gig..." Buck stopped mid-sentence, allowing Marsh to continue on with his train of thought.

"Well, they have not reached a deal on the overall value to the company, but they are getting close. Once that happens, then things tend to move pretty fast. BLTVDef absolutely can do the deal, but they will need to run the traps with Uncle Sam to make sure that everybody is on board. Then there is the due diligence, which is where the accountants and lawyers make their money."

"What about us? Any keepers? Are they going to offer anybody a job? Have they discussed it?" Buck wondered if anybody was going over to the new entity.

"Some back-office types, yeah," Marsh replied. "They have not discussed me. And they will evaluate the project once they take over, but don't get your hopes up. BLTVDef is a huge corporation. They have their own folks and their own way of doing business. You interested?"

Marsh was laughing at the apparent irony of Buck, a cocaine cowboy from a mom and pop shop working in a buttoned-down, large, high-tech Fortune 500 company.

"Fuck no. I just want out - are you kidding?" Buck laughed out loud. "When do they meet next?"

"Next week, just before Christmas. Dunno if they can hammer out all of the details by then, but we will see. I guess that, if this goes down, it will be six months at the max to wrap this up so we will need to push up the exit strategy by some three to six months."

"When are you planning to come into theater?" Kenny asked, concerned that the planning needed to start.

"Put together an updated exit strategy. I will get out there right after the first of the year, say the tenth of January. Let's talk then. Okay?"

Marsh continued. "Meantime, get with Khan and make sure where we are with the money in the Kuwait account. We are going to have to work up some projections on just how much we will have by, say, June or so. I want to make sure that we hit our numbers. If we are running short, let's discuss what else we can push out on convoys to Kuwait without arousing suspicion."

Marsh wanted to continue to execute. Buck thought otherwise. "What do we tell Khan?" he asked, wanting to know how to position this. He did not need things leaking out through Khan to Derya, but if they had to adjust their plans on the fly, Kuwait and the money was where it started.

"Use the Christmas holiday to get with Khan. I assume that he is there, correct?"

"Yeah, the last time that we spoke in Kuwait, he said that he would be there during the holiday," Buck replied, smiling to himself. He conveniently left out that a month prior, during one of his frequent trips to Kuwait, he and Khan had been taking turns banging six

Chinese whores aboard Khan's yacht in the harbor when the matter had come up.

"Okay. Just tell Khan that we are running some updated projections, given the new scope of work," Marsh said, referring to the additional twenty-five bases that had been just added to the original twenty-five. "Tell him we wanted to understand the delta between where we are, and where those new sites take us."

"Got it, yeah... but why don't we just cut and run, Bill? Just simply get to Kuwait. Resign, and pop smoke?" Buck did not want the risk. They had enough money in Kuwait to make everybody involved very rich right now.

"Yeah, good point," Marsh said. "But right now, everybody is asleep. Let dead dogs lie. We can always cut and run later, once we get closer to our numbers, or if things heat up. Until then, just keep counting the money and banging those whores on Khan's yacht. Do not worry."

Marsh tried to sound reassuring, but Buck's head was spinning a mile a minute. Marsh wasn't keeping things quiet in theater; Kenny Buck was! On some days, dealing with those "dead dogs" was like playing whack-a-mole. The little voice inside of Buck was telling him that this was a mistake.

"Talk to you about this next week. I am out." And with that, Marsh ended the call. That call was short, but not brief enough; others were listening. Inquiring minds wanted to know more about Khan's money. Much more.

CHAPTER 9
Let's Make a Deal

—m—

On the second day after Christmas, 2004, Jim Witt pulled his SUV off of Old Dominion Drive and headed north onto Chain Bridge Road in McLean, Virginia, towards Cork and Hammer's offices for a 9:30am meeting. Witt was the program manager for the team leading up the acquisition of Cork and Hammer. He hoped this meeting would be the culmination of some preliminary negotiations between the parties.

Jim Witt had worked at BLTVDef for a little more than twenty years. Like most senior management at the company, he came up through the engineering department. Unlike most engineers, Witt was more of a political animal than a technocrat, and so he decided early on to move into finance and eventually into program management, after receiving his MBA at the University of Virginia.

Witt knew little about Cork and Hammer before the war. Traveling to various locations supporting his equipment product lines early in his career, he serviced equipment in remote places where the CIA had front companies in facilities operated by Cork and Hammer. But BLTVDef was high-tech, classified computer hardware and software. You did not get higher tech than BLTVDef. Cork and Hammer was just the opposite; you did not get lower tech than Case Hammer's company.

What they had in common was that the United States government was, for all intents and purposes, the only customer for each. This was a condition the economists called monopsonistic - many suppliers, only one buyer. It didn't matter if your labor-intensive business was doing millions of dollars per year (as was the case with Cork and Hammer), or multi-billions in an entirely different industry (as was the case with BLTVDef). When Uncle Sam spoke, you listened, because Uncle Sam had you by the balls. At this point in 2004 and still early in the Iraq war, Jim Witt and BLTVDef had been listening for about eight months. Now they planned to do much more than look.

Witt liked what he saw. Most acquisitions were about valuing both hard and soft assets, along with associated synergies. To be sure, this was anything but a typical deal, but there were obvious synergies. BLTVDef was a hardware-driven, capital-intensive company with an associated service revenue stream that it derived from its equipment business, whereas Cork and Hammer obtained its revenue from low-tech logistics, moving stuff from A to B in places nobody knew anything about.

Cork and Hammer, although small and low-tech, was not a startup. They had a well-established book of business that threw off steady free cash flow with little or none of the shareholders' capital invested. And now with the war ramping up, the potential for free cash flow was on steroids, because Cork and Hammer's Iraq contract was cost reimbursable. Hammer and Marsh had negotiated the deal of a life time: a cost-plus award fee contract to provide logistics services in Iraq.

That contract allowed Hammer's company to be reimbursed in two different ways. One, they were reimbursed at a base rate of 2% on top of all allowable, allocable and reasonable costs incurred. Separately, they negotiated an additional award fee that could reach 7% annually, depending upon performance. The longer the war, the longer that annuity stream lasted.

How long, nobody really knew but the trend was up, and the timing was right. It was ultimately an easy sell to BLTVDef's top management because they were buying a service business that their client wanted them to buy, and would pump free cash flow into their capital-intensive hardware business.

Witt knew that he would have to replace the existing management, whom he regarded as nothing but mostly sub-par amateurs. Witt had guys with security clearances that would make the jump - buttoned-down, corporate types that he could depend upon - so no problem. Jim Witt also knew that Marsh and his merry little band of pirates were barely holding it together. He might be able to use Marsh in the short term, maybe sign him up as part of the deal. He would kick that one around a little more before he made a decision.

But, as he looked further into the deal, something just did not add up. Jim Witt wanted to ascertain why Case Hammer was shopping his company around just after landing a mega deal. By all accounts, it was a deal that would deliver an excellent return on invested capital. What he found was that, in the rush to war, the government had developed a sense of buyer's remorse. Well-placed sources confirmed that Cork and Hammer knew the business and had been ready - even eager - to mobilize in 2003, but it did not have either the deep pockets, or the ability to raise vast amounts of capital quickly. It also lacked what the government guys wanted in terms of top tier management.

In short, the boys on the Hill, at Langley, and in the Pentagon felt that Cork and Hammer had outlived its usefulness. It had been the small, reliable, low-cost producer who could mobilize quickly and get Uncle Sam into a theater without asking questions. With potential further expansion into Afghanistan, Iran, and possibly Pakistan, the government needed a much more stable company.

Like Cork and Hammer, BLTVDef had submitted a bid in the run-up to the war but was blown out of the water on price. Moreover, because they were newcomers to the business, by the time they put together a plan to get mobilized, the Iraqis would be throwing flowers at America's feet like France in 1944, and the war in Iraq would be over. Time-to-market was never their strong suit. But once on a path, BLTVDef was hard to beat.

Neither side discussed it much officially at the outset of the deal - that would come later - but there was another side to the synergies. That was the black box element of the transaction. Cork and Hammer provided the logistics and facilities for CIA front operations all over the world but lacked the secure systems integration capabilities in which

BLTVDef excelled. BLTVDef provided military hardware and software used mostly by the secret squirrels in both the Pentagon, at Langley, and at State. Merging the two, an unintended consequence of the war, created the perfect high-tech, global listening post. Those were the synergies that were pushing the prime customer of both companies into confidentially, but not so gently, facilitating this shotgun marriage

Witt knew one other thing as he sat down next to Case Hammer, muffin in one hand and a cup of black coffee in the other. Price was not going to be the issue here. If negotiations were driven chiefly by the three major elements: price, performance, and/or delivery, he was directed by senior management to focus on the latter, just get the deal done. He was not there to squeeze every last nickel out of this transaction, although he felt that Case Hammer probably would. This was, after all, Hammer's curtain call. Nor was he concerned about Hammer's team performance going forward. By the time he was done reshaping the company, it would be unrecognizable to Cork and Hammer veterans.

It was going to be all about delivery. The client wanted to expand the war, but they were not going to do it on a shoestring. They wanted deep pockets. They wanted professional management, technical capabilities, and they wanted them now. Less – as in time spent negotiating what for BLTVDef was small stuff, with a yesterday business - was definitely more here.

"Good morning, Jim. I think you know everybody around the table." Case Hammer gestured to the others in the conference room. In addition to Hammer and Bill Marsh, the attorneys for both sides were present, as was Valery Jenkins, the corporate attorney for the Cork Trust. The late Charley Cork's family trust owned twenty-five percent of the stock. The Cork trust was essential to doing the deal, and it had been on board from the beginning. With its twenty-five percent of the company, Hammer's thirty percent was more than enough to do the deal for this closely held corporation.

As with most things in life, there frequently comes a moment of truth. And so it was with this negotiation; a moment where both parties would definitely decide that they were going to do this deal. This was it.

These formalized business acquisition meetings had been held in confidence for more than a month now and had proceeded to a stage where the lawyers negotiated an agreement under which BLTVDef would purchase the assets of Cork and Hammer. Under the terms of the Asset Purchase Agreement, BLTVDef would buy the assets only, not the liabilities, for an amount to be agreed by the parties. It was BLTVDef's way of insulating itself from any land mines discovered in due diligence post-deal. The liabilities would be Hammers to resolve.

"Let's get right to it. As I see it, we have essentially two issues remaining to close this deal. The first one revolves around the valuation of Cork and Hammer. The second revolves around any compliance issues discovered post-signing but before close. On that last issue, how do you propose to handle it, Case?" Witt looked at Hammer intently.

In typical deals, that was a seller issue. However, since Cork and Hammer's principal assets - virtually its only assets - were government contracts, any previously undisclosed liabilities would be of interest to not only BLTVDef but also to Uncle Sam. Hammer knew that.

"We have discussed that here. What we suggest is this: let's get through the due diligence, government compliance and the like. As we get closer to getting this deal done, we will get a better feel for the estimated residual liabilities. We do not believe this is an issue," Hammer stated calmly but briefly, glancing at Marsh.

"We can agree to keep Cork and Hammer open in a non-operating mode, on paper only, with an agreed amount in funding on the balance sheet to offset the prospective liabilities. Then, as we mutually further quantify the liabilities, we can draw down the funding. But once we determine that set of liabilities, we want a firm ceiling. You okay with that?" Hammer stared back at Witt.

Both parties had an interest in a hard ceiling. Neither wanted second-guessing to set in, on either side. BLTVDef wanted the deal, but did not want to get left holding the bag for issues that did not occur on their watch. Conversely, the last thing Hammer's board wanted was an open-ended fishing expedition. Like BLTVDef, they needed to consummate the deal, especially if they could get that premium and move on. They just wanted some assurance on how high was up. This was where a good relationship with the client was worth its weight in gold, because both sides would need the client's OK on the deal.

"I can take that back to the board. Give me some time to work the traps at HQ, and I will get back to you on that. Let's talk valuation," Witt said smoothly, communicating that this could be a dead issue.

Cork and Hammer's worth was comprised of the present value of its future income streams. Before the war, that value totaled $3.57 a share based upon fairly predictable yearly earnings from its CIA front operations. Now, the income stream from the Iraq war had doubled Cork and Hammer's revenue in just one year, and that skewed its valuation. If peace broke out suddenly, the assessment of the company became one number; decades of war all throughout the Middle East - a far more significant amount.

"The board is prepared to accept $6.93 a share to sell," Hammer stated calmly, a 94% premium over its current value. War could be a very profitable business.

Witt did not blink. Actually, he would agree with Hammer on the concept that war was good for the bottom line. He had also been running valuation scenarios and thought this was cheap in terms of cost. Unlike Hammer, he defined cost not as an accountant would - the price on an invoice - but as an economist would - in terms of opportunity - and he saw a lot of it.

Small guys think small was what he was thinking at that very moment. *That is why they remain small, and other guys get big.* He certainly did not know it then, but Marsh, sitting next to Hammer stone-faced, had been inwardly screaming in rage over that exact sentiment.

Hammer valued the company using the proceeds from his present book of CIA business, in addition to the Iraq contract, whereas Witt had been running scenarios with different assumptions. Those assumptions included a much larger presence in the war in both Iraq and Afghanistan at a minimum, along with Iran and Pakistan, as well as a marginal increase in out-year CIA revenues. Witt also assumed some significant synergies on the computer hardware and software side, synergies that were unavailable to Hammer and his corporate band of buccaneers.

As a standalone business (and he intended to keep it standalone going forward), Witt had it valued at $10.02 a share. This is where size meant something because BLTVDef, with its deep pockets, stable management, access to capital, and high-tech product line extensions protected by its own intellectual property could do what Hammer could not at this point.

BLTVDef could take a small, low-tech company which had just landed the contract of a lifetime and grow it even further, to more than ten bucks per share. That was the opportunity. Shaking his head and closing his eyes to hide the pain of what was transpiring, Marsh would agree, for he separately had run similar scenarios.

"Look, I am pretty sure that you're basing those kinds of valuations on these conflicts going well into the future. If this thing ends tomorrow, we are stuck," Witt countered, failing of course to mention that he had himself done just that in his own valuations. "We can certainly consider a premium, but you are going to have to come down off of those numbers."

Witt was taking a chance. His boss, his board, and most importantly, his client, wanted this deal and was somewhat indifferent to the acquisition cost, given the circumstances. Nevertheless, Witt was aiming lower and so he would not just to cave into Hammer now, although if push came to shove, he would do just that.

"We had this valued at $5.41 a share. Why don't we look at a scenario where we split the difference; say, $6 bucks a share. Can you guys call me back in the next day or so with an answer?" Witt was trying to seal the deal. Something in Hammer's body language told Witt that he had hit the sweet spot. Hammer would never make any money in Vegas at the poker tables.

—⁂—

Visibly upset, Marsh walked into Hammer's office, sat down, and stared at the floor.

"Look, it's not my company, Case... but six bucks a share? Are you really serious? We've talked about this. All we have to do is keep moving forward into Afghanistan, and this is worth thirty or forty percent more. And that is, if you still want to sell." Marsh almost sneered at Hammer, his non-verbal's bordering on insubordination.

"I came here because you needed help in keeping things together during the downturn in the Clinton years. And now that the good times are here, you are jumping ship and leaving us all behind while you cash in," Marsh continued, not letting up.

"But what if Afghanistan or Iran or Pakistan does not ramp up, then what?" Hammer said, waving off Marsh's concerns.

"I have been chasing government contracts all of my life, Dr. Marsh. Paying bills, kissing ass, and staying one step ahead of my cash flow. We are paying 11% on our money now. If we have a single significant compliance issue in this small company, we are in serious trouble. You know how it works. All they have to say is that they are challenging a large invoice all set up in payables, and they do not pay it until the compliance issues are resolved to their satisfaction. That could take months. They could put us under in a New York minute."

Hammer stared at Marsh as the words sank in. Marsh never really understood the burden of having to make a payroll.

"The government is not going to do that," Marsh stammered. "At least, in a war zone. They'd be cutting their own throats."

"Bullshit. They do not have to make a profit. Don't kid yourself," Hammer shot back, the veins almost popping in his forehead.

Marsh conceded that Hammer had a point. "The big picture is that we are running on a shoestring, and you know it; as does the government. We probably could not manage a large operation in Afghanistan, let alone Iran or Pakistan. That's better left to the big boys. An expansion is great, but it can kill you. It's killed more than one company," Marsh said with an air of finality. Were Witt in the room, he would not disagree.

"I spoke to the board, and we have agreed to a special $1 million bonus for you, payable at the close, contingent upon winding down that Iraq project successfully. But it comes with strings," Hammer declared, staring straight at Marsh.

"I do not want any problems with compliance before close. You heard the conversation with Witt. We are going to agree to some sort of sinking fund available in case undisclosed compliance issues crop up; an extra bit of insurance. Your bonus is dollar for dollar tied to that insurance. No bumps in the night and you get the entire amount. And no leaks. I do not want this leaking until we close; just too much sensitive information." Hammer looked directly at Marsh, who stared back.

A million dollars? Marsh thought. *Gimme a break. That was chump change.*

CHAPTER 10
Into the Sandbox

IN THE SPACE of a few weeks the ninety-five passengers who cleared both the medical and background screening in Dubai had received offers of employment. They were going to go to work for a company they had never heard of prior to this, in jobs for which many had no experience. All had left home to do this work, something which the vast majority of American citizens had never done. They had endured a background check and were put through a medical examination with some, such as Frank, subjected to more than one.

Each of those passengers had received an orientation that few would ever remember. Some were forced to submit to a financial shakedown that further strained already tight financial resources. Moreover, they did much of this in a foreign state, and were now about to land in an active war zone unarmed in yet another country, to make more money than they had ever made before. Financially, at least, it didn't get any better than this.

The plane in which they were about to land was not your usual chartered aircraft; say, for instance a Boeing 777. No, this was an old Soviet-era Antonov AN-22. Entering the plane and looking around, Frank was getting a crash course on one reason why the Russians had lost the Cold War. Not only did it lack many of the amenities of a modern commercial aircraft but lots of the on-board equipment was garbage.

Before boarding, Frank noticed while stowing his gear that the tires were not only bald but were borderline flat. Some of the seats had handcrafted wooden backstops to prevent the seats from collapsing backward. The old electric onboard devices - there were no modern electronics that Frank could see - had long since quit working. The seatbelts, such as they were, looked like they had been added on as an afterthought, and the stained seat cushions had long since given up the ghost, so that Frank felt every ounce of turbulence during the flight.

As Frank and the passengers approached the aircraft single-file with their gear, they noticed a little bald man in a sweat-stained brown T-shirt. Wrench in hand, the little bald man had been banging on the engines while swearing to himself in Russian, seeking to induce life into the beast. Frank's co-passengers quickly named the Russian transport pilot Crazy Ivan because he was Russian, and looked slightly crazy. The talk on the aircraft was that Crazy Ivan was chosen for missions like this because he was accustomed to landing transport aircrafts in a war zone using various rolls and twisting motions designed to avoid surface-to-air missiles.

Satisfying nobody but himself that the matter was fixed, Crazy Ivan now became customer service. It turned out that Crazy Ivan was a real-life version of chef, cook and bottle washer: serving ambidextrously as mechanic, pilot, and now steward. His steward role consisted of handing out warm bottles of water at the beginning of the flight.

Sitting in the second row directly behind the entrance door to the cockpit, Frank soon noticed the pilot's bloodshot eyes, then got a good look at what appeared to be an open bottle of vodka sitting next to the co-pilot's chair.

This is great, Frank thought. *I am going to take the ride of my life into a war zone with a drunk Russian pilot in an aircraft that had been made by the best that communism could produce.*

Remarkably, the engines sputtered, then roared to life. Frank would have wagered whatever money he had left that the flight to Baghdad

International Airport would be his last. Entering the airport's airspace approximately two hours and thirty minutes after takeoff from Dubai, the old Antonov bucket of bolts with ninety-five civilians - none of whom had experienced combat before - went into a slow roll on the way down toward the ground in an attempt to dodge anti-aircraft fire. Sitting helplessly in this ancient metal tin can deathbed, Frank instinctively reached for his dysfunctional seat belt and closed his eyes.

"Welcome to Baghdad!" Crazy Ivan announced in a garbled Russian version of English, grinning like a man who had just cheated death once more as he popped open the rear of the aircraft, allowing the passengers access to their gear. As Frank opened his eyes, cold sweat streaming from his brow met the heat of the late afternoon desert sun. A new reality was about to set in for Frank and the other ninety-four who had accompanied him on this journey of a lifetime.

THE TRIP FROM Dubai to Baghdad was more than some of them could take. Until now, everything leading up to this moment had been conceptual in nature; the job offers, the work environment, the sights, sounds, even the smells. But now the cabin door would open, and a new life was about to begin, whether you wanted it or not. Some didn't want it, after all. Della Clark was one of those.

"I ain't getting off of this plane."

An attractive black woman who appeared to be in her early forties, Della sat in the aisle seat next to Frank. Crazy Ivan's war zone landing had left her frozen and unable to speak further. Staring straight ahead, she had the look of someone who had prepared to meet her Maker on the way down. Her chubby black hands were white-knuckled on the back of the seat in front of her, as if that was going to save her.

"Are you sure?" Frank knew little about her other than her name, and that she came from Atlanta. She and Frank had chatted briefly during the three-hour plane ride, but nothing seemed abnormal. Della had asked Frank about his job. She was going to be a logistics clerk; was he looking forward to the subcontracts job? Frank had been too deep in thought to process anything more than a surface conversation with Della, so when she froze it caught him by surprise.

"I am scared, baby," she finally muttered. "I just want to go back to the States. Now."

Frank wasn't sure what to do next. He was not in charge. Worse yet, there did not seem to be anybody in charge. The Romanian HR dude had escorted the ninety-five passengers as a group all the way through passport control in Dubai. He had micromanaged the ticketing, the baggage, and made sure that everybody got to the gate save for the inevitable few stragglers who had gotten drunk in a bar that night and missed both the bus to the airport, and the flight out. The Romanian had checked everybody off on a list and then said a perfunctory goodbye in broken English.

The plane had otherwise cleared and was now silent, leaving only Frank and Della staring at Crazy Ivan.

"She does not want to leave the plane," Frank called over to Crazy Ivan, who had just placed the last of the luggage onto the tarmac, not sensing the little drama that was unfolding in the front set of seats on the otherwise empty plane.

Frank had no idea how Crazy Ivan was going to resolve this, since Crazy Ivan was obviously getting ready to taxi the plane around on the tarmac to its final resting place. He could leave Della there, but she was in a visible state of shock. At that point, two other Russians arrived. From the looks of them, Frank assumed, they had orders to clean the plane. The Antonov appeared as if it hadn't been cleaned since the mid-sixties.

Frank lightly touched Della's hand and motioned for her to follow him. He stepped gently by her and grabbed a small bag that he had stowed under the seat.

"They want us to leave the plane. Let me at least get you to HR." He removed her still clutched hands from the seat in front of her and guided her towards the entrance way.

It was a good thing that they were in a group. As Frank and Della entered the airport with Della holding onto Frank, they both noticed the bullet shell casings that still lay on the floor, along with the bullet holes scarring the main entrance way where their group was forming a single line, attempting to clear Passport Control. Della's eyes grew wide at the bullet holes, sensing that this was no joke; there really was a war going on here. Her grip on Frank eventually loosened as she realized that all of the passengers seemed to be going through this together. She hadn't gone crazy after all.

It was here that the group met their HR representative, a cheerful Kosovar named Lavdim Sojeva, whose job it would be to get Frank's contingent through Passport Control to the baggage, then onto a bus bound for Camp Bradley. Lavdim expertly muscled the passport stamping through the Iraqi clerks inside of the airport, all of whom seemed unsure of how the process was working, but took pains not to cause issues. In minutes, the passports were rubber-stamped, and the new arrivals were on their way to pick up their bags.

"Lavdim, she wants to go home," Frank explained to the smiling Kosovar while unbuckling Della's grasp of Frank's forearm. She had been holding on so tight that it had begun to throb in pain. Della nodded in silent agreement.

"Yeah, we get that a lot. Twenty percent of all of the contractors that are put on a plane to Iraq, especially those from the U.S., never get off of the plane. She is in shock. I will take her to the HR office when I am done here, and we will process a ticket for her back to the States. Thanks for helping her get here."

Twenty percent? Frank let that sink in for a minute.

That was the last that Frank thought that he would ever hear or see of Della. Camp Bradley awaited.

Frank stared out of the window of the bus at the barren, moon-scoped Iraqi desert landscape during the thirty-minute drive from the airport to Camp Bradley. The weather was only slightly warm but predictably sunny this Iraqi winter day. That was good, since Frank and the others were wearing almost fifty pounds of personal protective gear, including a flak jacket. Moreover, the old school buses had no functioning air conditioning.

The drive had been just long enough to allow Frank to drift off to sleep. Now, the jolting of the bus and the screeching of the brakes told him that they had arrived at the camp's main checkpoint which, for security purposes, was a good two hundred yards from the main gate.

The third country national bus driver got out. He was replaced by American soldiers who instructed the entire contingent to depart the bus. They followed the soldiers into a small shed where each of the passports was matched to an itinerary. Each of the bags was painstakingly hand-searched for contraband, then Frank and his comrades were issued ID badges.

The camp sat on about two hundred acres of dry, flat, barren, sand swept real estate on the outskirts of Baghdad. It housed some twenty-two hundred civilians, not all employed by Cork and Hammer, but all of which were devoted to providing base support operations. The camp perimeter was encased by both barbed wire and twelve-foot high steel reinforced, blast-proof portable barriers made from concrete that were called T-Walls.

The buses lurched back to life an hour later, carrying Frank and his group from the main gate into the camp. They parked just outside of a set of containers with a "Billeting" sign attached. Billeting was where both expats and third country nationals were assigned a room while on camp. The billeting containers were a beehive of activity. Some of that had to do with new hires, although this time of the year, most of it had to do with the holidays.

Frank gazed in wonder at the scene. This was not your typical corporate headquarters. The minions exiting the bus (and all of them were minions, senior management had its own separate process) were issued living containers which had no indoor plumbing. Ex-pats were placed either two or four to a container. Many had just enough room in which to sleep on a cot.

Lower level management fared somewhat better. They received individual, albeit dry (lacking indoor plumbing) twenty-foot containers. Only the in-camp aristocracy – in this case, the senior staff - received first-class accommodations, which were double-wide forty-foot containers with indoor plumbing.

But for the little people, toilet and shower facilities were separate and not always close. Getting to them was sometimes a hundred-yard trek at night in a darkened camp lit only by individual flashlights.

Frank received shared accommodations in a trailer with three other ex-pats, two of whom had gone home for the holidays. Unfortunately, those accommodations would not come available for a day or so. In the interim, he would be placed in group accommodations. It was an adjustment, coming recently from a thirty-five-hundred square foot house in a beautiful subdivision in Cleveland, but this would not be the last time that he would have to adjust.

Camp Bradley had four large, pre-existing six-story stone buildings around which all other activity circulated. Those buildings, with offices like Kenny Buck's monster digs, housed the senior project management staff, including the colonel and his oversight team that supported both Camp Bradley and the external sites. The Army kept a small set of trailers, otherwise known as containers or hooches, nearby. Those containers housed some support staff, but the containers were reserved mostly for meetings with dignitaries visiting the base. The management directly underneath received their own trailers for offices, while the minions were allowed to share desk space in tight, shared office containers for their twelve hours per day shift.

Military operations, where most of the troops were housed, were directly adjacent to the camp. Travel between co-existing facilities usually occurred with inter-camp buses that ran continuously, stopping at designated places throughout the site. Camp Bradley had a typical base exchange called a PX where most common household goods were purchased. It had a twenty-four-hour gym, a motor pool, a laundry and a dining hall. In short, it was a self-contained, modest home away from home, normal for most military soldiers deployed to a war zone, but totally alien to Frank and other civilians who had never been up close and personal with military life.

Frank's living container, like that of all of the non-executives, was located a short distance to the east of the project management offices. To the west, almost the same distance from the project management offices, were the warehouse operations, along with the motor pool, laundry, PX, dining hall, and gym. A seven-hundred-man camp housing third-country nationals was built directly in between the operations area and the non-executive containers, but almost one hundred yards to the south of the project management offices.

Civilian and military vehicles also traveled an outer ring which traversed the camps, allowing access to both sets of operations. The roads were temporary; nothing more than gravel, sometimes nothing more than dirt. Almost everything that you needed was close, not more than a thirty-minute walk to everything on camp It was a self-contained world.

For most civilians like Frank, this was akin to entering another nation-state; actually, a nation-state within a nation - in this case, Iraq - but with its own rules and regulations. The U.S. military was an all-volunteer force of approximately one million three hundred thousand soldiers in a nation of three hundred twenty-plus million. China had a more substantial military presence; Walmart employed as many or more people.

In many countries, the military was deployed within the state; like China, for security purposes. By comparison, the U.S. military was deployed outward in more than one hundred fifty countries worldwide, with more than a quarter of a million at any time physically located outside of the U.S. Those who were stationed inside the U.S. were, for the most part, stationed either in military bases in the south or west and in locations typically not near large population areas. Entering that world as a civilian, particularly as a contractor on an army base in an active war zone, was a learning experience.

—m—

Frank's plane was not the only one to arrive on camp that day, so the housing queue was longer than getting in to see a rock concert in the States. Everything seemed to be hurry up and wait.

Frank sat in a place in the shade, his luggage, computer bag, and fifty pounds of personal protective gear parked next to him. As he hunkered down for what was going to be a long stay, his attention was drawn to the noise apparently coming from the laundry next to the billeting office. Frank could hear shouting; mostly a female's voice, some of it loud and not all of it in English, or at least English that he could understand.

Not having much else to do, and with a lot of time to kill, Frank left his gear in the care one of his fellow passengers so he could go ascertain the origin of the shouting. As he opened the door to the laundry, he observed what he later learned were five Filipino ladies. There was an older white man and a middle-aged black woman. They were all dressed in T-shirts, jeans, and tennis shoes, their ID cards hung from their necks and flapped in the wind as they engaged in a heated argument.

The older man carried himself with the look of an indifferent observer. He was trying hard to position himself as somehow above the fray, even though the ire was clearly directed at him. Seeing Frank enter and not knowing who he was, the voices immediately modulated, although the issue apparently remained.

The forty-something black lady, a foot shorter and almost one hundred pounds lighter than the rumpled white guy, was standing toe to toe with him.

"Look, Jim. There is nothing in the specification about ironing some State Department shithead's underwear. I do not care what his title is. He could be the Ambassador, or Paul *fucking* Bremer - I do not care. And we do not do dry cleaning. This is a war zone laundry. We wash and dry clothes. We have washers and dryers; nothing else, and you know that. If you want that prick's underwear ironed and his fifteen hundred-dollar suits dry-cleaned then we need more equipment and more people. And who the hell wears fifteen hundred-dollar suits to a war, anyway? I am not afraid to tell Buck all of this! Wanna go see him right now?"

"Well, but we are going to have to do it. Just work up some pricing for me." The white guy with the give-a-shit attitude turned to Frank. "And who are you?"

"Frank Davenport, the new subcontract administrator. And who is Paul Bremer?"

"Jim Parrish. I am the contracts manager on base. Bremer was head of the Coalition Provisional Authority, or CPA. They ran Iraq until the end of June, but he is gone now. Iraq has an interim government in place, such as it is."

Frank shook hands all around. At about six foot two inches and at least two hundred and thirty-five pounds, Parrish was probably in his late thirties to early forties, but he looked beaten up, much older than that. Overweight and out of shape from lack of exercise, he had a stoop to his shoulders which gave the impression that he was carrying the weight of the world on his prematurely aging shoulders.

"And I am Joyce Bailey; I manage the laundry." The black woman smiled at Frank, but when she turned to Parrish, her look darkened considerably.

Joyce's voice elevated. "I go into a meeting with the colonel, and he is like 'what the fuck; why aren't we doing dry cleaning'? And he is bitching me out in front of Buck and Taylor because we did not iron some pinhead's underwear. In a fucking war zone. So, when did we get a formal notice to proceed from the client on the dry cleaning?"

"About a week ago." Parrish grinned sheepishly.

"Did you notify us? Do you see any dry-cleaning equipment here?" Joyce wasn't giving an inch. "And yeah, I can get an ironing board and we can get an iron from Baghdad or Kuwait or the PX, but I have no people to sit around and iron laundry all day."

Frank was speechless.

"Well, they are not supposed to do that. They just cannot tell us to do it," Parrish countered.

But before he could continue further, Joyce reached up and grabbed Parrish's ID badges, hollering at him while pointing to the US flag which was prominently displayed on his ID badge.

"They are the fucking government. They can do what the fuck they want within the scope of an agreement on government contracts. It's called the Changes clause. And we have to comply, Jim. I know that much. Hell, my husband - now ex-husband after I caught him giving some fat Pinay chick with big tits the high hard one over in Subic Bay - did contracts for the Navy. Here I am running the freaking laundry... and I have to tell you what to do!" The sarcasm dripped out of her mouth.

"Well, we'll just get Frank to subcontract it out. Huh, Frank?" Parrish looked over at Frank, trying to enjoin the visitor into a conversation with which Frank had no intention of getting involved.

Frank looked down at the sand, trying to avoid eye contact with Joyce. He was beat, and this was a little too much information. He just wanted his room.

But Joyce just would not let up; the issue was clearly getting the better of her.

"Look, Jim if you do not want to manage the contract, just go back to selling used cars in Bakersfield. When I get written direction from your office telling me to do this, I will, to the extent that I can." Her look had an air of resignation, as if to say that she'd had it this with this guy who just would not get her point.

With that, Joyce closed the door to the laundry, with Parrish and Frank - mouth agape - on the outside of the laundry door, but not before all of the Filipino girls that worked there and who were witness to this little encounter began laughing among themselves.

—∾—

PARRISH AND FRANK strolled over to where Frank had left his luggage. The line had not moved appreciably.

Frank turned to Parrish. "You sold used cars before the war, Jim?"

"Yeah, sold used cars while working through law school. Then I couldn't pass the bar so I went back to selling. I took this gig to pay for student loans. They took me because I had a law degree." Parrish studied the ground while he spoke, evidently not proud of what he had become.

Frank reflected back on some of the corporate lawyers he had worked with on some of the acquisitions he did in marketing, and some of the corporate supply chain agreements. Those guys were very sharp, well-focused, and would fight over the placing of a comma in an agreement because a specific location could bring about a different meaning. He could never see Parrish going to court against guys like that.

"Is she right about that Changes clause?" Frank asked. He had a good, albeit layman's understanding of commercial law, but this was the first he had heard about a Changes clause as it applied to government contracts.

"Yeah, she is essentially correct," Parrish replied. "We had a conference call the other day with my boss, who is legal counsel for the corporation, and Bill Marsh who is the V.P. The client does this all of the time, just changes things on the fly. After all, it is a war and so it is not like they do not have other, more pressing matters. In this particular case, they just told us to proceed. We are going to have to go back and document the costs. We will get our allowable, allocable, and reasonable costs covered along with our fee. Just part of the game."

"But it sounds like we did not tell them that we could not perform," Frank replied.

"Yeah, well, you do not tell them that you cannot perform. They can make you perform."

Frank was confused. This was part of a new world for Frank. Most commercial agreements were bilateral in nature, which meant that both parties were bound only to the agreed terms unless changes to those terms were agreed to by the parties. Until now, that was the world that Frank inhabited. This new theater was a different paradigm.

In this world, the USG, through that Changes clause, had the right to unilaterally modify their agreement so long as they remained within the scope of the agreement. That meant that an agreement to wash clothes for fifty soldiers, for instance, could easily go to one hundred, or two hundred, or five hundred soldiers. At will. And on the fly. In a war.

"Okay, but did you tell them that you needed some time, in addition to the equipment and extra bodies?"

"That part fell through the cracks," Parrish admitted, somewhat sheepishly.

Frank now understood why the girls in the laundry were livid. He was not getting anywhere in the line for his room, and he was getting frustrated.

CHAPTER 11
A New Reality

—~~—

FRANK EXITED THE small, cramped ten by twenty-foot trailer which housed the site manager's office wearing a temporary badge. He had his luggage and directions to his temporary sleeping quarters. It was almost six in the evening, and Frank was recovering from jet lag. His eyes were open, but the rest of his body was beginning to shut down from a general lack of sleep brought on by the stress.

"Well, you made it," grinned one of the largest, morbidly obese people that he had ever met. Frank's temporary badge meant that, on this military installation, he was escorted everywhere he went until such time as he was granted a permanent badge. The person he was looking at, so large that he had blocked out part of the sun, was Frank's temporary escort.

"My name's Jimmy, but you can call me Jaba the Hut… or just Jaba for short. They all do," the fat man declared, grinning while thrusting out his large, sweaty palm.

The relative cool of the evening had begun to set in, on its way to being a cool crisp night in Baghdad's fourth winter day of 2004. Jaba looked to be around fifty years of age, although with rough, leathery skin and broken skin vessels in and around the eyes, probably from alcohol abuse. The years had not been kind to him.

The big guy was dressed in blue jeans, tennis shoes, and what looked to be a tent for a shirt. Jaba's white skin had become a deep shade of red from sunburn. Just standing there all but motionless, he was sweating like a stuck pig, even though Camp Bradley was located in a rapidly cooling desert with a relative humidity of less than ten percent. He had to be pushing around at least three hundred fifty pounds by Frank's eyeball estimation.

"The nickname comes from the *Star Wars* movie," Jaba volunteered, something Frank was well aware of, but at this point was too tired to discuss. The only thing he wanted to see at this point was the back of his eyeballs.

"Yeah, I know, Jaba. Hey, where can we go to grab something to eat?" Like most of the other new arrivals this day, Frank had had nothing to eat since a stale box lunch containing a baloney sandwich around midday, a couple of hours prior to the touchdown at Baghdad International Airport.

"We are going to drop off your stuff at the mass transit area. It is a sleeping area for those transiting through, until you can get a permanent hooch. And then I will take you over to the dining hall. It's called the DFAC here. You don't sound like you are ex-military, by the way, or you would have called it a DFAC or a dining hall," Jaba continued.

"What's your background, Jaba?" Frank asked as they both pulled up to the DFAC, preparing to enter the line into the large tent complex that resembled a huge auditorium that served as both a kitchen and a place to eat. The DFAC served a wide variety of foods all day and night during set serving times. The dinner this evening, Christmas eve, was set out buffet style. Once you signed in, all of it was available in unlimited portions. There were four different courses of meat, including shrimp and lobster, salads, vegetable dishes, fresh bread, drinks, cookies, and cakes; a veritable sea of food. That fact was not lost on Jaba.

"I have a degree in electrical engineering. I was designing computer systems out in San Francisco prior to coming over here," Jaba calmly informed Frank, reaching for anything and everything to eat within sight, as if this meal was his last. "I spend all day running parts, and escorting people on base who do not have badges, like laborers doing work on the facility, or subcontractors entering base to deliver parts."

Frank stared at the growing food pile on Jaba's tray, not comprehending what he had heard.

"Why are you here... and why do you do that?" Frank stammered.

"More money," Jaba replied.

Unbelievable, Frank thought to himself. He had dealt with engineering types in his former life at ImageSinc. He knew they were typically well paid right out of college, but they tended to plateau out unless they made it into management. Adding to that, it was expensive to live on the left coast. So maybe Jaba wasn't totally crazy...

"Are you sure you want to be running around here in the heat, Jaba? I hear it gets awfully hot here come summer," Frank looked at his escort, knowing from the weather reports exactly how hot it got. He wondered whether or not Jaba was going to survive a non-desk job.

"Well, I hope to lose some weight in the heat," Jaba said, unconvincingly.

"What about a job indoors, in IT?" Frank looked at Jaba.

"No security clearance, so it's fun in the sun for me. And what do you do?" Jaba managed to get those sentences out while devouring two chicken drumsticks, one in each fat fist.

"Subcontracts, Jaba."

Did you need to be a little crazy to walk - or in Jaba's case, waddle - into a war zone unarmed... just for some money? Frank was fast reconsidering that logic as he watched the big man devour enough food to feed four people. Frank flashed back to the ex-biker and the muscle-bound gorilla with the tattoos who struggled to complete the psychological profile without killing anyone. Maybe in the final analysis it was less about patriotism and more just about the money. Or, in Jaba's case, the free food combined with an undiagnosed case of clinical depression. Frank concluded that, in addition to the money, crazy was definitely in the mix.

—~~—

SHORTLY AFTER NINE in the evening, Jaba parked his white Chevy pickup outside of a large block building that served as temporary housing for those transiting in and out of theater. After grabbing Frank's gear from the back of the pickup, Jaba opened the door of the temporary housing quarters and shoved Frank's temporary badge at the clerk who stood behind the counter.

"Another one for the night, Mik," Jaba said to the clerk, a third country national with callow skin, cigarette-stained fingers, and brown spiked hair; possibly Bosnian, Czech, Romanian, or Hungarian.

Jaba turned to Frank. "Watch your shit in here. Lots of these fuckers are thieves. Make sure you lock up all of your shit before you go to sleep. And sleep light if you can, if you know what I mean. We should have some more permanent digs for you tomorrow. You should not have any trouble with incoming mortar attacks or with bunker drills waking you up. The roof is concrete reinforced. See you in the morning, and welcome to the sandbox." With that, Jaba was gone to his room for the night.

Frank surveyed the room. The temporary housing building was a massive facility set up to house transients from every contractor in Iraq. It was a central meeting place where those either coming into or exiting the country stayed while in Baghdad. Some were awaiting convoys out to other bases; others used it as a resting place in Baghdad until their connecting flights out of the country could be arranged. In Frank's case, this was home, for now, or until his new digs came available in the next day or so.

The facility itself looked to be formerly a large warehouse or motor pool left over from when Saddam ran the country. The ceilings were almost forty-foot-high, which was a good thing because the heat from the day escaped to the roof, rendering the floor space cool. Light entered from the floor-to-ceiling, barbed wire encased windows.

There had to be almost three hundred cots, all arranged in rows. It looked like a homeless shelter. Everything in the room was set up to be dissembled and moved quickly, so there were no walls or partitions for privacy. To cope, some of the transients made small makeshift barriers out of equipment that they had taken into theater. Bathroom facilities, or ablution units - a combination of toilet and shower - were outside, which meant that to use the restroom, you had to exit the facility in the dark to find them.

The area between the facility exit door and where the portable facilities were located had become a sort of impromptu meeting area for those wanting that last drag of a cigarette or, in some cases, a drink of bootleg whiskey.

"Your bunk is at C10 for the night," Mic said in his euro-accented English. "Lights out is in twenty minutes and that is quiet time. Keep your music off, or your headphones on... and no smoking in the facility, sir." Mic had Frank sign off for his bunk then reached for a cigarette; one last fix to be consumed outside in the area between the temporary housing facility and the ablution units before lights out.

Just then, Frank felt what had to be an iron fist gripping his shoulder blade as he bent down to pick up his luggage. He turned around to find the large gorilla with the tattoos that he had seen in Dubai with a bottle of whiskey in one large mitt which he was in the process of draining before lights out.

"You made it! How was your trip, dude?" The gorilla grinned at Frank as though he was a long-lost member of his family.

"Yeah, dead tired, man. How is your little biker friend; the one next to you in the test?" said Frank, trying to make conversation while looking for an excuse to part company, something he found was not possible as Mik had put him in a bunk right next to the gorilla.

"Didn't make it onto the plane, dude. He thinks that he failed the psychological profile. He said something about anger management issues. Dunno. Can you imagine that shit?" The gorilla downed the last of the whiskey.

"They allow drinking in the facility?" Frank offered, staring at the tattooed forearm gripping the whiskey bottle, hoping that if there were anger management issues this Christmas evening, he was on the right side of the gorilla.

"Nah. Military orders - no booze. Yeah, well, fuck 'em. It's Christmas Eve; got no pussy to fuck, I'm stuck in some hell hole in Iraq with you fucking guys, and I get to go to work in about seven hours. G'night." With that, the gorilla stumbled towards his bunk, empty whiskey bottle barely visible in the man's clenched paw.

Some ten minutes later, with Frank settled into his bunk next to the gorilla, it was lights out, and darkness prevailed except for the gentle glow in the dark from those who had portable electronic devices hooked up to earphones. An entire contingent of some three hundred transient workers was going to go to bed quietly this Christmas evening in a large, open-air facility, probably not knowing another soul in the facility. They would awake to Christmas day in Iraq, which would for them be just another work day in a war zone.

The darkness lasted less than five minutes. It seemed that as soon as the lights went out, they went back on. So much for quiet time.

"Merry Christmas!" cried a drunk, middle-aged and what looked to be ex-hippie who was tall with a Fu Manchu mustache and long blond hair that cascaded down his back longer than most women's hair. The rock star imitator at the light switch looked like he was holding guard on some military post.

Frank instinctively turned to the gorilla, only to find him now passed out in a drunken stupor, the empty whiskey bottle next to his cot. He was snoring like a freight train.

It was going to be a long night.

"Colonel's orders. Lights off at ten - sharp!" It had taken a minute for Mik, the Euro clerk who had himself settled down for the night in a bunk near the entrance, to make his short announcement to both the hippie and the rest of the facility while turning off the lights a second time. Except for the hippie, most were either now asleep or listening to music to block out the snoring in the now darkened facility.

"Fuck the colonel. Merry Christmas!" the hippie cried as the lights went on yet again after the ten o'clock at night lights out curfew.

"It's fucking Christmas. Let's celebrate!" yelled the long hair again, clearly intoxicated, but with his hand now firmly grasped onto what looked to be the light switch.

All eyes except for those of the gorilla turned to the cretin with the long hair. Unfortunately for the hippie, that included the colonel who, along with a small contingent of soldiers, had taken unannounced temporary quarters for the night in the facility. The colonel was not amused.

"Lights out, mister!" barked the colonel. He had been dressed in civilian attire, but nobody mistook the military bearing of the colonel for a civilian. Certainly not Mik, standing speechless in shock, nor the soldiers who rose to support their commanding officer. Watching this surreal spectacle unfold on the night before Christmas, Frank felt like an extra in a movie.

"When I tell you lights out, mister; I mean lights out. Get this man out of here!" growled the colonel, turning to the soldiers. Needing no further cue, two soldiers grabbed the hippie by the collar, yanking him away from the light switch, while another couple of soldiers entered the fray. The four dragged the hippie by the arms and legs from the facility and deposited him in the arms of the military police, with the hippie still yelling and screaming about Christmas.

With that, the lights went out and stayed out for Frank in those few nighttime hours before Christmas day of 2004. He stared into the darkness; quiet now overtaking the facility. It had been little more than six months ago, when working in a large corporation as a manager, he had a house, car, family, some investments, and a good job. Christmas would normally be spent with family, with presents under the tree, turkey dinner, and football.

Not this year. This Christmas would be spent in an open-air warehouse facility sleeping in a bunk next to a drunken, heavily tattooed gorilla of a person with an alleged seventeen-year prison term whom he would hopefully never get to know. Added in was some drugged up ex-hippie, a no-nonsense colonel, and a room full of transients in a war zone.

Ho ho ho! Welcome to the sandbox.

—∾—

THE INTERCONNECTED TRAILERS which, woven together formed an office pod in which Frank and his other subcontract administrators spent their day, were now vacant. The typical office banter had gone quiet at precisely seven in the evening as everybody closed down their computers and headed for either the dining hall, the gym, or their room. The options were limited most nights in this spartan environment, and this night would be no exception. There were a few, like Frank, who stayed behind to chat on the office phone with friends and family in the States, given the eight-hour time difference, but tonight he had the office all to himself.

Frank took a moment to reflect back on what had transpired. It had been a crazy few weeks, what with the mobilization through Dubai and all that. Frank had not only gone to work, he had gone on to another world; not just physically, but emotionally and intellectually. And he was having trouble with the transition. Too much change, too fast; a future hurtling at you faster than your ability with which to cope.

As a civilian and without a military background, being there was another, altogether different dimension - from the sights to the sounds, even the smells. Ordinary folks, many without either the necessary education or training, grappling with situations which were frequently over their heads and out of their control; looked for competent leadership, and found it sparse or non-existent. By the looks of it, most of the civilian ex-pats were not the best and brightest. But for the most part, they were trying; doing what they could, in a world gone mad.

In the US, most people got up each day with their family. They climbed into some sort of vehicle, left home, and went off to their other life, called a job; returning home at the end of the day to their real family. You knew your family. Together, they gave you an identity.

You even had an identity at work with what could be called your second family. That identity emerged gradually, and came from what you did; what you produced. For the most part, you were good at what you did; competition for limited positions in the workplace, if nothing else, required it. You belonged to that other family because you added value.

You were attached to your community. You went to baseball games, got involved with your passions, like art or music. You lived life; that was your identity.

By contrast; here, you had no real identity. Nobody knew the other person sitting next to them, nor did that other person know you. You had no idea who was competent, and who was not, nor did it appear that there were consequences for either competence or incompetence given the overtly political environment.

Living arrangements were transitory, by design. You could wake up in one camp, and by nightfall be both living and working in another location. You were seldom alone, but you could be forever lonely.

There was neither the time nor the energy or the ability to work on a skill set or to indulge a passion. Days melded into nights; weeks into months, with no end in sight. You could be forgiven during those mind-numbing days for believing at some point that this was a permanent state of affairs; war as a civilian ex-pat career. Except that everybody knew that their work was project based. Everybody also knew that projects ended and unless you somehow latched onto another project; when it ended - and it could end quickly - then so did your cash flow, not to mention your identity.

He thought that he had heard something strange. Frank glanced at the alarm on his watch. It was almost four twenty in the morning. He had the alarm set for four thirty, so the alarm had not yet gone off. It was always a struggle to get out of bed at that hour, but Frank wanted to get at least an hour workout in the gym before heading over to the dining hall for breakfast at six thirty. As he turned off the alarm, he glanced over at Jason Meeks, his roommate, and found out what he had heard that was strange. Meeks wasn't alone.

This was Frank's second night in his new room. Frank had no idea who Meeks was, or was with, but from the sounds of the screams, she and Meeks were apparently going at it hot and heavy. Frank marveled at how people in this environment could work twelve to fourteen hours a day, seven days a week, and yet find both the time and the energy for the extra-curricular activities. It was all that he could do to drag himself away from the computer at the end of the day, get to the dining hall, and crash. *If only I were twenty years younger*, he thought and smiled to himself.

"Do not mind me, dude, but I need to turn the light on so that I can get to my stuff. I am going to hit the gym," Frank called over to the bed next to his which contained two writhing bodies.

"Yeah, whatever." There were chuckles under the sheets.

Minutes later, Frank was headed in the gym in the moonlit Baghdad night.

"Sorry about that." Meeks grinned at Frank as they clicked through the columns on the Excel spreadsheet some four hours later.

Frank and Meeks had been pouring over a spreadsheet that contained a list of Meeks' subcontracts. Jason was about to leave for his holiday, planning to return in about two weeks. Frank was attempting to get his head around the details contained in forty or so agreements. He needed to get up to speed and learn in about a day and a half what Meeks had been working on for the better part of six months.

"Sorry about what?" Frank looked up at Meeks.

"The chick in the hooch; an Army security chick here on base. She likes us ex-Special Forces guys, for some reason."

Frank had just gotten there but wondered if that type of fraternization was allowed. He really did not care what either of them did on their own time; he just did not want to get caught up in it. Besides, he was too tired to care.

"So, Jason. What is your background in subcontract administration?" Frank had been pouring over Meeks' work and was surprised that anybody could make sense of what he was doing. The paperwork looked like it had been written by a high school sophomore which, as it turned out, was Meeks' education level.

"None. I had been digging ditches with my brother. He runs a construction company in Homestead, Florida, but work is slow right now, so when one of my buddies called and asked me if I wanted to go to Iraq, I jumped on it."

"Yeah, no problem, Jason. But tell me, what do you like about the gig, besides the money?"

Meeks smiled. "Yeah, the cash is good. Rust is one squared away dude," referring to Kevin Rust, the vice president and former two star general, also a former Special Forces guy. "But if you want my opinion, you need to watch ole Kenny Buck. He is one motherfucker. I stay away from that guy. I have seen what he does to those who cross him; just fuck with them, and then they are gone. I have heard from some of the guys in the warehouses that he is running some kind of scam, but I just stay away. I have told Janey in compliance, but I guess she does not want to hear it, so I do what he wants. He runs this department, not Coleman."

CHAPTER 12
High-Touch, and Terrorism

IF YOU WERE looking for some good weather in mid-January 2005, Kuwait City was a beautiful place to be. Sitting at the northwestern tip of the Persian Gulf, and within an easy drive of its neighbors Iraq and Saudi Arabia, Kuwait City offered a nice respite from the long, dark arduous winters on the European continent. The high temperature hit seventy-eight degrees Fahrenheit this day with a mixture of sun, some clouds, and a bit of humidity, which at this time of year was not unpleasant.

Derya Ali had things other than the weather on her mind as she parked her designer sunglasses between her firm, upraised breasts and swung her long, sinewy legs, housed in tight designer jeans, out of the rear of her chauffeur-driven white Infiniti QX 56. At 5'8" and 125 lbs., with a flawless olive complexion and straight, jet black, carefully manicured hair, her rock-hard body had been chiseled from years of climbing mountains in Turkey as a young girl.

Not slim; she had sensually wide hips with a flat, firm stomach on a body best described as voluptuous. Combined with a smolderingly easy smile at first contact and dark, wide mesmerizing eyes so hot they could melt steel, she was most men's dream. And she knew it.

At first blush, she could easily pass this day for just another very wealthy Kuwait City lady stopping by to see her husband at work before a day's shopping trip, with nothing more on her mind than buying some gold and getting a manicure and pedicure. Only nothing could be further from the truth.

Approaching her twenty-sixth birthday, she stood in the parking lot outside of Khan's office not far from where his 105' Sunseeker Yacht was moored. Derya was a woman on a mission. She had planned to meet Khan in his office, located in an older, nondescript, large brown sandstone six-story complex on a side street three blocks from the Persian Gulf. She liked that building; it also housed dress shops, convenience stores, and a manicurist on the first floor.

Derya Ali was not only unmarried, she had never been married, and had neither children nor a boyfriend in the recent past. Possessed with an engaging personality when she deigned to use it, she cared little for the general chitchat from women her age about men or movies. In those rare moments when she did talk to others about her family, it was always limited to her brother Jamal and how much she loved him and wanted to see him.

The scion of a wealthy Middle East construction magnate of both Turkish and Jordanian heritage, her now thirty-two-year-old brother had gone on to graduate school in London for business before moving on to a career in international finance. She had gone to live with her mother in Jordan after her parents split in 1998, finishing a degree in economics in Amman. Still, she continuously kept in touch with her brother by phone. It was through him that she still had a family; her father having passed away last year, and her mother now infirm. Jamal brought back happy childhood memories before the divorce that she now treasured.

Their careers kept them both very busy and on the move. Jamal was the cerebral one; she the pragmatic, task-oriented one. When meetings could be arranged, they were especially sweet, so she planned them well in advance. There were cool summer meetings hiking in the gorgeous Halgurd Mountain near Erbil, in the Kurdish region of Iraq where wealthy families vacationed to escape the worst of the summer heat. Their next meeting was tentatively scheduled for late summer or early fall, depending upon circumstances and, if all went well, this meeting would prove equally sweet.

At an age where most women were thinking about family and babies, Derya had recently immersed herself in a job managing the project for Jabil Khan's contracts in Camp Bradley. Cork and Hammer had a mountain of reimbursable overhead tied up in subcontract administrators, purchasing agents, and logistics clerks at the contract level. By contrast, Derya, to whom most of that work was directed through Buck, got things done with a small team on the camp by working longer, harder, and with constant attention to detail.

Derya Ali had initially been recently referred to Jabil Khan at the not-so-subtle behest of his Kuwaiti sheik financiers. Khan, like most men his age, automatically presumed that Derya's age and sex precluded her from such a responsible position, only to be pleasantly surprised. Khan found Derya unusually mature for her age. Wars tended to do that to a person.

Unlike those at Cork and Hammer, who tended to go through the motions, there was an air of energy about Derya, an approach to work so intense that it bordered on fanatical. In the States, talents like hers would carry her far: a large salary, bonuses and possibly stock options. But this was a Middle East war zone, and there would be no shares of stock, so she would measure her return on invested capital much differently.

And yet, as good as she was tactically, Jabil Khan wanted more, and that was what was on the agenda for today. Good project managers were more than just managers of people or processes. They functioned in foreign countries more like State Department liaisons, or ambassadors, as much intelligence analyst as day-to-day administrator, a role that consumed much of Derya's time. Intelligence was the lifeblood of Khan's business, and so that was what she had traveled from Baghdad to Kuwait City to discuss.

—ɱ—

Jabil Khan had been pouring over the financial statements of the Baghdad project in preparation for his meeting with Derya. Khan originally scheduled his meeting with Derya for his office but, with the good weather, had asked her to board his yacht so that both could enjoy the backdrop of the harbor as they spoke.

As he waited for Derya's arrival, he reflected on what he had accomplished since Marsh and Buck brought him aboard at the inception of the war in 2003. Working with Cork and Hammer had been painful at times. But like most things in life, it was not just about what you knew, it was about who you knew, and what they could do for you. Peering up from the numbers to look out at the ships docked in the harbor, he would conclude that, so far, Cork and Hammer had done a lot for him.

At forty-seven years of age Khan, of Pakistani origin, was tall and slim with horn-rimmed glasses shielding his dark eyes. He had greying black hair with a receding hairline and a mustache, both of which he kept trimmed short. A prototypical Middle East trader, Khan would broker goods, guns, money, people; in short, anything and everything of value. Khan had taken up residence in Kuwait on the eve of the war to be appropriately positioned, and had aggressively marketed his project management services to Marsh.

Jabil Khan had gotten to know Marsh through his work on several smaller, independent Middle East projects. But those earlier requirements were mostly small-time brokering services, using Khan's connections all over the Middle East for miscellaneous goods and services in return for which Marsh provided Khan a negotiated profit. To his credit, Khan had produced, and Marsh had not forgotten when it came time to implement Plan B.

Now, almost two years later, Khan smiled as he checked the latest balance of the slush fund. It was that $200 million balance, along with what he was going to do with his 30% cut of the take, that Khan was contemplating as Derya entered the room. And yet, as good as those numbers were, those were not what Khan wanted to discuss. Those were yesterday's numbers. In the corporate world, shareholder value tended to equate to the here and now, and so he wanted more - *here and now.*

Although Khan and Derya had roughly two-thirds of the current work in Baghdad and were assured of that same deal with additional sites, they had none of the work at the border sites. Khan wanted it all, and for more than one reason. He also wanted more time, something he felt was going to be in short supply soon. Unconfirmed rumors had started in camp, where rumors always bred like flies, that Cork and Hammer were going to sell.

If so, that could bring an end to his cozy relationship with Marsh and Buck on camp. He wanted more; he needed to know more; indeed, his sheik financiers were continuously pressing him for more, and yet Buck and Marsh were being silent on the sale of Cork and Hammer in his own private conversations with them. That was where Derya came in handy.

—m—

"Good afternoon, Mr. Khan," Derya smiled, staring straight at Khan while settling into the posh digs on his yacht. They were in a spacious cabin with large glass windows which not only let in the abundant early afternoon sunlight but also afforded a postcard view of both Kuwait City and the Persian Gulf.

A secretary wordlessly delivered bottles of cold water then left. At that point, there were only the two of them.

"Good afternoon to you, Derya. I hope all is well with you. And send my best wishes along to your brother," Khan said.

He was always formal, smiling obsequiously. It was an air of deference unusual anywhere in the world, but most of all in the Middle East; Khan the aging entrepreneur deferring to a young, hard-charging female executive.

Both parties had gotten used to this peculiar aspect of their arrangement early on because in any business relationship, particularly in the Middle East, the first thing to understand was that nothing of any consequence got done until both parties understood the power dynamics: where the power came from, and who had it. In this instance, both parties not only understood the power, but also who had it. And Derya had it.

"My brother has managed to review the financial statements that you have sent him," Derya said. "Like you, he wants more, especially coming from that border region with Iran and Iraq." She made no pretense of small talk. She had not driven from Baghdad to Kuwait City to sit in an air-conditioned room on a ship to kiss some low-life Pakistani broker's ass, somebody who did not give a damn what happened, as long as he got his cut.

"He thinks that both financially and strategically, we need to get more involved near the border. I have been dealing with both Marsh and Buck, and I tell them that I want to participate in that work. They push me off onto Colonel Harper, who told me that the Army Corp of Engineers has control over those agreements, due to the sensitive nature of the area.

"Buck has also told me that the border region comes under another part of the military chain of command, outside of Cork and Hammer's scope of work. I have been discussing the issue with Colonel Harper on more than one occasion but so far have not been able to get any movement on this." She left unsaid just how and where she had been discussing that issue with the colonel.

"I plan to continue discussing this with both Marsh and Buck, and with Colonel Harper, but I also plan to discuss this with Coleman when I get back. Coleman is useless, although I usually manage to get what I want. I am not sure how long Coleman will last. They seem to get rid of them one after the other, in short order," not realizing as Derya said it, that Kenny Buck was preparing to do just that - terminate Coleman - to cover his tracks.

Derya regarded most of those working at Cork and Hammer as worthless. They did not believe; they just went through the motions. Not that it bothered her, but most were mere pawns in the game, and yet made more in a day than some Iraqis made in a year for doing virtually nothing.

"Yes, of course, Derya. I assumed that you were on top of it. And yes, that has been very important to us also for some time now." Khan did not mention the issue explicitly, but subtly reinforced the fact that he had been pressing the lost opportunity at the border with Marsh and Buck since shortly after the mobilization in 2003.

He had learned not to micromanage Derya. Doing so only got her mad.

Khan had never learned how to deal with women, not to mention women in power, and he was not going to find out now at this stage of his life. For him, women were servants, useful only if they were providing a much-needed service which for him always seemed to revolve around either domestic work or sex and not necessarily in that order. But this was an exception, and he would deal with it. It was always all about the money with Khan, and the money was good.

The next ninety minutes or so were spent on various tactical issues: coordinating the response to numerous bids, getting different sub-tier suppliers paid, and transporting money back and forth to Baghdad. Moving money was always problematic, not only because the banks in Iraq were non-functional and had themselves been infiltrated by criminals, but also because of the incidence of crime in a population with high unemployment. It was then that the conversation turned to the issue of Cork and Hammer leaving.

"I met with Kenny Buck a few nights ago," Derya informed Khan, again leading him to believe that this was an ordinary business meeting. It was anything but; it was more aptly described as a social event conducted alone with Buck in his trailer under circumstances that Derya cared little about discussing.

"I told him that I was hearing from others that Cork and Hammer was going to sell. If that was true, then you and I needed some idea whether or not our services would be continued under the terms of a new supplier." She paused, and then added, "Because if that is true – if our services are no longer required - we may need to wind up our financial affairs, closing that account in Kuwait. We may also need to re-evaluate our relationship in Baghdad in general. Buck knew what I meant, *because I can be very persuasive.*" The tone in Derya's voice raised an octave with each of the last six words, referring to the fact that while the account was in Kuwait, getting to the proceeds of that account could be challenging.

One obvious but not insurmountable problem with this logic was that Buck and Marsh had set up Khan's account to be "For Deposit Only" meaning that he could deposit money into the account, but he could not withdraw unless all parties consented. Neither Buck nor Marsh were going to do that until the end. And Khan knew it.

Derya was playing hardball by creating a psychological if not physical barrier to that account in Kuwait. Both parties knew that the Kuwait account had been created illegally through kickbacks. Marsh and Buck would certainly want to access quickly the funds in that account if the end came unexpectedly. They just wanted that ending to occur on their terms.

Re-evaluating the relationship created the impression that Jabil Khan might be open to unilaterally pulling out before the end. Doing so meant not only killing the continuing source of cash flow but causing all sorts of logistical nightmares when your single source key supplier went south on you. Derya was telling Khan that she had essentially informed Buck: "We are crazier than you are."

It was a heretofore unspoken source of leverage, but one designed to push Kenny Buck into disclosing just what he knew. It was high risk because, at that point, both parties needed each other. But that is how the game was played between two thieves between whom there was no honor.

"And Buck; what did he say to you?" Khan removed his glasses to clean them while he contemplated the consequences of that negotiation position.

"I think Buck is a liar, but he continues to say that he knows nothing. Taylor says he knows nothing either, but his eyes lie to him. I am getting this from some of the Euro-trash bitches that work in Coleman's supply chain group. They can't keep either their legs or their mouths shut, although I hear they suck cock like the good whores they are. I will continue to press Buck and Taylor, and also the colonel."

Derya motioned to Khan as she said that, indicating that it was time for her to leave to get on the road back to Baghdad.

Khan rose to show Derya out the door. In doing so, his mind was working the angles. As a broker, he was always working the angles. On one level, he knew that the threat to not only create barriers to the money but to also threaten a pull-out would have a limited effect on both Buck and Marsh. Their nuclear response to this could be as simple as turning Khan's group over to the U.S. Military on fraud and kickback charges. But that wasn't going to happen; nobody wanted to kill the goose that laid the golden egg.

On another level, Khan admired Derya's continuing efforts to get at the labor work on the border that was crucial not only to him, but to her brother. And her brother was no ordinary associate of some Kuwaiti sheiks.

As Derya turned to leave, Khan pressed a sealed note into her hand. The envelope said simply 'important'. Moments later, Derya disappeared into the elevator.

But as she sauntered away, the Pakistani middleman could not help but admire the goods from a distance. He thought that Derya's ass was one of the finest that he had ever seen, and in forty-seven years he had seen his share. More importantly, he knew that he would never touch that ass; not because a strong, charismatic, intelligent, highly educated and motivated woman was much more than he could handle, which it was, but because that was one sure way to wind up dead.

Khan could get ass just about everywhere - mobs of Chinese and Russian whores choked the streets of Dubai - but he could not get the kind of money he needed to finance this operation just anywhere or in the amounts that he needed, during a war. To get that kind of money, one turned to a particular class of investor, what the American investor class would describe by its slang expression: a "hard money guy".

Hard money guys made loans that came in handy when the banks, being normally risk averse, would only loan a certain percentage of the money needed to complete the financing on the construction or rehabilitation of a large structure, forcing the developer to raise additional capital to complete the deal. Some of them were little more than loan sharks. They provided the equity or so-called bridge financing; capital that if you were sane, you approached with great care and caution because it was usually costly, short term in nature, and almost always came with strings attached. Derya's brother Jamal Ali was that particular class of investor, and then some.

Jabil Khan would not show this kind of hard money on his Sources and Uses of Funds section of his financial statements, to the extent that he ever bothered to create one. This was the ultimate off-balance sheet financing, something that for obvious reasons he shielded from Dr. Marsh and Kenny Buck. Derya's brother Jamal was the chief financial officer of Al Qaeda, and he definitely had strings attached, none of which included Khan fucking his only sister.

Instead, those strings consisted of an informal, albeit deadly covenant to the financing. Khan's hard money deal contained a side agreement whereby seventy-five percent of Khan's total take from the kickbacks from each transaction would travel through that Kuwaiti bank account back to Al Qaeda, where it would be used to fund terrorism worldwide.

As Derya's driver closed the rear door to the Infiniti QX 56 in preparation for the long ride back to Baghdad, she reached into her bag and pulled out the sealed envelope that Jabil Khan had given her. The note had been passed to her from her brother through Khan via a Kuwaiti sheik intermediary. Letters like these were rare, given the geographical disparities; she in Kuwait City, and he somewhere in Afghanistan.

It was a short note, urging Derya to keep pressing for information about the listening posts at the border. He was starved for real-time intelligence. How she was doing in camp with Buck and Colonel Harper, and what else she was learning? Had she had been successful in getting more work at the Iran border which would allow his people to learn more about those listening posts? He had been in contact with Khan but did not trust him which is why he sent his only sister.

He wanted a note from her when she could afford it, just something short. And although they were both busy at the moment, he needed to tell her just how proud of her he was, and hoped that they could meet up later in the summer or in the fall as planned. Staring out of the window at the brown sand dunes she passed by on the flat, empty, seemingly endless desert terrain, she broke down and cried.

She was far away from him, so far away. And while she had worked so hard and done so much, she feared that things were spinning beyond her control, which in fact they were. She was proud of her brother who had given up riches, a beautiful house in London, and all of the creature comforts that the son of a now-deceased Middle East magnate had to offer, because he believed in what he was doing.

This fight with the West that Al Qaeda had been fighting had never been her fight, but because it was his fight and she loved him, then his fight was now her fight. She hated the Americans in particular, and wanted them to just leave the Middle East, never really stopping to wonder what would happen if they actually did. Derya had never considered whether or not the fight to which she had applied herself was itself right. She relied on her brother and her brother hated them. Now, through the force of his personality, so did she.

Grabbing the cell phone tucked away in her computer bag, she dialed a number that only she had. Derya's brother had warned his sister several times not to call unless absolutely necessary. Jamal was never sure who was listening, but the handwritten note hand-delivered to Derya from her brother via Khan had overtaken her sense of caution. She anxiously waited for him to pick up. Chance would reward her on this day, and for that brief period in time, less than five minutes, brother and sister were reunited over time and distance; the childhood memories flashing back as they came together on a delicious phone call that they had not shared in weeks.

Her brother had been right to be cautious. Brother and sister had been together for sure, but they were not alone, for everything they said had been bugged by Big Brother - as in, the CIA. Derya's cell phone, her computer, her computer bag, her luggage, her room - they were all compromised. They would have jammed a bug all the way up her ass until she choked on it if they could have gotten to it.

Lady Luck would smile on both Derya and her brother on this particular day. The call had been too short to obtain coordinates necessary for locating the financier, but the CIA secret squirrels would continue listening and looking for the coordinates, prosecuting the electronic war both on the ground and in the air with vigor.

The secret squirrels knew that, in addition to making a little money, Derya's brother wanted access to the base camps in the north because Al Qaeda had, at that point, been providing tactical cooperation to Iran for at least a decade. All of the parties knew that the Army Corp of Engineers had been constructing those camps near the Iraq border with Iran. It was one of the reasons that the Iranians kept armed divisions camped along that border with Iraq, in the event that the newly constructed base camps morphed suddenly into the spearhead of an invasion.

It was also the reason that, despite Khan and Derya's best efforts to enlist Marsh, Buck, and even the colonel in their cabal, it would be a bridge too far, destined to fail from the beginning. It would be a battle of the CIA secret squirrel's twenty-first century high-tech versus Derya's drop-dead gorgeous, sensual-but-deadly twelfth-century high-touch. The smart money in D.C. was on high-tech.

Jabil Khan's people, working directly for Derya but acting at that point as Al Qaeda proxies, would never see the light of day at those border camps. Case Hammer had seen to that, assuring his high-level CIA handlers of that fact as a part of his deal with the Agency. Those relationships were something that neither Marsh nor Kenny Buck would be privy to, let alone Jabil Khan.

The CIA secret squirrels wanted the Al Qaeda financier; the money man. They wanted him so badly that they had invested $25 million in Hammer's small front operation. It would be debt financing; money that Hammer would sign for both personally and as a part of the company, a company that was now for sale.

The secret squirrels were also playing a dangerous game with military assets in a war zone. Using Hammer's company, they were dangling contract opportunities in front of the terrorists, attempting to manipulate the Al Qaeda financier's love of his sister in order to lure him into the open, where they would most assuredly kill him and everyone around him, with malice aforethought.

CHAPTER 13
A Country Chick, and the Drifter

—᠁—

"You know how I like it." Taylor grinned as he dribbled out the words in his deep Louisiana drawl, stretching out his corpulent six foot, two hundred thirty-five-pound frame on the sofa in the forty-foot double-wide trailer he called home in this part of the world.

"Sure, baby. Coming right up," Janey Lynn Reed replied, applying a hint of Coca-Cola to an otherwise tall glass of Jack Daniels. Jack and Coke was their nightly ritual in this desert wasteland that they called home. Alcohol was prohibited on the camp of course, but that was for the little people. Everybody on camp was equally subject to the same regulations, it was just that some were more equal than others. Taylor was the deputy project manager. Reed was both the compliance manager, and his live-in girlfriend on base, which made them both more equal.

Jabil Khan's people had smuggled the whiskey onto the base. It was an open secret at the senior staff level; a compliance issue to be sure. The automatic answer to that: rank had its own privileges - do as I say, not as I do - and so Reed would get drunk virtually every night of her life in Iraq, never confronting the apparent paradox.

Born in Metairie, Louisiana, Reed was now forty-three years old but looked older. Like Taylor, her plump five-foot-three frame had never seen the inside of a gym or a track. She was fighting a losing battle with the effects of alcohol aging her skin by slapping on makeup in a way that conjured up images of Apache Indians applying war paint before battle.

Early on, Reed had gone to work for NASA in Huntsville, Alabama as a buyer, but eventually drifted into a low-level compliance officer job. A control freak by nature, she found that she enjoyed the audit work. Unfortunately, government work did not pay enough, so she took a part-time job in a local bar where she supplemented her income. It was there two years ago that she met the soon to be unemployed shrimp boat operator she was now sitting across from in Iraq, having found solace in each other and their miseries, through a bottle.

Taylor was an agreeable sort by nature which is what attracted her to him. Reared in a trailer park not as lovely as the one in which she and Taylor currently lived by abusive alcoholic parents, Janey Lynn Reed had a violent temper when drunk, which was often. By contrast, Taylor possessed an outwardly cheerful disposition which masked the churning that he felt inside, having to deal daily with Kenny Buck. He liked her fighting spirit; she his calm demeanor. So, she camped out in that hooch with Taylor night after night, secretly making plans to marry Taylor when both had saved enough money to leave Iraq.

She hadn't consulted with Taylor about whether or not he wanted to get married. She was now in her mid-forties and, in her mind, had entered that nightmare zone where many women go when they are over forty and never married and discover that their prospects for marriage were somewhere between slim and none, and Slim was leaving town. She was desperate. She wanted a house with a yard, a picket fence, 2.5 children in the yard, and she wanted Taylor, in that order.

She had taken this job when Taylor called needing a manager of compliance. She wasn't sure if he just wanted a compliance officer, a bedmate, or a wife, but she used the war to negotiate a leave of absence from NASA to find out. She was now drawing down an excellent six-figure salary, doing less work than at NASA, and sharing a bed with the man she planned to marry.

—ꝏ—

Terry Taylor was your basic drifter. Now in his mid-forties, he had essentially grown up on a shrimp boat. Taylor had a brief run at owning his own ship, but the hours and the hard, dangerous life of a Louisiana shrimper - battling the seas, having to go further out to sea to catch shrimp, dealing with the competition, while struggling to keep dependable help - got to be too much. In time, Taylor lost the boat and wound up drifting from job to job. He was briefly married, but that lasted all of about six months when he just decided to move on.

It was in that earlier life as a shrimper where Taylor and Buck met, two good old southern boys that just liked to have fun. He had even introduced Janey Lynn to Buck briefly in some dive of a bar but the two of them were like oil and water. Janey Lynn, the control freak, and Buck with the psychopathic personality, did not mix. So, it was Taylor, outwardly jovial with an even temper but without the agenda that made things click earlier when they were drinking in a stateside bar, and now in Iraq.

Taylor had been doing odd jobs, drinking his life away with Janey Lynn Reed, when Buck called from Iraq asking him if he wanted work there. Taylor had never worked on a project before. He did not own a passport and had no idea where to get one, but the money that Buck promised for a laundry foreman's position was almost six figures. That was more than someone with no education or training, let alone management skills, would ever make in one year, either before this job, or after, so he accepted immediately.

Now, less than a year later, he had been improbably promoted from overseeing a bunch of very affectionate Filipino girls doing laundry all day long to a deputy project manager reporting to Buck. Borderline homeless not so many months ago, he was now living in a double-wide trailer with more apparent status than he had ever had in his life. What he had could be taken away immediately, but he owed Buck for it, so when Buck wanted something, Terry Taylor did it without questioning why.

—ʍ—

"BABY, HOW MANY times have I told you about those hooches. The rooms are too fucking small." Janey Lynn Reed had a foul mouth that reflected her trailer park upbringing, nasty under the best of circumstances, and it got worse when she was drunk. The more she drank, the more she swore.

"I told Coleman about that," Taylor said. "He said that Khan was working on it, but wanted more money. He wanted a change in scope to do the work. He said that Khan was not going to restructure anything without more money."

Taylor was exhausted, but he did not disagree. Not that he understood the contract issues, he just did not want to discuss them. What he really wanted to do had nothing to do with work, but Reed often brought her job home with her and was not in the mood for fun and games between the sheets, especially after she had downed one or two cold ones. He was doing his best to tune her out, but it was not working.

Taylor and Reed had just returned from a scheduled inspection of the subcontractor's hooches that housed third-country nationals, otherwise called TCN's. The TCN's frequently came from other countries outside of the United States; like Turkey, Kenya or Kosovo. They cleaned toilets, put food on the table, and delivered water and performed other mostly blue-collar tasks.

Reed and Taylor had been accompanied by Coleman, the supply chain manager, Derya Ali who represented Jabil Khan, the subcontractor who had constructed the man-camps, and Johnny Burke, who was the quality assurance manager but in this instance was doubling for the health and safety manager who was on vacation.

The barbed wire-encased seven-hundred-man camp which housed the third-country nationals was perched on a small spit of land not far from the little management village housing the colonel, Buck, Taylor, and others. The distance was not great, less than a kilometer. In terms of living conditions, it was like comparing a slum in the Philippines or Brazil to Beverly Hills.

The inspection started at two in the afternoon and went on for three hours, much of it outside in the heat. The team trudged from building to building inspecting furnishings, looking for health and safety violations. They found some small infractions, but the eight-hundred-pound gorilla in the room always came down to the living area. It was an old issue, dating from the original construction of the man-camp.

Their client had imposed health and safety rules and regulations as a part of the agreement. In typical government bureaucrat fashion, some government regulations were usually either vague or confusing, or conflicted outright with other provisions. But that would not be the case here. The client had very clearly and consistently set forth fifty square feet as the minimum for living space per person in the man-camp.

The problem for Cork and Hammer on this one was that they had never converted the requirement into a subcontract specification. That defective specification was something that Cork and Hammer had accepted in writing via Buck upon the camp's completion, and they had long since paid Jabil Khan for the work. As a result, people were crammed six to a room that should have housed only one. The situation was a poster child for a media driven public relations nightmare. Buck knew that, and was not going to do something about it unless he was forced.

However, if - God forbid - either the outside government bureaucrats or the media decided to look at the man camp, then the rules of the game would change. The bureaucrats would wake, aroused with a vengeance.

For their part, both Khan and Derya Ali were adamant when they got around to discussing that issue for the hundredth time as they all stood outside in the heat, tempers short: if no more money, then no multi-million-dollar modification of the facility, at least on their dime.

To be sure, Marsh and Buck had no problem paying Khan for the extra work. Their problem was that they did not ultimately want to pay for it: they wanted their client to pay for it in a reimbursement. That was risky, because if this extra work was placed with Khan as reimbursable, but audited correctly, some or all of both the original work and the rework stood a chance of being thrown out by government auditors. Cash flow issues aside, Cork and Hammer would most likely wind up on the short end of that one, paying for a massive man-camp modification.

Now that he was pressed, Marsh handled this the only way that he had ever intended. He sent a note to Reed saying that Cork and Hammer would pay for the work without getting reimbursed. Buck instructed Taylor to sign the paperwork. He would leave his fingerprints off of this for plausible deniability purposes, of course. Taylor was to instruct Coleman, who was clueless as to the rights and responsibilities here, to draft a change to the scope and pay Khan for the work.

In the process, Buck also informally told both the colonel and Rust, the VP and program manager, that the work was being done for the account of Cork and Hammer. The paperwork in the file would show that the work was to be done by and for Cork and Hammer, knowing that Reed, like Buck a control freak, would verify that the correct paperwork was in the file in anticipation of an audit.

Months later, after the modifications were completed, the invoice would come. It would be sent directly to the client for reimbursement with some fraudulent paperwork attached - Marsh's email to Reed on the matter notwithstanding. Cork and Hammer were not going to pay for this issue. They had no intention of ever paying for it.

The colonel would quietly, in a matter-of-fact manner, inform his superiors but would only say that the camp had been slightly modified to comply with the specification. He would craft his correspondence in such a way as to convey the impression that he was the one driving the issue, when that was not the case. That low-level missive would not itself kick out an audit - at least not now - so his ass was covered. Khan, Marsh, and Buck just increased the revenue stream; they were happy. And BLTVDef would get a man-camp that was to specification.

Marsh and Buck had washed their hands of the issue. Hammer simply tacked this issue onto the broader set of outstanding claims. He had a plan to deal with issues like this later, in his own way as a part of the business closing negotiations. But the little people, like Coleman or Reed and her boyfriend Taylor, would not be so lucky. In addition to the client, in time they would all pay.

CHAPTER 14
Benign Incompetence

—~—

EATING AT A dining hall, otherwise referred to in military jargon as a DFAC, was more than a place to eat in a war zone. It was a unique experience for a civilian. On most bases, it was one of the only places to eat. DFAC's were air-conditioned, which was not a small thing if your job required you to work in the heat. For the most part, the dining halls were clean, neat, and the food was safe and ready to eat.

To someone coming from a stateside, civilian background with no government experience, the scene was a little surreal. Arriving there at noon for lunch when they were most busy was to be witness to a strange menagerie; a colorful mixture of civilians, military, third-country nationals, and the occasional VIP, all huddled together over the same food. Eating in this cramped, air-conditioned makeshift tin can of a restaurant in the desert, enjoying a respite from a January day that was abnormally hot, even for Iraq, tragicomically reminded Frank of the bar scene in the original *Star Wars* movie.

The dining facilities themselves were little more than forty-foot trailers strung together not far from Frank's warehouse operations. The place was propped up on cinder blocks and encased by concrete T Walls to protect it from a rocket-propelled grenade. Each of the metal, laminated fold-out cafeteria-style tables came with hard-backed plastic chairs. Overhead televisions blasted out mostly cable news or entertainment programming, allowing its patrons to keep up with some of the news and/or sports while drowning out the usual midday chatter.

All of the dining halls were run by local contractors, businesses theoretically managed by Frank's group. The contractors did not supply the food which came from USG sourced and delivered contractors. They provided the labor in the form of third-country nationals who cleaned and stocked the food lines, not unlike a buffet-style restaurant, except in a war.

Frank's table was near one of the self-service serving lines. Those lines served a variety of meats, fruits, and vegetables but also endless portions of ice cream and cake. There may have been folks there on a diet, but judging by the number of people who came back to the line repeatedly, Frank did not see any Weight Watchers devotees.

And yet as hot as it was this day, it was nowhere near as hellish as it was going to get later in the year, in more ways than just the weather. Frank knew all about hell, coming from Pittsburgh. Called the Steel City due to its steelmaking heritage, it was a place that in its earlier steel glory days was described as "hell with the lid off."

That moniker owed itself in part to the smog and pollution that spilled out of the nineteenth and twentieth-century mill town factories; sulfur dioxide mixing in the rain and snow to form sulfuric acid. It was a mixture so potent that when it snowed, the snow was black; so toxic that it ate away auto bodies as they sat in your driveway, not to mention your lungs. The term also had its roots in the organizational Darwin-like existence in those mills where only the strong survived.

Twenty percent of all male deaths in Pittsburgh; mostly immigrants, had come from those mills in the late nineteenth century. An annualized list of mill-related deaths compiled by local writers of that era judged it comparable to a battle in the Civil War. Just working in those mills, where the life expectancy was forty, was itself a version of hell on earth.

In the coming months, Frank would face his own Darwinian version of hell on earth. Outside, in the desert where America would fight a war, he would come to grips with temperatures so extreme that he would swear he could see his own Middle Eastern version of "hell with the lid off" as the searing heat radiated through the desert, torching everything and everyone in sight.

Inside the office where Frank's own personal war was waged, much like that of his mill worker ancestors, he would face a different struggle to survive in a war zone landscape, unlike anything he had ever managed. There were long hours in an organization run by incompetent psychopaths, with few rules consistently enforced, much like the Pittsburgh steel mills of more than a century earlier.

Frank was good at what he did, but that alone was not going to be enough to emerge unscathed and with his dignity intact from this hell on earth. He could manage up the organization, and he could manage down the organization. But today was about managing around, getting to know the organization and its players. It was how you diversified your risk; cheating Darwin in a sense, which was why he was here planning to eat lunch with Jim Parrish, the contracts manager.

FRANK HAD JUST settled into his chair at the dining hall when he noticed Contracts Manager Jim Parrish approaching his table, his tray stuffed with food. Frank had been in camp for what felt like ages. In fact, he'd met Parrish only a couple of weeks earlier upon entering Camp Bradley. The last two weeks had been a blur, most of it intra-organizationally. Frank had been assigned a set of subcontracts by Coleman to read over and administer. He was also placed on a list, along with a room full of subcontract administrators, to get new subcontract actions.

Frank Davenport had come from a big company in a competitive environment. His job in a previous life - not to mention his bonus as a supply chain manager - was mostly based on cutting costs. That meant finding ways to leverage his supplier base for better terms. He'd quickly discovered that this was going to be a much different environment.

Frank found there was little if any attempt to actually administer agreements. There was no attempt to wring savings from the suppliers.

More troubling, it did not appear that many of the subcontract administrators knew how to interpret the language in the agreements, or how to implement that language. This was probably because, like Jason Meeks, many of the subcontract administrators had no background in subcontract administration.

Since the fish rots at the head, these deficiencies pointed directly to management. In those initial weeks, Frank had a chance to take his measure of Jim Coleman, his boss, and he quickly discovered what everybody else already knew: Coleman, besides being incompetent, was borderline illiterate.

Coleman had trouble with the basics. He could not craft a subcontract agreement. He could also barely understand the language used in those subcontract agreements; agreements that he was required to manage seven days a week. That fundamental disconnect explained the total lack of subcontract management.

Frank had informed Coleman early on that in many of the subcontract agreements that he audited, the subcontract administrators were modifying the corporation's General Terms. Those terms were outlined in small, almost unreadable four-point type that lawyers inserted into every agreement to protect the corporation. Anybody with any background knew that the lawyers, who generally lacked a sense of humor when it came to such matters, expressly forbade changes to those terms without the advice and consent of the legal department. The general terms were like the Ten Commandments; they were carved in stone.

Frank asked Coleman if he had gotten the legal department's approval for those changes. What Frank got was a blank stare in return. Not only did Coleman not know, Coleman also didn't know that he did not know. More importantly, he did not care.

But this was not his former life. This legal department was overseen at a local level by a guy that reportedly had been selling used cars before the war. And so, for Frank, the purpose of this lunch was to get to know more about Parrish and his role in the organization.

Was he actually competent? If so, was he friend or foe? In an active war zone, it was a world without rules, an environment devoid of fact-based management. This was management by force of personality. Parrish did not have to be a friend, but it would be nice to ascertain that, at worst, he was another Coleman; meaning, benignly incompetent.

—⸙—

"So HOW DID the laundry thing ever work out?" Frank looked over at Parrish, who was intent on devouring his plate full of food as if it was his last meal.

"Oh, it should be okay," Parrish mumbled. "Once we gather up our costs, we will submit a request for equitable adjustment up through corporate. That will get negotiated out with the ACO, along with a hundred other things. That is the way it works with a cost reimbursable contract in a war zone, Frank."

"Did they give us a good original scope of work for this?" Frank was referring in this case to the laundry.

"Hell no." Parrish laughed. "They just looked over at us, and told us to dry clean laundry, and then wondered why it wasn't done... like the other day." Parrish was laughing, but beneath that exterior grin, there was a good deal of stress which translated directly into what he ate and how fat he was becoming.

"Do you have experience in cost reimbursable contracts, Frank?" Parrish was trying to understand Frank's background, while changing the subject.

"I ran a global supply chain for a stateside medical products company before moving into marketing and business development," Frank replied. "But it was all fixed price work."

Frank stared back at Parrish, trying to grasp how this worked exactly.

"But isn't that a lot of risk? How much dry cleaning, for how many soldiers? What clothes get dry cleaned?"

Frank had lots of experience negotiating multi-million-dollar fixed price contracts in the States, but in those agreements, the scope of work was clearly defined ahead of time, and agreed to by both parties. Here, it seemed that everything was being done on the fly. "Just git 'er done" was something he had heard a lot since arriving.

"Yeah, I understand where you are coming from. We do kind of work at risk in the short term because we have to perform."

"Really? Without so much as a letter telling you what to do? Wow."

"Yeah, sometimes, Frank. You must perform in a war zone. That is what we signed up to do." Parrish mumbled out the words while gnawing away at a fried chicken drumstick.

"So how it works is like this: Buck, Marsh and I will sit down and sketch out a basic plan, which includes extra labor, along with the equipment and material. We will get you guys in procurement to price out some equipment, along with any miscellaneous items like special cleaning fluids. We already have pricing on labor; we will just add a couple of heads. Our overhead rates have already been negotiated with the government. Those numbers form the basis for the equitable adjustment."

Frank stared back at Parrish. "So essentially, you rewrite their scope of work for them and get paid for it?"

Parrish smiled, while stuffing his mouth with a second helping of ice cream and cake.

"Yeah, pretty much, that is how it is. In their defense, you go into a war with one thought in mind, and then things change. Quickly. The original statement of work was only intended to get us into theater."

"So, what do you do?" Parrish inquired. "No company is going to take this kind of risk on a fixed price basis. That would be suicide. And the government knows that, which is why they chose a cost reimbursable type of arrangement."

Parrish continued. "Buck will run that plan, which is essentially a revision to our statement of work, up through the office of the ACO, who administers the contract for the government at the local level, for a sanity check, along with Colonel Harper. Depending on how much this particular modification costs, and the laundry thing is small stuff, the decision on whether or not to proceed stays local. Big dollar changes go up the chain."

"And so, they just accept your numbers?" Frank asked.

Parrish smiled wearily. "Would be nice if it were that easy. There is always some griping about price, performance or delivery."

"We are going to have to show that the additional equipment, materiel, and subcontract labor was sourced at the market price, unless there is some sort of emergency. That is where your team comes in. Like I said, the government already has our overhead rates on the labor. Those rates were negotiated at the outset. Assuming that we do that and the government is convinced by our proposal that the costs are allowable, allocable, and reasonable given the circumstances, then the government signs off on the equitable adjustment, and we proceed."

Parrish grimaced as he spoke. "The problem is that there are hundreds of these, all day long. I report directly to Michael Beck, our corporate counsel, but I am also matrixed to the VP's Rust and Marsh, as well as Buck for the day-to-day. There's me... and my staff of one TCN... to help with the paperwork. There ain't enough hours in the day."

"It gets to be a pain in the ass," Parrish continued. "Tracking each one, developing modifications to the statement of work, negotiating each one out and implementing the changes in a sea of chaos, not to mention a drain on our cash flow because you have to spend the money up front in order to get it returned in the back end."

"And that assumes that there aren't any hiccups like an audit. Then things really slow down, which is why you need deep pockets financially. A war like this can break a company if they don't get paid in a timely manner. And to be fair to the government, they do have a fast pay mechanism which means that you can get paid in ten days, but like everything in life, sometimes shit happens."

Frank was getting a crash course on war zone contracting. "What do we get from all of this?" he asked, wondering if the risk was really worth the reward.

"We get a 2% base award fee on top of our costs. There is also a separate award amount based upon a judgmental evaluation by the government, sufficient to provide motivation for excellence in contract performance. It is called an awards fee, and it can go as high as 7%."

"Management meets regularly, sometimes quarterly, with the government. That board, which is made up of the government's contracting officer who is the ACO, Colonel Harper and others, recommends the award fee up the chain, which is why you see management chipping in, helping craft the modifications to the statements of work for the laundry. The government factors stuff like that into the award fee, especially with new work, like the twenty-five sites that we are adding now."

Frank thought long and hard about what he had just heard. "Wow. That is a sweet deal."

Parrish looked back at Frank, incredulous. "You think so? Two points, with the possibility of an additional seven percent ... and you think that is a good deal?"

Typical lawyer, Frank thought; always looking at a mountain of risk, but never understanding the reward side of the equation.

"Yeah, if what you say is true. Gotta remember, Jim, it is about return on the investor's capital here. If you are getting all of your costs reimbursed and they throw a couple of points your way, it is a bit like printing money. You got no capital invested to speak of so, where is the incentive to control costs?"

Parrish grinned. "Yeah, the key word there was 'if'. So long as the costs are allowable, allocable, and reasonable, everything is good. But all that it takes is for them to start disallowing costs, and your profit disappears. For a long time. And even if we file a claim, and let's say that upon appeal those costs are ultimately found to be reasonable, your cash flow takes a big hit."

Frank concluded that while Parrish was certainly not a financial genius, he was not stupid. It was not hard to see that Coleman and his supply chain group could be a weak link in that just described scenario. Materials and subcontract labor made up a large share of Cork and Hammer's costs. Disallow some of those costs, even a little, and you are on the road to bankruptcy. Frank was right; Coleman was a weak link. But what he did not know yet was that Coleman was a weak link *by design*. And he was not the only weak link, not by a long shot.

—~—

"By the way, are you getting settled in?" Parrish smiled, recalling his early days entering a war zone as a new employee of Cork and Hammer. Like Frank, Parrish was a civilian contractor in a non-governmental for-profit corporation. Everything seemed to be in a state of barely controlled chaos in those early days. At times, it bordered on an out-of-body experience. Even now, things had settled down only a bit. Indeed, coping with that out-of-body experience served to bond colleagues together. It certainly wasn't management that took any interest in assisting with the transition to wartime contracting.

"Yeah, a little," Frank ventured, thinking back to his time in Dubai. "The work for me is the easy part. Knocking out subcontracts is nothing. But I find it a little surreal that they have these little contractors running around here when the military probably could, and should, be doing this work. After all, these contracts are not high-tech weapon systems. Gotta wonder why we are here."

"Well, I can tell you that the logic I hear from Rust and Colonel Harper is this: the brass wanted the fighting forces to concentrate on what they do best; fight, not clean toilets. But..." And here Parrish smiled. "It also allows military personnel to transition to the private sector - the revolving door - while keeping them busy. For example, generals like Rust in the military transition to vice presidents in the private sector. It's crony capitalism. Everybody is getting rich."

"How so?"

"This is about campaign contributions, Frank. It is keeping your big donors happy. The guys on the Hill all need to get re-elected, and so they need a steady supply of money. Cork and Hammer has been at this since after the Second World War. In one shit hole after another, doing the government's dirty work. I guess that Cork and Hammer knows, and has somehow contributed to, every politician affiliated with the Armed Services Committees, at a minimum – despite a long-standing ban on this 'pay to play' stuff. It is an incestuous business."

"Some of it is also about plausible deniability; fronts for the CIA and the like. They get companies like Cork and Hammer to do things that the government either doesn't want to do, or does not want it known that they do. It can be a shitty life chasing government contracts, but if you survive and they reward you with a contract like this - you win - and you die a rich man. It is a bit like a modern-day version of the East India Company."

"The East India Company?" Frank had been more or less listening to Parrish, but could not help being intrigued by the reference to one of the earliest large, public-private corporations.

"Yeah," Parrish replied. "Formed in the early seventeenth century as a joint-stock trading company, The East India Company eventually created a private army and ruled over much of India. The word 'loot', which is Hindustani slang for plunder, comes from those times."

"By 1803, their security force had grown to 260,000 men - twice the size of the British army, by the way - and could marshal more firepower than any other nation-state. That firepower subdued an entire an Indian subcontinent. At one point, the East India Company was generating almost half of British trade."

"The conventional paradigm was that Britain had seized India, but in reality, it was a dangerously unregulated, private company that did the work. They were the original corporate raiders. The plunder derived from its unabashed looting not surprisingly made Robert Clive, the sociopath who ran the company, the richest self-made man in Europe at that time."

"Cork and Hammer and their likes are not that much different now. The big donors, mostly US corporations, are driving foreign policy. It would not surprise me if companies like Cork and Hammer acquired their own private armies at some point, not unlike the East India Company. It's the tail wagging the dog, know what I mean?"

"So, whatever happened to them?" Frank asked.

"Oh, they loaded themselves up with debt and then went crying to the British government for a mega bailout. Their debt was so large that when it became public, thirty banks collapsed, bringing trade to a standstill. The Brits eventually bailed them out, but then were forced to rein them in through regulation. It was the first example of a nation-state regulating a private concern," Parrish replied.

Frank knew a little about the East India Company from his high school history classes. He now knew more than he ever expected to learn. But Frank hadn't come to the dining hall on this particular day for a history or civics lesson.

"So, what do you think about Coleman?" Frank asked, changing the subject.

Parrish answered the question without answering directly. "Coleman is a nice guy. But Buck is constantly ranting about Coleman to Rust; not having the right stock, or screwing something up. Rust is the VP and the rainmaker. He is an ex-general who was hired to make sure that the military brass is satisfied. They provide us with our award fee, not to mention more work."

"Rust won't put up with it for long. He has to answer up the chain to the military and, the way they see it, they pay us to take care of these problems. Our problem with Coleman is not their problem. I do not get involved in the supply chain details; I stay in my lane. I hear Buck ranting about Coleman all of the time."

Parrish paused, then said, "Sounds like you have the background that they want in the position. You sure you want something like this? Buck leaves me alone, but he can be tough to work for."

Frank was slowly losing his appetite. Dining hall food never inspired an appetite. One just ate it to avoid starvation. What had caused the loss of appetite was observing that, between generous portions of food that were rapidly migrating to his waistline, Parrish was confirming his worst fears about Coleman and Buck and the hell into which he had arrived.

"Have you had a chance to meet Derya yet?"

Parrish's question snapped Frank back to the dining hall and reality. "Not yet, although I have heard the name."

"You will. Derya works for Jabil Khan as his on-site project manager. From what I understand - I wasn't here then - Coleman single-sourced all of the initial agreements to Khan at the onset. You will meet her."

Based on what he knew about Coleman, Frank found it difficult to believe the man could implement any strategy, much less a simple one that essentially threw all of the business to one supplier.

"Where did Khan come from, and how did Coleman decide on Khan early on?"

"Dunno, Frank; I wasn't here then. That was a while ago. The government is most likely going to want to see those agreements re-competed. Otherwise, they can disallow our costs. Trust me, every time that I go into negotiate an equitable adjustment now, the ACO is bitching about our cost basis."

Frank considered what he had just heard. Re-competing all of the agreements, while simultaneously completing the sourcing for twenty-five additional sites in an active war zone, with a client already upset about Cork and Hammer's ability to deliver - and his boss couldn't read or write. It was enough to strain even competent project management. This was not that. Frank's appetite was gone.

CHAPTER 15
"Asset Management"

—⁓—

THE SUN WAS setting in the mid-January sky. It was just about 7:00 p.m., quitting time. Conditions were cool this time of the year in Baghdad, especially when the sun went down. The high temperatures during these mostly sunny days reached the mid-sixties, falling into the mid-forties on the Fahrenheit thermometer at night. If you had to work outside, these were nice days to do so. Camp Bradley's central warehouses were little more than a very large set of sheds with gates, a lock, and some fans blowing around the air. Without heat or air conditioning, you were essentially working outside.

The warehouses held equipment and replacement parts for the six existing sites, as well as for the additional nineteen sites for which construction was in progress. The parts in these warehouses were generally purchased in theater. Early on in the war, that meant mostly from Kuwait since there were no other suppliers identified. And by Kuwait, that really meant Khan or his surrogates. As the war progressed, there was a push to source parts in Iraq but, like Kuwait, those were mostly front companies - Khan's front companies.

The warehouses were also the central destination for the other planned twenty-five sites. Cork and Hammer employed a typical hub and spoke concept. Camp Bradley was the hub, meaning that one of its crucial functions was to supply the other sites. Those other sites kept a minimal supply. They placed daily demands on the central warehouse for parts. These parts were ordered through a central computer system, shipped, and billed to the outlying sites where they were consumed.

In a normal setup, the supply chain manager had the cradle to grave responsibility for maintaining the optimal inventory. Normal commercial supply chain managers minimized their weeks of supply in the pipeline because they had the organization's capital at risk. Normal supply chain managers kept a host of metrics available to tell them when their inventory was out of balance.

Jim Coleman, the supply chain manager, was not a normal supply chain manager. What made him anything but normal was, besides knowing nothing about advanced metrics - he had trouble with basic math - none of his people reported to him. They reported to Buck. Coleman had all of the responsibility, just none of the authority to do something that he knew nothing about. Buck wanted it that way; in fact, he and Marsh set it up that way.

Unlike a normal supply chain manager, Coleman's organization merely processed orders for materials through the system once the materials were ordered by project management. Coleman's people's job was to get the parts on order, follow the orders through the system until the parts arrived at the base, place the inventory into stock, and disburse the parts when project management required the parts.

Buck set this game up knowing that he alone controlled the client's capital at risk, and so he kept much more than enough inventory for normal demand. He did this for three reasons.

First, his client was not monitoring inventory levels. They did not care how much inventory he had. They lived for the crisis of the day; crises that popped up constantly. You got no points for having an optimal inventory that conserved capital, but you were held to account for not having the right materials at the right time. Unfortunately for Coleman, it would be he, not Buck, that would pay that price in meetings with the client and, ultimately, with his job.

Second, demand was increasing, given the growth in the outlying sites. That meant that he kept safety stock on hand for shipping to outlying sites; safety stock ostensibly set up to feed the new sites that were just now being built, and were capital-intensive in the construction phase. The problem was that much of that inventory would never make it to those sites.

Third, Buck also knew that the more parts he ordered, the more parts he would use. The more parts that he used, the more parts he would bill. It was all part of defrauding his client in a cost reimbursable environment.

The third-country nationals that ran the warehouse operations had begun to put down their equipment at the end of the day. They were in the process of stowing the Bobcat utility vehicles on which they jockeyed through the narrow aisles each day stocking shelves when a scrawny creature with a British accent arrived. The TCN's, mostly from Hungary, Bosnia, Kosovo, and other parts of Eastern Europe all knew each other, but nobody really knew the Brit. And the Brit kept it that way.

They knew where he worked, in the office next to Kenny Buck. For them, the appearance of power was everything, so when he asked for a list of parts to be pulled and placed into containers, that list with Taylor's signature at the bottom said it all. Nobody said anything.

Barry Kliskey was the Brit. Working for Buck, he had acquired all of the trappings of a good ole boy from Louisiana, minus the Cajun accent. He wore the typical patriotic red, white, and blue ex-pat uniform of the day: a raspberry-red neck, a white collared shirt, and blue jeans. Kliskey's faded blue jeans covered his skinny ass but did little to conceal his distended pot belly, earned from countless nights crawling home from a corner pub in a London ghetto. Rounding out his southern fried get-up was the requisite matching ball cap over mirrored sunglasses and a pair of ill-fitting cheap imitation alligator leather shit-kicker boots.

Kliskey's dull-witted yet intense stare befitted someone slightly deranged. His cartoonish American expat outfit, coupled with his demeanor and the connection to Buck, communicated to the mostly European TCN's that he did not need to take their crap. He just wanted the parts.

At the end of a long day and ready for dinner at the dining hall, the TCN's were only too happy to oblige. They would hand over the keys to the warehouses on their way to signing out for the day. Kliskey took over from there, directing his own team that, in the process, helped themselves to whatever they wanted in that warehouse.

Minutes later, a trailer convoy pulled up, and the evening's work began. Kliskey's team knew what it was looking for, and began pulling inventory from stock: electronics, plumbing, and air conditioning parts, all ostensibly destined for a covert operation the military was rehabbing for use as listening posts near the border with Iran. Only this stuff would never make it to Iraq's border with Iran, or to those listening posts.

Kliskey's team pulled parts without regard to their consequences. He was not concerned with stock shortages, nor with correcting paperwork, or that his deliberate, malicious draw down of stock would adversely affect vital operations. He and Buck owned the people; they had their own agenda, and they were managing through force of personality. It was Coleman who answered for the process. Coleman would have to answer to Buck and the colonel in stock shortage meetings.

In turn, the colonel had to answer to his counterparts in the military – especially near the border where construction was going at a feverish pace – and he did not like to hear that he did not have inventory. The colonel wasn't stupid; he knew what Buck was doing. He just ducked the issue up the chain for now, and with good reason: it was difficult to get a man to understand something when $3.5 million in bribes coming from Buck depended upon his not understanding it.

—ɯ—

IT WAS APPROACHING nine-thirty in the evening when Kliskey's guys put the final lock on the trailer convoy. Ex-pats just leaving work in the camp would exchange one ten by twenty trailer where they spent twelve hours a day for another container of the exact same drab gray color and shape that had a small cot where the desk sat. Leaving work, they would fumble around, walking on uneven ruts on rough roads in the dark while seeking out the dining hall on the way home. Small flashlights were necessary equipment because overhead street lights attracted rockets, and rockets meant sirens.

Sirens meant bunker time. Bunkers were concrete shells, small, re-bar reinforced fortresses with twelve-foot high T-shaped concrete walls. Those T-walls, along with the one-hundred-ton crane assisted installation, had been supplied by local Iraqi contractors who had grown instantly rich in the process. Bunkers dotted the camp where both civilian and military personnel assembled day or night in ill-fitting helmets and flak jackets, waiting for the all-clear.

Nobody liked bunker time. It was like sitting in a furnace during the heat of the day and being relegated to one late at night messed with your sleep. Still, it was the price you paid for the ability to escape the effects of rocket-propelled grenades in a war zone.

There were no bunkers in the no man's land outside of Camp Bradley that was called the Red Zone. Accordingly, bunker time existed only inside relatively safe areas like Camp Bradley or what would be called the Green Zone, and so there was no bunker time for the convoy leaving Camp Bradley this night.

Terry Taylor poked his head around the corner of Jerry Ballow's office, grunting while handing Jerry a stack of paper.

"Here's the paperwork for tonight's convoy. Make sure that we get this out before you go home."

Eyeglasses in hand and still staring at his computer, Ballows peered up at Taylor with a wan smile. "Yes sir, we will get 'er done."

A little more than three hours later, Ballows himself provided the paperwork to his Army liaison, a corporal young enough to be his grandson. The distance between Baghdad and Kuwait City was approximately 350 miles, a distance normally traversed in about six hours on well-maintained roads and at high speeds. The travel time to Kuwait for this military protected convoy was projected to be eight arduous hours.

This trip was not ordinary; a seventy vehicle, up-armored convoy traveling back roads at night on a circuitous route through terrorist-infested terrain. The goal was to get there as quickly as possible without getting killed in the process. As a result, they did not stop for anything, animals crossing the road, cars in the way, even civilians/could-be terrorists stupid enough to insert themselves between moving vehicles. Less concerned with precisely what was on the manifest, the mission of the Army convoy commander was to get from point A to point B, and he was going to accomplish that mission.

As the logistics manager, it was Jerry's job to know what was on each and every manifest. One wall of his ten by twenty trailer-turned-office was papered floor to ceiling, covered with charts pinpointing each delivery. Jerry was not overly concerned with the contents of this outbound shipment. Some of the trailers were empties and the rest carried scrap equipment that would be disposed of in Kuwait per Army regulations. Once in Kuwait, the empty containers would be loaded up for the return trip back to the camp.

Shortly after midnight, the Army convoy commander received his all-clear to move, and the Humvee-escorted convoy departed into a cold, drizzly Iraqi night. The rain was a good sign, hopefully portending a quiet, uneventful night. Nobody liked working in the rain, not even armed terrorists on the hunt for a convoy to ambush.

The convoy commander would not be so lucky, for about twenty-five minutes out from the camp, one of the trailers developed trouble with a tire. The convoy commander would never know that this particular tire had been sabotaged, cut to induce a small leak almost immediately. Not once in the Red Zone would he attempt further due diligence.

Stopping only long enough to disconnect twenty-foot Trailer No. 4668854 from the convoy, the troops quickly shoved the now semi-mobile trailer awkwardly to the side of the road with an up-armored

Army transport truck. Style points didn't count here. Speed was of the essence, and orders were immediately barked - Move out!

Passing the trailer and gaining speed quickly so as not to be a target any longer than necessary, soldiers tossed grenades in an attempt to disable, if not destroy, the trailer that they thought contained only scrap equipment. In what seemed like an eternity, but in reality was only minutes, the convoy had stopped to amputate a life-threatening appendage and had promptly disappeared into the blackened, misty fog, otherwise unhurt, and still on track to accomplish the mission.

Others, while not terrorists, did work this night. Almost like clockwork, minutes after the military convoy had disappeared towards Kuwait, a small convoy of pickup trucks appeared. Quickly setting up shop next to the charred remnants of what was minutes ago a fully functioning trailer, and with mechanic-like precision, they pried loose the rear panels of the container using bolt cutters to cut away the chain and lock holding the door panels together.

Once inside, they proceeded to disembowel the metallic carcass. Fortunately, the contents were undamaged, for it was this specific trailer and this particular set of goods that they were seeking and for which they had gotten soaked in the now driving rain. Unlike the manifest, which described the contents as "Other Miscellaneous Non-Hazardous Trash/Scrap Materials," Trailer No. 4668854 contained hundreds of those expensive electronics, plumbing, and air conditioning parts which had, only hours before, been sitting in Camp Bradley's central warehouse.

Those goods, all brand new, were negotiable on the open market in Turkey, or Kuwait where the parts were initially purchased. It did not take long, thirty minutes at most, to empty the full trailer. Then these Arabs in the night disappeared as quickly as they came, with the rainstorm pounding the sand dunes, forever erasing any forensic evidence of the incident.

Thirty days later, a scrap ticket writing off the contents of the convoy arrived on Frank's desk. Accompanying that ticket would be a separate ticket scrapping the trailer itself. Stapled to the card scrapping Trailer No. 4668854 was an incident report from the convoy commander detailing the incident. That paperwork was what Frank needed for the auditors who might eventually, in a day of reckoning months or even years later, pore over the contents in an audit, satisfying themselves that the contractor had done its job.

Frank had noticed that there was an entire, separate paper file that had been kept for scrap tickets just like this. The file folder had hundreds of scrap tickets, all documented in detail with an accompanying written report from the U.S. military about the loss of assets in the Red Zone. Frank could not know that the "scrap" described on the paperwork had not so long ago been part of his inventory. It was inventory that had been requested by Buck for repairs that were separately authorized, allocated, and expensed for reimbursement, but that never occurred.

Instead, the parts would be returned to Kuwait and recycled, sold back to Khan for pennies on the dollar. Replacement parts, for which there was now an apparent demand, would be ordered by Coleman's group. Khan would ship those same parts back at list price. For now, Frank would not question either Buck or the military commanders. He had been told that life in the Red Zone was tenuous. He believed it.

For the civilian contractor foot soldiers, dazed and numb from consecutive twelve-hour days pushing scrap ticket paperwork and the like, this was a necessary evil, a job to do which kept the larger than usual, war-related paychecks coming. For Case Hammer, that paperwork, which documented a cost of goods to his government-imposed overlords, was his revenue stream.

Those government fog-of-war costs were his fountain of gold. They were his wet dream. Those dusty files sitting in some forgotten filing cabinet represented an ejaculation of hard currency, a stream that had only grown as the war ground on. These were soaring revenues on which the valuation of his company relied on in the now pending sale to BLTVDef.

There would come a day of reckoning for the contents of those files. But that day was tomorrow's business, something over which government auditors and company compliance bureaucrats would do battle. The contents of Trailer No. 4668854 were today's business, and so of a much more pressing nature for Marsh and Buck. That immediate concern took the form of a bank account in Kuwait. In the thirty days that it took Frank Davenport to receive, review, sign, and forward those same scrap tickets to a silently smiling Kenny Buck for countersignature, the net proceeds of Trailer No. 4668854 would accrue to Marsh and Buck's Kuwait bank account.

"NEXT ITEM ON the list: bottled water. We have been running out of bottled water. We can't keep doing this." Kenny Buck scowled over at Coleman, with the colonel and Buck's lynch mob of staff looking on like birds of prey sizing up their next meal. The critical part, left unsaid, was that it was Buck and Taylor who were placing the orders. Coleman was apparently just processing them. Frank was struggling, trying to get his head around why, if Coleman was only processing orders, he was the subject of such ire.

The meeting was a regular expedite meeting where management sat down with the supply chain types to go over stuff that was out of stock. Frank had been in a thousand of these meetings earlier in his career, although most of them had been devoted to improvements. In the real world, once a defect was discovered, time was dedicated to getting to the root cause, along with a plan to get better. In this case, Buck should have been asking why they were out of stock, but he knew better. This was just a show trial.

"I will check into it, Kenny," Coleman replied, looking at the floor like a beaten dog.

"Buck is the one placing the orders," Frank whispered to Janey Lynn Reed. She silently motioned approval at Frank.

As they exited the meeting, Frank sauntered into Coleman's office. "Hey, can I ask: how many weeks of supply are you budgeted to have on hand for bottled water?"

It was simple math. Weeks of supply for a particular item was a function of the demand for that specific item, given the inventory in stock for that part. If Coleman had ten units in stock for anything in which the average weekly demand was ten, then Coleman had one week of supply on hand.

Frank could tell that this stuff was like rocket science to Coleman, who did not have "rocket scientist" tattooed on his forehead. Coleman had no budgets; he had no idea of how to draft a budget, and he did not understand the basic math.

"Let me go down to the warehouses and do some checking," Frank said to Coleman, then he disappeared.

Back at Frank's office, Jason Meeks was closing up his computer, preparing to depart the camp by bus for the trip to the airport for his holiday. "Speak to Keni. He runs the warehouse," Jason hollered as he boarded the bus.

Minutes later, Frank had negotiated the sand-covered craters that passed for roads on the camp and connected his office containers and the warehouses. Now he was standing face-to-face with Keni Mehmeti, a Kosovar, who was the lead warehouse operator.

"Bottled water, Keni. Any idea of why we are always out of stock?" Frank knew that the Kosovar wasn't managing the warehouse; Coleman was. Keni was just a guy who pulled the stock items off of the steel shelving. He also supervised a small crew of Kosovars who also pulled parts. That was his proper role.

In an organization devoid of processes and metrics, the unofficial pipeline was where you stood the best chance of getting answers. And the Kosovars who ran the warehouse were the informal pipeline. Frank's problem was that he did not know any of them. It was an excellent time to meet them.

"Frank, we just pull orders that come from Buck and Taylor. We do not get into why we have stock or do not have stock. I can tell you that stuff leaves here at all hours of the day and night, even after my guys leave."

"Who is coming in here after hours, Keni?" Frank was stunned at the lack of security around the warehouses.

"Kliskey. He sits next to Buck. Buck tells him what to do. Yeah, and the colonel is pulling bottled water out of the warehouse all of the time, just to water the grass in front of his living container. Ever wonder why his grass looks so green... in a desert?" The Kosovar laughed. "Shit like that goes on all of the time around here, Frank. Welcome to the funny farm."

"You are kidding me."

Five minutes later, Frank was in Coleman's office. "Jim, I just spoke to Keni Mehmeti in the warehouse. He says that stuff is leaving after hours. He also says that the colonel is watering his lawn with bottled water."

"Hey, Frank. Did Jason give you his company-issued cell phone on the way out?" Coleman had utterly changed the subject.

"Yeah, why?"

"Because the U.S. Marshals were just in the hooch that you share with Jason. They found seventy-five thousand dollars in his wall locker. They are going to want to examine the contents of that cell phone."

Frank was stunned. He had never really gotten to know Meeks and, from the sounds of it, he never would.

Meeks would not be the last to leave.

The daily expedite meetings, where parts shortages were discussed at a senior staff level, had become increasingly long and contentious as the stockouts increased, just as Buck had planned. For his part, Coleman, not the brightest of bulbs by any means but not altogether stupid, had begun to suspect that he was being set up.

He wasn't the only one.

—~—

"What is going on? When we last spoke, you were telling me about the shakedown in Dubai, correct?"

Larry was just getting up to speed in what was a fluid situation. He and Frank had been sending emails back and forth during Frank's initial days in camp. This was a chance to sit down for just a few minutes on the phone in an attempt to bring some clarity to a fluid situation.

"Yeah, what a long, strange trip it has been," Frank laughed, referring to one of the Grateful Dead's more famous lyrics. "And I have been here less than two weeks. So, let me give you the brief - I am going to call it the 'USA Today' - version of what has been happening since I got shaken down in Dubai. Fucking surreal, but here goes."

"Really. How are your digs, man?"

"It is tough to describe to somebody who had never been outside of the U.S., let alone traveled to the Middle East," Frank said. "It is a bit like a trailer park in the California desert, only in the Middle East, surrounded by a bunch of military guys with guns and a bad attitude."

"They put the little people like me in what they call dry hooches; living containers with no bathroom facilities," Frank continued. "But they did not have one the first night, so I got put into group accommodations, which was nothing more than what looked to be a homeless shelter with lots of cots."

"Lots of snoring going on." Larry laughed, trying to make light of the matter.

"Yeah, until one of the 'inmates' began to jump nasty with the guards. On Christmas Eve, no less."

"Oh shit."

Frank continued. "For beginners, we get to Baghdad from Dubai in a Russian bucket of bolts piece of crap left over from the Cold War, dodging anti-aircraft fire on the way down, with a pilot who was fucked-up drunk. Freaked out the lady beside me so much they sent her home."

"Yeah, and the next day, while I am in line to get my digs, the lady in the laundry gets into the face of a guy who turns out to be the contracts manager about not doing his job. Turns out that the client has imposed new specifications down onto the laundry, but nobody told her, and now the client is in a rage. Don't know the contracts manager obviously, but he does not sound like the sharpest knife in the drawer, at least not like the guys that I was dealing with in the medical products business."

"My God. Who is running that place over there?" Larry asked. Frank was asking the same question, only it seemed that Larry had gotten to the nub of the issue from nine time zones away a lot faster than he did.

Frank laughed. "Yeah, funny you should mention that because I have the same question."

"I no sooner get here than I go into a meeting with my boss, and he is getting beaten up about some bottled water. They have been running out of bottled water. I check into it, and it turns out that his boss is the problem. His boss has been ordering it; not my boss. And then his boss has been snatching it from the warehouse; a warehouse run by my boss - but with guys that do not report to my boss - if you can understand that. Oh, and by the way, what bottled water that we do have is being used to water the freshly-mowed grass in front of the colonel's hooch. In a fucking desert, during a war."

"And blaming it on your boss?" Larry sounded concerned. "That sounds familiar; taking the fall for somebody else's mistakes." Larry knew Frank's history, of course, and the pain of that chapter in his life.

"There is more. We had an issue with a man-camp, which is where some third-country nationals live. That camp was built out of spec with the client's requirements. Turns out that project management gave my boss the wrong specification, but they want to blame it on him."

Larry gasped. "Jesus. What do you know about your boss?"

"He appears to be flat out incompetent. I have had a couple of conversations with him, but he has no background, no training. They appear to want it that way. It gets a little technical to explain on the phone, but trust me, he is clueless."

"How are you with that? You have a long way to go there."

"Going to keep my head down. I need to get up to speed on how the government handles things, but I know what I am doing in an economic sense," Frank said. He was whistling through the graveyard, knowing full well from experience that competence alone would not save you.

"The scary part is that there is a lot of money floating around; government money. I am not going to prison for them," Frank said, reflecting back to Meeks and the wall locker money.

Frank was also having flashbacks to how his earlier job had ended. He realized that he still had not adjusted to that event in his life, not to mention his divorce. And now he was caught up trying to survive in no man's land.

"I know you, Frank. You will do the right thing. If you get into trouble, just listen to that little voice inside of you. You and I have discussed that many times. Don't ignore it; you know that."

It was an excellent way to end a short, stress-reducing conversation with a good friend.

"Good advice. Got to go now; got to get to the laundry, and then to the dining hall before they close. Thanks for listening." And with that, Frank began to turn the page on his career, and his life. Somehow, he sensed that the transition would not be as smooth as just collecting a paycheck.

CHAPTER 16
Force of Personality

—∾—

JIM COLEMAN'S FATE was no anomaly; he was just another in a long line of managers at Camp Bradley that been welcomed into the proverbial NFL - Not for Long - under Buck. It was how the fear and intimidation part of the plan worked. Coleman would soon be shown the door after being tortured long enough in meetings so that both the colonel and Buck had a paper trail justifying his release.

Colonel Rick Harper would inform the general to whom he reported that he had forced the contractor to make a change. While not true, that spin on events served to cover his ass. It also sent every other bureaucrat higher up the organization chain who was complaining about the shortages right back to sleep. Marsh would inform Hammer that Buck had solved the problem, praising Buck for his managerial skills in the process. Buck would just bring in another victim, and the game would continue. That next victim was on the agenda today.

"Let's talk about some HR issues." Buck grimaced, pushing his chair back while reaching for another cup of coffee.

"I know what you are thinking." Marsh smiled at Buck.

"Coleman's replacement?"

"Yeah. That guy was as dumb as a fence post, which I had been good with until now. But that latest blow up on the man-camp modification combined with the parts shortages; those were the straws that broke the camel's back. Were you fucking with him on that man-camp specification, by the way?" Marsh laughed, implying that Buck had deliberately set up Coleman to fail. "I read the reports from Janey. Christ, did I read reports."

"Yeah, well ... a little." Buck smiled slightly, understating the issue while sipping his coffee. He wasn't going to bullshit Marsh, who not only knew this stuff backward and forwards, he knew all of the games. Buck knew he was to blame here; it was just the psychopath in him coming out.

"Well, at the end of the day, that change order was big bucks," Marsh said, "and Coleman either knew or should have known about that man-camp specification because Janey told him, so we need to get rid of that guy now. The client needs a scalp so that they can go back to sleep. I also think that it is a good time to change horses there. We do not want anybody getting too comfortable, especially right now, if you know what I mean."

Marsh was referring not only to the supply chain manager's position but also with an eye to Khan and the money in Kuwait. He did not want Coleman waking up to what was going on around him; not that either Marsh or Buck thought that he would.

"Yeah, well for some people, dumb is forever," Buck concluded. This, for Coleman, would be the epitaph carved onto his corporate tombstone. "Any thoughts on a replacement? We are going to need somebody in here quickly. Lots of work with those additional man-camps. What do you think about Davenport?"

"Janey took a look at his resume. He was a corporate supply chain manager in a previous life. Has an MBA, and Janey says that he appears to be very smart. And everybody else here in Coleman's shop is worse."

In other words, Marsh was saying that he was over-qualified. In another situation, in another corporation, and at another time, Frank would fit in perfectly.

"Did you have a chance to chat with him about the position?" Marsh knew through emails that Buck had planned a short meeting.

"Not yet, but I will. Seems to know his stuff."

Frank had just arrived, and while Buck and Marsh had met him, they had not gotten a chance to vet him or his skills, not that they actually wanted somebody with some qualifications. What they had was a resume and a recommendation from Janey Lynn Reed. Buck knew that Coleman could be managed; he was not sure about Frank.

But they did need somebody who could handle the extra work that the client was shoving at them. The corporate valuation was, in part, based upon the projected revenue stream from additional projects such as the other sites. Those sites needed to function. It was a delicate balancing act.

They wanted somebody just good enough to manage short-term while they were expanding the sites, but not good enough to catch on to their scam. They also did not need a repeat of the Coleman situation blowing up in their faces late in the game. In the final analysis, Marsh decided to take a chance on Davenport, figuring that by the time that he caught on, if he caught on, they would be out the door. Buck thought that was a mistake. He did not know Davenport, but he did know Reed, and if she liked him, Buck by definition did not.

Buck would be proven right.

"Okay," Marsh said. "Make an offer to Davenport. And one more thing while we are on this supply chain thing... Re-competes. When we bring on Davenport, what do we want to tell him about re-competing Khan's stuff?" Janey Lynn Reed had been complaining to Marsh privately that Coleman was not pushing harder to re-compete Khan's subcontracts.

"Let me handle that," Buck replied. "I did talk to Davenport about that. We are going to have to show competition in the new sites. I spoke to Khan. He assures me that he has Iraqi front companies for all or most of the goods and services that we buy. We can give the appearance of competition, which will satisfy both internal audit and the external auditors for the additional twenty-five sites. As for the original sites, Derya has been quietly negotiating with the subcontract administrators. She has some of those extended, but not all."

Buck left out the part explaining just how Derya had completed those negotiations. What Buck also did not say was that he would drag out the remaining re-competes for the original sites as long as possible, hoping that events, like the transfer in ownership, would overtake a small thing like the re-competes. The last thing he wanted was anybody getting any closer to those subcontracts than necessary.

Buck did not want somebody like Frank, who looked like he knew what he was doing, negotiating down pricing or getting into the details. He also did not want to listen to both Khan and Derya, who were continually complaining about wanting more business. He just wanted this all to end.

"Okay. Good stuff. What else do you have? It has been a long day, and my back is killing me."

THERE WAS A knock at the door of the Colonel Harper's forty foot, double-wide trailer that served as his home away from home in theater. The colonel's hooch had all of the modern conveniences: a king-size bed, large screen television, and a large wet bar for meetings with staff both during and after work. Unlike the little people, it also had maid service, as in full-service maid service.

"Who is it?" the colonel asked, peering up over his glasses. He'd been reading a letter that his daughter had written to him about a kitten she had just gotten at a pound, complete with a picture attached. It was just before noon, and much of the staff would be at the PX, at the dining hall, or in the gym working out.

"Housekeeping," a small voice called out from outside of the green metal door to the trailer.

"Okay, c'mon in." He grinned, removed his glasses, and placed the letter and picture of his daughter and kitten on the nightstand.

"This can't take long. I have a meeting in about thirty minutes," Harper informed her in a manner not unlike he would when addressing one of his non-commissioned officers for whom he was lord and master.

Not that she cared, but that was good news for she was not there for pleasure. The act itself would be construed as an act of joy if one were to observe it from a distance, but to these two what would transpire next was every bit as much of a business transaction as if both were sitting in a boardroom.

She understood her customer now and knew what he liked. Wordless, for time was a factor, she unzipped his zipper to his pants, ambidextrously reaching for his very erect penis while unbuttoning her top, all the while maintaining direct eye contact with the now faintly moaning senior officer. She smiled at him, and then placed his hands on her still firm breasts. Her large, brown oval eyes flashed at him before she proceeded to the task at hand.

She liked him touching her breasts, not because it felt pleasing to her but because in doing so, the time shortened between what she did with her mouth and what he managed to deposit into a napkin that she provided especially for this occasion. The sum and substance of the act lasted less than two minutes, during which time her eyes never left his.

Like her, the colonel understood the commercial nature of what they did and had always done. And yet, for all of the ritual nature of the act, he never failed to get off when she made eye contact as she did. In bringing the colonel to climax, Derya managed to convey an impression that there was no fear, like an animal, no sign of weakness, and he liked that.

In his mind, he was the aggressor. He barked orders, and people obeyed without hesitation. Aside from the act itself, it was what he liked about what they did; a conquering sadistic sexual predator and his surrendering prey, if only in his mind and just for a brief few minutes. He wanted those eyes to succumb at some point, to convey a sense of fear.

But that would never be the case.

The eyes that stared back coldly and unemotionally would not relent; they did not convey either a sense of foreboding or of fear, only a basic, primal urge. Capturing the spoils of this little psychological war in her eyes, Derya's gaze intensified, the roles reversing. The predator had long since become prey. She was in total control of her now captured game, toying with it like an animal before the kill.

Dressing quickly, she reached for the handle to the trailer door. On the way out into the white-hot brilliant sunlit blue one hundred ten plus degree Fahrenheit heat of the day, she looked back; not as a victim, but as a man-eater taking stock of her now caged victim. She would return - she wanted to return - to play with her toy. She owned his cock, but more importantly, she owned his ass.

"Oh, and one more thing, colonel." She shut the door briefly to prevent the blast furnace that was the midday Iraqi heat from entering the building.

"What is it, Derya?" The colonel's eyes met hers, trying to ascertain the nature of the quid pro quo that was sure to come; quid pro quo being a fixture in this part of the world. Nobody ever did anything for nothing, he thought, as if what Derya just did was because she found him handsome and irresistible, like some rock star.

"We have been supporting the U.S. military, and have been doing it successfully. No?"

She still had her sunglasses on in the colonel's darkened hooch, shading those gorgeous eyes that now seemed to come alive, especially since she was discussing an issue in which she had an abiding interest, which was the work at the listening posts along the border with Iran and Iraq.

"Yeah, I guess so; at least from what Buck tells me. Why?"

"Well, you have some work going on at the border, and we would like to do that work, as well. Can you talk to Buck for us? I have spoken to him, but he just puts it off on his supply chain people, and we are not getting anywhere, colonel." She smiled sweetly, her eyes gazing down at her prey.

—ꝏ—

"Let's get some chow and have a chat," Marsh called out to Buck as he set down his carry-on bag containing his laptop and briefcase alongside his suitcase. Marsh had the executive quarters at Camp Bradley; a double-wide with all of the electronic toys which was situated between the colonel's and Kenny Buck's trailer. Unlike the minions, it had daily laundry service, a brand-new vehicle at his disposal, a full wet bar and a built-in jacuzzi.

"When does the DFAC close again? I am hungry," Marsh said wearily. It had been a long day.

"Twenty hundred hours," Buck responded, looking at his watch as the skies darkened and the nighttime desert air cooled. "We have about thirty minutes; plenty of time."

"By the way, how did your little impromptu meeting with Rust go?" Marsh had been grabbed by VP Rust, along with his chief of staff, Charlie Bates, on the way into camp for an impromptu meeting over the scope of work modifications for the twenty-five new camps. Marsh had arrived about five in the afternoon but had been in the conference with Rust and Bates since about that time, so this was his first opportunity alone with Buck, and he was starved. As the project manager, Buck was usually in those meetings but had been driving back from Kuwait when Marsh arrived.

"Oh, he is happy. The client wants those additional sites up and running yesterday. Rust, Bates, and I spent two hours this afternoon holding their hand, assuring them that we were on track. We have some issues, as you know, but nothing we aren't in the process of handling."

Rust's job was the care and feeding of the client. It was something that he liked to do. He did not overly concern himself with operational matters below him; he focused on what was going on above him. That was where Marsh and Buck entered on the organizational chart. Rust was only too happy to turn the operational issues over to Marsh and Buck, and they, in turn, liked it that way, for a good reason.

Marsh and Buck entered the dining facility just in time to grab a plastic tray, fill it with food, grab some silverware, and retire back to a small, quiet conference room that adjoined the facility. Most times, that conference room was booked for client meetings with Iraqi dignitaries or State Department officials touring the facilities. It was empty tonight, and so Marsh and Buck used it to meet. The days were long and ended late, and so meetings like this were frequent, but that was life on a busy project.

"Did Rust bring up those sites up north?" Buck asked. Marsh knew that Derya and Khan had been bugging Buck for more work, especially up north near the border with Iran.

"No deal. That work stays in-house with the client, the Army Corps of Engineers. Rust was pretty adamant about that."

"Roger that," replied Buck, leaning in closer to Marsh so that he could lower his voice. "That bitch is making noises about causing issues with getting to the Kuwaiti account, if you know what I mean. Not sure that she can do that; we control the accounts. She and Khan want that work up there - I get that. But I have told her no, the colonel has told her no, but she just keeps it up." He was referring to that earlier conversation in Buck's hooch where Derya had been playing hardball with Buck without consulting Khan.

"Did you have a talk with Khan about her while you were in Kuwait?"

"Yeah, the little fucker is dealing out of both sides of his mouth. I tell him to control the bitch. I tell him that we appreciate what she does for us, but 'no' is 'no.' And I told him that we were not going to listen to any negotiations about the money. He knows how much we have in that account. And hell, we are doing another twenty-five camps. What the fuck is his problem? He says that they are concerned that Cork and Hammer is being sold which could leave him out in the cold."

"And? What did you say about the sale?"

"Told him that I could not confirm anything at this point, just like I told her." Buck turned his attention back to his steak.

"Look, Khan isn't getting anything from those accounts until we all get something, which is when this thing ends. I understand his concern about the game possibly ending a little earlier than planned. You need to make that clear to him. And to Derya." Marsh wasn't in any mood to play "let's make a deal" after a long flight from the States, combined with some of the usual client hand holding.

"What do you want to do?"

"For now, we just keep on going." Marsh was trying to keep Buck calm and focused. He did not want the wheels coming off at this point. "We tell them nothing until right at the very end, which is when we check out through Kuwait for the last time. They will suspect things; that is OK. She will see people on camp; rumors will swirl. Tell Khan that we still have a deal. If he expects anything at all from that account, he needs to stick to the deal. Next issue."

"What is your plan with Janey Lynn?" Buck hated the mouthy bitch. He had hated her from back in the States, but this is where his hatred for the woman was getting in the way of their little mission.

And Marsh knew it. He had been refereeing the little intramural skirmishes with Buck and Janey over Coleman for some time, with Taylor as sometimes go-between stooge. Buck wanted to bring managers into theater, chew them up, and spit them out. It was simpler that way. In his view of life, people were disposable. It was a cold attitude common to hardcore drug addicts. Getting a fix mattered; little else did, and druggies like Buck don't feel your pain. Marsh just brought a more strategic approach to the situation.

"Look, we need her right now, if for nothing else than appearances. She has been through the files and knows what is in them. Now, to be sure, she does not know what is going on with Khan and the supplier base. But if Witt's boys and/or the client show up here and start poking around into stuff, we need her to be able to pull files and talk to the issues. Hammer is counting on that."

"Well, do we have anybody at corporate that can fill in?" Buck was pressing the issue. Marsh could tell that the man-camp problem had gotten to Buck a little more than he was letting on. Or maybe it was just the stress. Either way, Buck of all people did not need to appear to be in a panic mode.

"Not now. Are there any other time bombs that I should know about?" Marsh was getting a little concerned.

"No," Buck replied in a manner not all that convincing, his mind churning a mile a minute. And then he began to smile.

He recalled that Taylor had been banging the Filipino girls at the laundry. He also knew that Janey Lynn was jealous as hell and - envy being one of the seven deadly sins - he would use that against her. Janey Lynn Reed was going to pay for her big mouth. He needed Taylor - for now.

Buck and Marsh began their trek back to Buck's office in the cool desert evening. They were all alone in the large compound's parade ground, a perfect time and place to discuss what Marsh wanted to talk about next.

"Oh, let's talk time ... and money," Marsh said, turning to Buck. "We need to speed up the shipments to Kuwait. I want to make sure that we are on-budget when we pull the plug on this thing. I know that we have those additional sites to manage, but we are on borrowed time now. "

Marsh looked directly at Buck, with a look that for a millisecond almost intimidated his psychopath of a project manager. Then he continued.

"They are getting close on this deal, as you know. Hammer and Witt at BLTVDef have been meeting on the acquisition. They have been working steadily on it, and both sides are committed to the deal. I do think that it will go down, but you need to keep that confidential because when it does happen, it will be a rush to the finish. Both sides will want to close this really quickly."

"How quickly?" Buck was concerned about doing all of the due diligence on the acquisition at the same time they were expanding into the other twenty-five sites. He was also keeping his eye on the Kuwait account, which for both Buck and Marsh was the holy grail.

"I want to hit budget, and then some, if possible. Where are we with that, by the way... the Kuwait account? How much do we have now?"

"Yeah, I did check on that," Buck said. "We are still more than $100 million short of our $350 million goal, so we have some work to do to get there."

"Well, you are going to have to get with the colonel and tell him that we are going to have to speed things up. We can create additional bogus demand on our end, but he is going to have to work his end to move those materials to Kuwait. We need to increase the churn of materials going in and coming out of those warehouses. Got it?"

Moving materials in and out of a war zone was not nearly as simple as shipping goods in the States, something of which all sides were painfully aware. Trucks were blown up all of the time, so convoys were carefully planned and scheduled with military vehicles to guard against terrorist attacks.

"Tell Khan to get an offshore account set up for the colonel, with the account number. Present him with the account number when you give him the instructions to coordinate the speed-up on his end. He will get pumped up when he senses that he is a little closer to $3.5 million. Set up the Kliskey account at the same time. The money is going to keep 'em focused."

"Once you get the green light from Colonel Harper, start ramping up the demand for parts from Khan and his front companies. Start pulling even more stuff from the warehouses. Those warehouses need to be picked as clean as we can over the next few months before we check out. Use the additional sites as cover to explain the marginal increase in demand."

Marsh looked at Buck, who had a stressed look on his face. Buck was all in with the plan, it was just that there were not enough hours in a day, and this was crunch time. Marsh was leaving the details to Buck, but it was those details that Buck, the micromanager, was struggling with, trying to keep all of the balls in the air at the same time.

"Roger that, sir. Trust me, I am on it," Buck said.

CHAPTER 17
A Monopoly on the Legitimate Use of Physical Force

—∞—

It was just after six in the morning, and Frank Davenport was on his way to get breakfast before heading off to work. The sun was up, but the comparatively mild heat of this January day had yet to arrive. The air was delightfully crisp and usually quiet this time of year during the daily two-hundred-meter walk to Camp Bradley's dining hall.

Most expats on base, still mostly asleep from the night before, stumbled through that trek almost half-conscious. It was another typical Groundhog Day; a bit like going for coffee before heading off to work in the States. Only today would be different, providing a stark reminder that they were "not in Kansas anymore".

Frank had no sooner left his hooch than he heard it: the rat-tat-tat of machine-gun fire, followed by screams. As he looked up, Frank quickly determined that the noise appeared to be coming from a top floor of a nearby apartment complex not far from the T-walls which encompassed the base. As Frank entered the main road, which led to the dining hall, the machine-gun fire got louder. It was then that he saw the signs.

The signs were basic, but right to the point, which is how things tend to get communicated here. One said NO and pointed one way, which was how Frank typically traveled to the dining hall. Another said YES and directed the expats in the exact opposite direction. Just in case that some expats had trouble understanding the definition of NO, a Humvee with an armed soldier stood directly in the road, motioning the expats in the direction of YES.

As Frank and the six other expats with whom he was sharing this short but memorable walk turned towards YES, Frank looked up again in the direction of both the gunfire and the screams. The apartment building had been close to the outer T Walls, so close that machine gun shells had entered the camp over the T Walls.

For most of the expats, YES was just another detour on the road to getting something to eat. But there were those, like Frank, who took a moment to marvel at what they had just seen. Like most civilians, Frank had never seen or heard the sounds of raw, unvarnished killing. And especially before breakfast, for that was what was going on not far from their base camp respite. For those who had, the death occurred in a highway accident or even a homicide. Those killings were rare; they were likely illegal, and there were consequences for violating both community norms and the law.

Following World War 1, Max Weber, the German philosopher, defined the state as an institution that claimed a monopoly on the legitimate use of physical force in a given territory. This was state-sanctioned violence, but in a state which had lost its former monopoly on physical force, also something with which American civilians almost never get up close and personal. And it was occurring right in front of them in real-time, not on some CD or DVD.

There would be no station breaks or advertisements for coffee or smartphones before returning to the action. There would be no Hollywood-style crescendo of sound in the background as the bad guys died on screen in slow motion while customers ate popcorn at home or in a theater. Moreover, the screams of death did not occur on normal business hours; as if something like that exists where one human being is called on to search down and kill another. The screams and the gunfire would continue in some nameless, faceless apartment complex - until it didn't.

As Frank approached the dining hall, the noise from the apartment complex receded, replaced by expat chatter about what they had just seen and heard. It was then that Frank noticed that the soldier in the Humvee had left his post. That was a sign that the violence had stopped, at least for now. For most of the expats, the incident would be quickly forgotten amid the clamor for bacon, eggs, and toast, along with the opportunity to bill for another twelve hours.

But there were those who, like Frank, understood how significant what they had seen and heard was. Thomas Hobbes said four centuries ago that life without government would revert to a "natural condition of mankind" in which there was no civilization, no laws, and no common power to restrain human nature, and would be "solitary, poor, nasty, brutish, and short." Close-in killing in an apartment building, which had to be some of the most dangerous work that there was even in peacetime, let alone in a war, was that "natural condition".

As he entered the dining hall, Frank looked back one last time at the now quiet apartment complex. What Hobbes had described: life in a man-made jungle, utterly devoid of rules, of government – a failed state – was what he had just witnessed. He thanked those who did the kind of work, sometimes under extreme conditions, that created rules where there were no rules and fashioned order out of chaos, thereby allowing him and others to do what they did.

—ɱ—

"Do you mind if we sit with you?" Frank looked up from his lunch to find two beautiful women, along with a small, chubby Hispanic fellow wearing a Yankees baseball cap. All had just been through the dining hall serving area and were standing there in front of him, trays in hand.

"Sure. C'mon and sit down." Frank smiled at the two women while he shook the Hispanic guy's hand, motioning all of them to the other three seats at his empty table.

Coleman had introduced Frank to his staff when he arrived, but he had obviously whiffed on a few. That belated introduction would occur now.

"I am Frank Davenport, new subcontract administrator. What do you guys do?"

"I'm Zoe Nagy. Nice to meet you, Frank. I am from Hungary." Zoe Nagy was a statuesque blonde, late twenties by her appearance, almost six feet tall, with a deep voice and a sultry European accent, although she spoke fluent English.

Zoe motioned to the other blonde woman next to her, putting down her tray next to Frank.

"That is Daniela Novotny, Frank. She is from the Czech Republic. We both do subcontracts." Zoe's voice lowered, as if for emphasis. "But I am warning you now, Frank. She is my bitch, Frank. So, stay away." With that, she looked over at Daniela, and both women began to laugh.

Daniela was about five foot six, lean, dressed in worn form-fitting, low-riding jeans, revealing a taut stomach that said "Love Ya" in red letters. That suggestive bit of marketing had been engraved at a point just north of where those hip-hugging jeans ended, but south of her jewel-encrusted navel. HR had duly advised Daniela that the jewel in her navel did not comply with the dress code, but Buck and Taylor liked to look at it, so HR had long since dropped the issue.

Frank looked over at the Hispanic dude.

"My name is Jay Hernandez. I am a project lead at one of the new outlying sites. I am just in for some orientation. Nice to meet you, Frank." Hernandez laughed. "And yeah, Daniela is her bitch. But they won't let us watch. Isn't that right, Zoe?"

For the women, the decidedly not sexy Hernandez would only witness both women up close and personal in his wet dreams.

"No, Jay. You cannot watch," Daniela interjected, as both women began laughing again, smiling at each other in the process. It wasn't all a joke. "Now Frank, on the other hand..." her voice trailed off suggestively, and both women chuckled.

Frank was not going to take the bait, at least not yet. "I room with Jason Meeks, and when I woke up the other night, he was banging some

Army security chick. Or so he said. I mean, I could care less, but… is that all that goes on around here?" Frank smiled at both women then got back to his food.

Zoe turned to Frank, again lowering her voice in that husky European accent. She pointed her fork at Frank. "We are from Eastern Europe, Mister Davenport, so let me tell you a little story about what went on during the Russian Revolution…Frank."

Zoe paused for dramatic effect.

"Stalin was legendary with the women during the Russian Revolution. Rumors had it that he and another guy had impregnated forty percent of an entire town. Years later, they asked Stalin why he did it. Y'know what he said…Frank?"

"No, what?" Frank found it a bit surreal that he was sitting in the middle of an active war zone with some beautiful Euro women whom he had never met, and one was rattling on about Josef Stalin and sex.

"There was a lot of downtime during the Revolution…Frank," Zoe said.

"Yes, there is lots of 'downtime' in a war, Frank. Gotta do something; know what I mean?" Daniela interjected, looking back over at Zoe, laughing again at their little improvised sex-comedy routine.

Frank thought back to his conversation with Parrish in the dining hall. Yeah…eat, sleep, check email…fuck. *I signed up for a year of this*, Frank thought.

"NICE MEETING YOU, Jay." Frank shook Hernandez's hands as the four of them stacked their dining hall trays. They headed for the dining doors, Jay in one direction, Daniela in another, leaving Frank and Zoe alone together walking back to the office on foot, sunglasses on, ID badges dangling from their necks. It was a fifteen-minute trek through the off-white sand to their open-office digs and air conditioning.

"Tell me a little about yourself, Zoe," Frank asked.

"I come from Budapest, Frank. I studied in London, getting an undergraduate information technology degree, and an MBA. I worked for a small import/export company in Budapest before the war. I was dating an American ex-pat in Budapest. The American contractors had offices in Budapest, so he got me a job there. They taught me subcontract administration. That is how I started. Then, when Iraq opened up, I put in for it and with my background, they hired me. I have been here for about six months. Daniela and I just got back from a ladies-only R&R, doing some shopping in Dubai."

"Sounds like you should be running the place, what with your resume," Frank said, again ignoring the sexual innuendo, his curiosity about both her and others in the organization getting stirred.

Zoe looked over at Frank with a pained expression.

"They do not like women in positions of power, Frank. And they really do not want Hungarians telling the American ex-pats what to do. Like Coleman. He is an idiot; everybody knows it. I saw your resume, Frank. You may be who they want to replace Coleman."

Frank let that sink in for a few moments. He had only recently just arrived, and people that he did not know were already scheming to replace his boss. Not that Coleman, or for that matter anyone else that Frank had seen was anywhere in the same league with the CEO for whom he had just recently worked, not by a long shot. What with all that had gone on, he just wanted to work, get paid, and go home.

"Yeah, I had an earlier conversation with Coleman about weeks of supply. Pretty simple, but he did not get it. He was getting beaten up in a meeting with Buck and the colonel about not having bottled water. Sounded really strange how this all works around here. I managed a large supply chain in the real world. It does not work the way that it was being described."

"I just met you, Frank, but you seem nice. Just keep your head down." Zoe did not say more about that; she changed the subject. Zoe went back to that low, husky European-accented English. "The system here is basic, Frank. Nobody here does any real demand forecasting.

They are just going through the motions. Buck does all of that. But I am warning you. Nobody wants the information."

Frank wanted to know what was so evil about some demand forecasting. He was on a path to finding out more than he wanted to know.

—∞—

THE APPOINTMENT WAS scheduled for one forty-five in the afternoon. Frank had received a call from human resources asking if he had about fifteen minutes to be interviewed for the supply chain manager's position. Frank did not officially know that the job was vacant, had not applied for the position, nor had he had substantive discussions with anyone in management about it.

In most large corporations, HR is responsible for posting a position for employment. They describe the requirements of the job in detail in writing, and they accept resumes well before the interviews begin. To someone who had grown comfortable with this more conventional approach to recruiting candidates, what was happening here was odd. The warning signs were flashing red.

Even still, curious to explore the matter further if only to meet and take his measure of the principals with whom he had only a couple of meetings to date, Frank consented to the interview. He had been given a heads-up of sorts from Zoe Nagy early on that this sort of thing might be coming. Frank had been led to understand that he was the only one being interviewed, and so the call from HR confirmed what he had already ascertained on his own, that management talent was non-existent here. Frank was advised to be on time. He was told that the interview would last fifteen minutes, because Kenny Buck had another meeting with the colonel at two sharp that afternoon.

What Frank found when he entered Buck's cavern of an office was unlike anything that he had encountered in more than two decades in a corporation. Frank found himself alone with just Buck and Taylor. He was motioned to a chair directly in front of Buck's executive desk.

Frank had previous meetings in Buck's office, but all of them were at a conference table where he had witnessed the savage beatings being administered to Coleman.

This inquisition-as-interview would be done with just Buck and Taylor, with Frank sitting directly in front of Buck's desk.

As Frank sat down, he found that to speak with Buck, he had to look up. Upon further examination, he discovered that Buck's desk and chair had been constructed on a pedestal, which meant that to meet Buck's eyes, one had to look upward. It was an obvious, non-verbal way to show who was boss, to wordlessly intimidate.

But there was more.

As Frank sat down, he simultaneously noticed that the front legs of the wooden chair in which he sat had the legs shortened, an inch or so. Shortening the front legs further aggravated the angle at which eye contact between Frank and his protagonist could take place. It was an awkward position which, in addition to the intimidation factor, got painful over time. Which was precisely the point.

Frank settled into the chair. While waiting for the interview to begin, he reflected back on how Coleman would have handled this, a circumstance that psychologists describe as fight or flight. *Coleman had been cowed by this sort of behavior*, Frank thought.

It was in those watershed moments in life where crucial decisions are made in an instant, where things change in the flash of an eye but with repercussions that could be lasting. Call it experience. Chalk it up to a gut feel or even instinct, but Frank had taken stock of where he was and had decided that, based on what little he knew - and he knew very little - that he was not going to be bullied. He had risen up high in a large corporation, had seen hardball politics played in the major leagues, and was convinced that this was not the majors. He would be satisfied if they just let him do his current job and cash the checks while working for another moron.

Buck silently shuffled the papers in front of him, appearing to glance over Frank's resume which HR had provided for the interview. As he studied it, Frank silently struggled to resist the rage fighting for control of his otherwise reasonable side. Frank knew that the head game was what Buck wanted. He would not submit to this sophomoric attempt at fear and intimidation.

Frank Davenport decided right then and there to act, not to react. While he was not going to talk himself out of a job altogether, he was not going to talk himself into this one, either. As a marketing guy, talking people into products had been his life, and he was good at it. That was not going to happen here. Frank's reasonable side would win, and rage would lose.

"You know Terry, correct?" Buck gazed down at his victim.

"We did meet." Frank glanced over at Taylor, then back at Buck without emotion.

"So, it says here that you have an MBA from Case Western University in Cleveland. Huh, Frank?" Buck's eyes never left the paper except to glance down disinterestedly at Frank over a set of reading glasses.

"Yes, I do." Frank smiled upward. "Yup. Case Western. So, where did you get your MBA, Kenny?" suspecting that he knew the answer just from Buck's general demeanor.

Silence.

"Janey has seen your resume. So has my boss, Dr. Marsh. We would like to speak with you about the supply chain manager position."

The words were few, but the non-verbals sent a clear signal: Buck was cold, calculating, someone who, when you looked into his eyes as Frank had to do when he was forced to look upward, you felt you were looking into the eyes of a dead shark.

Buck continued.

"We need somebody who is a big picture guy, Frank. Can you be that guy? We are going to have to let Coleman go; much too detail-oriented."

Are you kidding me? Frank thought. Supply chain management was all about details. Good supply chain folks understood a larger corporate picture, to be sure. In fact, the great ones used that strategic thinking to create supply chains that became a formidable offensive force, a severe competitive advantage in its own right.

He and his former colleagues in the profession immersed themselves in a thousand and one details, surrounded by a staff dedicated to wrestling with those details. It was how their chosen strategy grew wings and came to life. Coleman, on the other hand, was not only no good at details, he was also clueless as to a big picture. He was just clueless.

"I have written business plans that have been approved by a large, highly technical corporation's board of directors, Kenny. I can see the big picture," Frank stared up at Buck, smiling coldly.

"I have also put together strategic supply chain strategies. I know the numbers; I also know the metrics. I can solve things, as I did with your little bottled water issue, Kenny." He was staring right at him, not backing down. He pondered whether or not to go further into details, citing examples of what he had done in the past, but decided against it. Buck didn't want to hear about the details; that much was clear. But Frank had made his point.

Recalling an earlier conversation with Janey Lynn Reed, Frank continued. "Janey said, when I spoke to her, that it sounds like we need to re-compete the agreements. I can get that done and, by the looks of it, we can cut costs."

Frank knew that supply chains, if done correctly, wound up costing the corporation little or nothing because they existed in large part to save the organization money.

Buck was not impressed.

"Okay, good. But we are in a war with a lot of product to get, and typically we need that product in a short amount of time," Buck countered. "The client cannot prosecute its mission if we do not have the right stuff. Cost does not mean anything if you do not have what we need when it matters."

Frank thought back to Coleman and the bottled water fiasco. There was no use in debating the issue. He changed the subject.

"Before we get to the re-competes, I would like to take a look at the resumes of my direct reports, to get some idea of their strengths and weaknesses."

At that, Taylor chirped up. "You own the process, Frank. You do not own the people; we own the people."

"What do you mean? How can I implement something, manage a process and be responsible for those results, if I cannot both manage and hold accountable the people who are charged with getting things done? You cannot separate the authority from the responsibility. The system will break down," Frank stated, glaring at both Buck and Taylor. He had never heard of anything so patently ridiculous.

Buck's face twisted. His eyes flashed and his voice thundered, reverberating throughout his high-walled office cavern as he glared angrily down from above. "Because you are the manager, Frank."

At that, his voice got quiet, barely audible in his now otherwise silent office. "And if we do not like you, Frank, I just find alcohol in your room, and you are the next one gone. Get it?"

With that, the door to Buck's office opened, and the colonel entered with his entourage. It was a signal for Frank to leave.

CHAPTER 18
Money Talks, and BS Walks

—∞—

"SO, WELCOME TO the management here," Janey Lynn Reed said as she sat down in Frank's new office. It was Coleman's recently vacated office, stocked with what appeared to be government surplus desks and chairs, big enough for an executive desk and a small conference table with chairs and a refrigerator. While it was a significant step down from the executive suite with the cherry-wood furnishings and the reserved parking space located in a pristine office park, it was a step up from the digs he had recently shared with other folks who battled it out in the noise and congestion while sitting all day in shared accommodations.

Frank had not had time to redecorate, not that he was the redecorating type. As a former marketing guy, he knew that image was everything, but right now the time was better spent getting acquainted with his direct reports and what they were doing, and so he had been up to his neck in more pressing things. And besides, in a war zone, you did not get points for having great looking digs; that is, unless you were Kenny Buck. His one small concession to the redecorating was to pitch his Penn State Nittany Lions baseball cap onto the hat rack in the corner. He would tend to his image, but he would do it by cultivating relationships like the one sitting in front of him, rather than through cute toys on the walls.

"Just getting up to speed, and you?" Frank asked, motioning to the files on his desk. "You were right, nothing here was competed, and most of this stuff is getting to be almost two years old."

"We want to re-compete this stuff every year, Frank. The client understands that we mobilized into theater in the spring of 2003, and so a lot of the justification for what we did was based on that. But the game is different now, so we need to get the business that you have out for bid. Pricing needs to start to fall, or we are going to have to show why not," Janey said. She pointed to the pile of paperwork that had been stacked onto Frank's conference table, waiting for his review.

"I get the issue with the re-competes," Frank said. He pointed back at the stack. "All of this stuff looks like it has Khan's name on it."

"It looks like they did some or most of everything through him. Is that about right?" Frank had been looking through files all morning but had yet to find one without Khan or his project manager Derya Ali's name on it. The approved supplier list he had received from Coleman's document control department had been both incomplete and just plain wrong, like so much of what Coleman did, which forced Frank to look into the files.

"The way that I heard it from Terry," Reed was referring to Terry Taylor, "was that Khan was around at the beginning. Buck and Marsh had known Khan from other projects, so they knew him; knew what he could do."

Reed didn't know the whole story; neither did Taylor. Only Buck and Marsh did, and they kept it that way.

"It was a rush just getting into theater," she continued. "There wasn't a lot of time for forward planning. The client wanted things done yesterday, and you had to deliver. Much of the specifications were not fleshed out. It was 'just deliver,' and we will make it up as we go. And so, they went."

Frank was starting to understand the short-term mindset that drove the cost reimbursable attitude here. No planning, just deliver - somehow.

"What do you think of Khan's work?" Frank asked Reed, who in all fairness was the wrong person to ask. She did not have to get someone to perform; Taylor and Buck did, but it was nice to get her opinion since he knew her relationship with Taylor.

"They do a pretty good job," she said. "Derya is a bit of a witch."

Frank smiled. Having both seen and spoken briefly to Derya, who was stunning to look at, he suspected that Reed's evaluation might be colored by some jealousy.

"She has been pressing a lot lately for some work at the Iranian border. The client handles that, but she will not take no for an answer. Terry has told me that she keeps coming to Buck looking for that work. We send some parts up there occasionally when the client needs something, but the work itself is being done directly by the client."

Frank nodded, changing the subject back to the question of re-competes. "I have spoken to Buck about the re-competes, but he does not seem in a real hurry to do anything. I will keep bringing it up to Buck when I see him."

"I would also like to get Khan to no more than fifteen to twenty percent of the business or so. We are way too leveraged with somebody like Khan here. What happens if he just goes bankrupt, or disappears? We would be in terrible shape. I never leveraged my supply chains with one supplier for more than fifteen or twenty percent of the business."

Frank could tell that Reed had never considered that side of the risk equation.

However, he listened intently as she described in detail how things worked there.

"Here is the problem: Buck likes Khan and what he does. But in the government, the client is not just one person. You have to satisfy more than one set of stakeholders. The colonel is just one stakeholder. The audit agencies are another, as is the administrative contracting officer, or ACO, and his group. They all have a different agenda.

"The colonel is a bit like the operations guy; he needs to get mission-oriented stuff done. The ACO manages the contract real-time, handling the finances as well as the operations, and does so following our contract. He handles the administration of new work as well as changes to the existing work."

"The audit agencies are in the background; looking over people's shoulders, a bit after the fact to make sure that we did what we said we were gonna do. Those stakeholders are indifferent to who we select, so long as we satisfy their requirements. And one of those requirements is that we continually test the market for the best combination of price, performance, and delivery. If they find that we are not performing, they could take away our approved procurement system."

"That means that we could be forced to get government approval each time, even for small things, like toilet paper. Stuff like that could bring us to our knees. And worst case, they can snatch our cash; literally, place a hold on our money - our receivables - until we justify what we did. That could get expensive, not to mention time-consuming."

Reed ended her schoolhouse lecture, convinced that what she said was correct given the circumstances. In theory, it was.

Frank could tell that he and Reed were on two different levels. Reed was an auditor. Her understanding of risk was at the granular level, limited to the cost side, with no consideration of the revenue side. Auditors got into the weeds trying to find evidence of risk. Hers was a well-meaning focus, on not doing things wrong - from small things like filling out a form correctly to other issues like no competition - because you got punished by the government for doing things wrong. That is how she defined risk; in a tactical sense.

On the other hand, senior executives who create products were more concerned with doing big things right, and in that process learned to live with risk. They did not like mistakes any more than an auditor but were comfortable with uncertainty. That was because, unlike an auditor, they were required to turn risk into reward. But on another, non-granular level, at a strategic or systemic level, risk scared them.

Frank was the business guy, and the systemic risk here scared him. He got the schoolhouse lecture. What was left unsaid was why, with that much risk on the table, did they let somebody like Coleman and Buck operate the way that they did? And why put all of your eggs into one basket, more specifically Khan's bucket, without a plan to immediately diversify? Could it be as simple as a lack of time, too busy? Possibly, but given the risk, good management finds the time.

Companies spent a fortune trying to manage systemic risk. And this was probably more than some intramural skirmishing in a busy calendar. What was going on between Buck and Coleman would have gotten both of them fired in other organizations because it put all of the revenue - potentially the entire contract, as well as the financial health of the company itself - at risk.

Reed was thinking small picture. Frank was trying to get his head around the big picture.

"So why keep Coleman around if he was not getting done what Buck wanted?"

"Coleman was the third supply chain manager here. You are the fourth," Reed replied.

Frank had heard that from others upon his arrival. Coleman was incompetent, but Buck was contributing to it. When there is excessive turnover, there is always more to the story. Four supply chain managers in less than one year? Frank felt that was excessive. It would be in his interest, since he was the fourth one, to find out why.

THE VICE PRESIDENT'S senior staff meetings occurred once a month and on a Tuesday. Unlike the expedite meetings, these were more formal affairs with a written agenda derived from the events which typically flowed down from the client to the project management office or PMO. As such, they were internal affairs, without the client listening in, or participating.

Chaired by Vice President Kevin Rust, the meeting included Kenny Buck and his senior staff of seven which, in addition to Frank, meant Terry Taylor, Jenny Miles from HR, Johnny Burke who represented quality along with health & safety, Julie Tuck who managed both accounting & finance and project controls, Janey Lynn Reed from compliance, and Jim Parrish, the contracts manager.

This was only Frank's second such meeting, but he had quickly discovered that meetings like this were not where issues were actually managed, or even really discussed. These meetings were about control, rather than having anything to do with substance. The purpose of this orchestration was so that Kenny Buck could assure Vice President Kevin Rust, an ex-general to whom he reported to on-site and whose sole concern was looking good in front of the client, that all was well down below. In doing so, Buck kept Rust, who like Marsh reported directly to Case Hammer, out of Marsh and Buck's business.

It was a delicate dance which served both party's interests. Buck got his agenda but, if anything went wrong, Rust knew that he could just blame it on Buck and Marsh. It was a concept called managing up whereby middle managers manage their bosses. It was an excellent concept in theory, except that Rust spent all of his time managing up. He responded to the client, along with Marsh and Hammer who were his bosses, and showed little interest in managing down, or around the rest of the organization.

The items which made it to the agenda resulted from conversations between Buck and Rust's chief of staff, Charlie Bates, in the days leading up to the meeting, with Buck serving as the gatekeeper for all agenda items. Unlike Rust or Bates, who saw their role as the client's good news fairies rather than problem solvers, Buck and Taylor knew who to talk to and what to ask, or not ask. As a result, the meeting itself was more of a reaffirmation of what had been decided behind closed doors, merely a forum for putting things on the record.

Frank's agenda item had been to brief Rust on the progress that had been made in supporting the construction of the twenty-five additional sites. It would be a short summary of the procurement actions let, progress on subcontracted services, as well as the status of the materials. It was an overview, one that Rust could take to the client. Rust was not into the details.

It was just enough to give Rust a warm and comfortable feeling that all was well down below, allowing both parties to declare their version of success. The implicit assumption was that Rust would do his part in playing the game by not asking hard questions, or getting curious. And Buck would do his part, not having to lie in public and in front of the entire senior staff to the ex-general's face.

"Agenda Item #10: Progress on Construction of the Additional Twenty-five Sites: Supply Chain," announced Charlie Bates. It was Frank's agenda item; his signal to brief Rust and Bates.

For the next twenty minutes, Frank ran down a set of briefing slides, providing Rust an overview of his progress to date. Unlike Coleman, Frank prepared the slides himself, providing Buck and Taylor a correspondence copy of slides before the meeting. It was a typical dog and pony show; something that Frank had done many times. Midway through the presentation, Rust went off script when it got to the part of the program which dealt with the subcontracts.

"We do have everything either out for bid, or we have bids in now... is that correct, Frank?" Rust asked.

"Yes sir, we do. We have competition for all of the services. We should be able to bind agreements on everything that we have within the next week or two." Frank said this not knowing that Khan's shell companies were providing that appearance of competition.

Buck smiled slightly.

"What about base access?" Rust said, turning to Buck. The suppliers were of no use in a war zone if they could not get base access. This was Buck's lane. The approved suppliers had to be vetted by the client up front to gain entrance.

"We will get 'er done, sir," Buck replied in his sugary sweet Cajun drawl.

"And what about the subcontracts on this base, in addition to the other twenty-four sites? Where are we on re-competing them?" Rust looked at both Frank and Buck. That part was not in the script.

"You mean Camp Bradley, sir?" Frank asked.

"Yes." Rust stared back at both Frank and Kenny Buck.

"Some of those are complete," Frank said. "The rest are coming up for re-bid in July, sir. I have spoken to both Janey Lynn and Kenny about this." Frank said this without missing a beat. "We want to reduce Khan's footprint here. We also want to take out costs; maybe ten to twenty percent. Right, Kenny?" Frank looked over at Buck, whose smile had quickly disappeared.

Janey Lynn Reed nodded in agreement. “Policy does require a re-compete after twelve months, sir. That is unless senior management signs off on the extension and provides an explanation for the file so that we are covered in a client audit.”

Buck stared over at the finance types in the meeting. All of them were getting a little green at the gills. Like Buck, they knew that reducing costs in a cost reimbursable agreement was tantamount to committing suicide one cut at a time. They also knew that Rust either knew or should have known how to play the game by this time.

Rust did not know much about the financial end of a business. He had no education or training in this area, nor did he express an interest in learning how to manage financial risk. The finance guys joked that he seemed to fall asleep on the monthly profitability calls with corporate, and did not think that he had the business acumen to balance his own family budget.

What he did have was a six-figure bonus, based on gross revenues. It was a number simple to understand. It was also as simple as the organization could make it; less total revenues equaled less bonus. So why was this sort of thing even being discussed seriously?

Buck, on the other hand, did not qualify for a bonus at his level on the organization chart. At least not officially. He had no intention of allowing a re-compete to the existing agreements, but he also did not want Rust into his business. Right now, Khan was providing Buck and Marsh with some nice cash flow on the kickbacks in Kuwait from the existing agreements. Even giving the appearance of competition by using Khan’s front companies would potentially reduce prices and could thereby reduce his cash flow, something that both he and Marsh were reluctant to do, especially now.

Buck wondered where Rust came up with this line of questioning, seemingly out of the blue. He made a mental note to speak to Marsh. But right now, for purposes of this meeting, he would try to kick the can down the road.

“A lot is going on, what with the new construction, sir,” Buck replied. “We have been all bowed up getting the other twenty-five sites online. I was thinking about short extensions on all of the local subcontracts so that we could concentrate on the new business. That said, we can revisit the issue."

It was Buck talking out of both sides of his mouth.

Rust looked over at Frank. Frank smiled. "We can walk and chew gum at the same time, sir. We can get it done."

Buck smiled when he heard that. *Good luck with that*, he thought.

"Okay, I will allow you to work that issue," Rust said. "Let's move on. Charlie, next agenda item."

It was just past seven in the evening on the fourteenth day of February 2005, a Monday. It was also Valentine's Day, but in a war zone, it was just another long, twelve hours plus slog. Daylight began just before seven in the morning, which could be brisk in the desert this time of the year.

Sunset occurred approximately eleven hours later. That meant that these days, frequently sunny and pleasantly warm, started around sunrise but ended long past sunset. Veronica Esposito, Terry Taylor's administrative assistant, had just finished putting together some computer-generated slide presentations for project management summarizing her reports that she had submitted. Her job was to process the mountain of required weekly or monthly reports which were a part of the contract data requirements list, which was a part of the agreement between Cork and Hammer and the United States government.

Some of these reports were weekly, some monthly. They covered everything that someone thought was meaningful. The sum and substance of those reports varied in scope from meals served, tanks of water delivered, to the number of buildings constructed, and the status of engineering projects. Once completed, they would make their way to Jim Parrish, the contracts manager, who would dutifully forward them along to his counterpart, who was the ACO.

Mind you, Cork and Hammer would attempt to extract little value from these reports, except to sing the praises of Cork and Hammer in quarterly meetings with the client when they went begging the client for more award-fee-generated revenue. Otherwise, Cork and Hammer never did much with the reports unless or until somebody asked.

For the most part, nobody asked.

There was no action plan to unilaterally use any of the reports to manage more efficiently or effectively; to get better, faster, or cheaper to save the taxpayers some money. There would be no six-sigma defect tracking, no quality circles enjoined, no quality driven leadership teams established. Nope. They weren't that stupid; they were there to maximize their own shareholder's value, not their client's stakeholder value.

The primary stakeholders were the U.S. taxpayers and, by extension, the U.S. Military. It was the job of their client - not Cork and Hammer - to save the taxpayers money, or at least that is how Cork and Hammer saw it. And so, when Veronica hit "send" on her computer that night, they had "checked the box" which was bureaucrat jargon for doing something. This allowed the organization to go right back on auto-pilot, waking again only when it was time to hand their client another bill for delivering those reports. Sending the client an invoice was a totally different matter. That would happen with something akin to world-class, German-engineered timeliness and precision.

CHAPTER 19
The Candy Man

—᯾—

VERONICA ESPOSITO - or Roni, as she was called by her friends - was thirty-eight years old, and would have been a dead ringer for Jennifer Lopez if she were a couple of years younger. Roni had been on-site in theater at Camp Bradley for six months and, although well-liked, kept to herself. A single mother of three children, she hailed from Houston, Texas where, before the war, she worked at a Wal-Mart part-time as a cashier.

With three young children to feed, money was beyond tight, so when she was offered an administrative assistant position paying almost five times what she was making at Wal-Mart with benefits for both her and her children, Roni thought that she had died and gone to heaven. Roni had no administrative assistant experience, but that did not seem to matter much to the recruiter. Job titles and experience frequently did not go together. They wanted warm bodies to mobilize for Iraq immediately. Roni assured them that she fit that bill.

Roni had placed her children in the custody of her mother six months ago with a promise to call home every night after work to maintain a connection with her children. The nine-hour time difference meant that she usually missed her oldest son who was in school when she called, but she caught up with him on the weekends. It was a grueling schedule, dealing with work seven days per week, and then managing a household from a world away, but Roni needed the money.

Besides, she was really looking forward to this, her first Valentine's Day call away from home.

From her cube, she could hear doors slam as her co-workers exited for the evening. One of the locals who worked there filing paperwork, an Iraqi woman in her early twenties, stopped by to chat briefly with Roni about her own Valentine's Day plans before quickly running to catch the bus. Then the noise receded, and the office was quiet now.

Roni locked the door to the small office next to her cube so that she could not be disturbed. She reached for the office phone to call her mother when the pounding on the door began. Putting down the receiver with the call still in transit but not complete, she asked who it was.

"Kliskey," came the answer.

She opened the door to find Barry Kliskey, the skinny Brit who was Buck's assistant, standing just outside of her door carrying a large duffel bag.

Kliskey occupied an office next to Buck, but he did not exist on the organization chart. That much Roni knew, for she both comprised and updated the organizational charts every month. Kliskey had access to all of the computer systems - she had been instrumental in arranging for that with IT - but he appeared to have no formal role in the organization. Kliskey never went to meetings. He had no ex-pats or locals who officially reported to him, and he was frequently either not on base or not in his office. He chatted briefly with the other managers who reported to Buck, such as the contract manager, but had no apparent friends on the project and appeared to like it that way

Roni also knew that Kliskey occupied a forty-foot double-wide trailer next to Buck. It was one of only five on the project outfitted like that. The others were for Buck, Taylor, the colonel and Rust. This signaled that Kliskey had all the trappings of power. By contrast, the little people like her all lived in dry, mostly shared twenty-foot trailers, or hooches.

Roni had long noticed Kliskey looking at her. He always made it a point to leer at her ample breasts while she was making copies, taking every chance to make small talk. That attempt at small talk would extend to lunch where Kliskey would make an attempt to interfere with her lunch with friends. He would hint around at wanting to date her, possibly marry her. She would always smile and laugh it off, pretending it was just some joke.

Until now, she had minimized this sort of behavior as standard with many men with whom she had worked over the years. Keeping her work and home life separate, she just never gave them any encouragement, hoping that they would go away, as many did. She also did not want to go to either Taylor, Buck, or HR with this subtle form of harassment. Absent any clear physical evidence, she and not Kliskey would wind up the victim, isolated from the good old boy's network. In a worst-case scenario she would be sent home, which she could not afford financially at this point.

But this knock on the door felt different. Denial was about to meet reality.

"Yes Barry, what can I do for you?" Roni blurted in a slight Hispanic accent, all the while staring at Kliskey, trying to comprehend the sight before her. Keeping one eye on Kliskey, she glanced at the clock on the wall which told her that she was now late for her call, and soon her mother would be calling her. Cork and Hammer had installed a direct line back to the States and, while it had a DC area code and rang in DC, being charged for calling from DC to Houston was a lot better than her mother calling Iraq from Houston.

Kliskey's eyes were bloodshot. He was unsteady on his feet, his body swaying back and forth, trying to control the duffel bag that he finally put on her desk in that small office, partially obscuring her telephone. His breath smelled of alcohol.

If she did not know better, she thought, maybe he was demobilizing from the base and had been celebrating that fact by getting stinking drunk. If that was the case, perhaps he was harmless, after all. Maybe he just wanted a friend with which to drink, now that he was leaving to wherever he was going. She did not drink - on this base or anywhere else - and was not about to start with this guy. No maybe about it.

She did know better, or at least she thought that she did, because she and her colleagues managed the official travel itineraries for those leaving the base. His name was not on the latest daily report. She also knew that, around Buck and Taylor, lists like that meant little.

"Barry, do you mind? I need to call my family. It is Valentine's Day, and they are waiting for my call."

With that, Roni attempted to extricate the telephone from underneath the duffel bag, but Kliskey was not buying it. Instead, he grabbed her hand roughly, almost violently, and shoved it down into the duffel bag. He had never touched her before.

"What are you doing?!" she screamed. Feeling paper as Kliskey forced his hand down deeper into the bag, she removed its contents and discovered that she was holding wads of $100 bills, all of which to her untrained eye appeared to be real. Shocked, she peered inside the bag. It was all currency; a three-foot high green Army-issued duffel bag filled full of money.

The office was silent. It was just the two of them now, and Kliskey was balanced unsteadily against the door, making it impractical to push by the drunk Brit, and leave. The alcohol from his breath seemed to permeate the stale air in the closed, cramped office.

"I want you, baby," he stammered, his red eyes staring at her and her breasts, intentionally drawing out the heavy British-accented pronunciation of that last word "baby" in such a manner that reminded Roni of a low budget imitation of a British movie. She was not amused.

"I have wanted you for a long time. I...I can take care of a lovely bird like you. Come have another look, love - see?" And with that, Kliskey ripped open the drawstrings of the bag so that she had an unobstructed view of the bag and its financial contents. Roni had heard of people's lives flashing before them but never knew that it could be so real. Or that it could happen to her.

"We could get married, live in Mexico. Anywhere," Kliskey continued, tapping at the bag with his fingers. "I can get more. Much more."

"How much is in there?" Roni dropped the money and withdrew her hand from the bag.

"A million dollars."

"A million...fucking dollars, Barry? Are you shitting me?"

Roni had never seen a million dollars, had never counted a million dollars, couldn't even conceptualize an amount like that in her bank account. All she knew at that point was that she wanted out of her office. She made a move to get up, but Kliskey continued to look at her breasts and did not move.

"What are you doing with that amount of money here?"

The project had been virtually cashless since very early on; it had certainly been cashless in the six months since she had arrived. All of the civilian expats, for instance, as well as all of the suppliers, were paid electronically. The only cash that she had seen had been either at the small PX which dispensed soap and other assorted personal hygiene items on base, or at the accounting department in small amounts, and then only for those who were departing for a holiday and needed some ready cash.

"For my mates, baby. Like the colonel... and the sergeant major. And your boss. I am the Candy Man, baby."

Kliskey slurred his speech, making all of the familiar gestures of someone who was either drunk or was smoking a joint. Growing up in a poor family, guys like this were all around her in Houston; hopped up on some shit talking trash as a prelude to wanting unprotected sex, just like this guy.

The rage boiled up inside of her, recalling her first and only marriage to a guy that ended when, too shiftless to get and keep a regular job, he turned to drugs to make ends meet. She had left him to care for her kids without a job and, for a time, with no place to stay for her or her kids but with her mother. She thought that, with the new job, she had finally outrun both the drugs and the losers but now, sitting in an active war zone listening to some inebriated freak, Roni suddenly realized that she could beat neither.

"I have to go." With that, she got up to leave, but Kliskey continued to block the door. Sensing he was not going to win the argument, the seedy little Brit attempted to change strategies on the fly, resorting to an out-and-out solicitation.

"Well look, if you are not going to marry me, how about if we go back to my digs and get comfortable. How much of this do you want? I can give you some of it if you need it; as I said, there is more where that came from." He reached again for her breasts.

But as he reached, the instability caught up with him, causing him to lose his balance and, in the process, providing an opportunity for Roni to get to the door. She took the opportunity, pushing past him towards the hall.

Kliskey grew desperate.

"Taylor and Buck aren't going to do anything, baby. It's your word against mine, and I take care of all of them, baby. Taylor, Buck, the colonel - others. We are tight cause I am da Candy Man, baby! C'mon baby, give me some of that!" He reached between her legs as she exited the room.

And then he started laughing. She could still hear the laughter as Roni exited the building, heading directly towards her hooch. She swore to herself that she could still hear him laughing as she opened the door to her quarters - and threw up all over her bed.

It had been a long day, another twelve-hour day of never-ending days back-to-back in a war zone that could wear on anybody. Frank had spent the better part of this day-turned-night in the warehouse along with Keni Mehmeti conducting an inventory. It was their cat and mouse way of surviving: staying one step ahead of the inevitable raping and pillaging done Buck and Kliskey.

Exiting out of the warehouse towards the DFAC, he noticed Roni Esposito heading in his direction, coming out of the DFAC. He had been introduced to Roni in Terry Taylor's office and had exchanged pleasantries so it was a surprise when she wanted to see Frank outside of the office.

"Hi, Roni. How are things?"

"OK, Frank. Hey, can we talk for a minute?" Roni had a worried look on her face.

"Sure Roni, what's up?"

"Do you happen to have any job openings in your department?" Roni cut to the chase, not even a mention of small talk.

"I do. Why?" It was a question to which Frank knew that Roni, who kept track of personnel for the entire project for Terry Taylor, knew the answer before she asked it.

"I need to get out of there," Roni stammered, staring straight down at the sand. Her eyes filled with tears.

Frank had job openings, although the ex-pat positions were few. Most of the opportunities that he had were for local nationals, which paid far less. But Frank's problem wasn't job vacancies; those he had. It was taking a secretary from Terry Taylor. And not just any secretary. Roni was Terry's personal secretary, and that had enormous political overtones.

It was well known that Roni was Taylor's eye candy in the office. She sat just outside of his office, in a cube that afforded Taylor an easy glance at her all day long, not to mention Buck and Kliskey, who always seemed to be leering in her direction. Frank was not sure how Roni was with that, but he had heard from both Daniela and Zoe, who took delight in monitoring things like that, that his girlfriend Janey Lynn was anything but pleased with the arrangement. All the more reason to stay far away, thought Frank.

"I guess that I could check my requisitions on what I have open," Frank stated carefully, "but what is motivating you to make a move? You appear to have a pretty good gig with Taylor. Not to mention that, but if I find something for you, Taylor would have to agree to the move. Are you sure that you want to do that?"

Frank looked down at Roni. He noticed that her hands appeared to be shaking, almost uncontrollably. *Stress, or just a long day?*

It was then that Roni unloaded on Frank the incident where Kliskey had come to her seeking sex, waving a bag full of money as collateral.

Frank had seen enough with Coleman and Buck that he was not surprised to know that this would go on, although the scale of what she was describing did shock him.

"How much do you say that Kliskey had in cash?" Frank was getting sick at his stomach.

"A million fucking dollars... *in cash...* Frank." She stared into his eyes. Frank could tell that she was lost.

He surmised that Kliskey and, for that matter Buck and maybe Taylor, had been wanting sex like dogs in heat, but Frank had trouble getting his head around that much cash floating around in a system where he could find little if any evidence of hard cash. All payables and receivables had been automated, he thought. Even holiday vouchers where employees would draw money from their accounts to enable them to travel on vacation were, except for minimal amounts, wire to wire bank transactions or, in a worst-case scenario, paid out in the presence of a third party who signed for the cash. All documented.

"I had spoken to Zoe about you, Frank. She thought you were a pretty good guy, which is why I came to you," Roni finally uttered after what seemed to be an awkward moment. "But I did not tell her all about the Kliskey thing, just that I wanted to make a move."

"Do you think that she or anybody else know about the cash?" Frank asked. "What is the cash for? Who would need that kind of cash?"

"Not sure. But that is a lot of cash to be floating around here, so somebody knows. I cannot sleep at night, Frank."

She wasn't the only one.

"Do you want to talk to Taylor about moving you?"

Roni started to cry. "I am confused right now, Frank. And I am scared. People in my neighborhood back home would kill for a small piece of that kind of money. I need this job because I have kids, but I am not going to fuck Kliskey for my job. I am not a whore, Frank. But Buck is a prick. And Kliskey is one crazy fucker."

She became very quiet, just staring into his eyes, seemingly helpless. The cold desert night air now flowing across the DFAC parking lot accentuated the chill that had crept into their conversation, as both Roni and Frank's mind wandered off in different directions.

"I will let you know."

Roni began to walk away, but as she did, she turned around, again staring him right in the eye, only this time the look was different. Gone was that "help me out" look; in its place was "look out below."

"You watch yourself, Frank. You saw that they did to Coleman. I think that they respect you, but they do not like you. Don't take that too personally. They don't like anybody."

And with that, she was gone.

What was somebody doing with a million dollars in this place? Frank ran supply chains. He knew the answer, at least conceptually. He just did not know how. At least not yet.

CHAPTER 20
The Game Within the Game

—⁓—

IT WAS A typically busy morning in late February, in a part of the business that never seemed to slow down. Frank reached for a bottle of water in his office refrigerator, thinking back more than a month ago to the bottled water incident that still seemed so fresh in his mind. In some ways, things had moved on in a positive direction, but in other ways the more that things changed, the more they remained the same.

Frank had accepted the position, along with the fifty thousand dollars per year increase. In that sense, life was getting good, and fast. He had thought it odd that they would throw so much money at him so early on. Most companies took a more measured approach to pay increases. Not here. They were glad to pay him the extra money. After all, he was part of the revenue stream. More costs equaled more profit.

Life was not all bad with his boss, either. In the intervening month, Frank and Kenny Buck had established a bit of a cold civil war, with neither side wanting to antagonize the other. The routine expedites, which had delved into a weekly savage beating under Coleman, were replaced by stiff, but cordial meetings focused on the issues.

Knowing that he did not have ownership of his direct reports Frank, with help from Zoe and her girlfriend Daniela, came prepared to the first meeting. He produced a list of materials; where each stood in terms of inventory, what needed to be done, and more importantly, what Buck's guys needed to do, in terms of stock level. That simple, low-tech list, updated weekly, sent a message.

Frank's list, something that Coleman could not do, told Buck that he knew how to manage. It also said that there would be no more savage beatings; no more Spanish Inquisition-style slow-motion torture. Unlike Coleman, Frank was pro-actively engaged. Officially deferential to the position, if not the person, he also did not succumb to the head games. His staff quickly took notice. More importantly, the colonel saw the change in the quality of the work. He even commented favorably once or twice, something not lost on Buck.

Frank was not going to change Buck, but he made him back off, if only temporarily. He made Buck blink. In an organizational, Darwinian sense, Frank had established his turf. The raids on the warehouses did not change. What did change was that they were better coordinated with Keni Mehmeti and the Kosovars in the warehouses so that the stock-outs were minimized.

Buck was a psychopath and a criminal, but he was not stupid. He needed those extra twenty-five sites up and running, and quickly. The colonel was reporting on the progress toward getting those sites functional - doing it daily - huddling with Rust and Buck constantly. There were roads to build, walls to construct, troops to be mobilized, entire small militarized cities to create in a short amount of time. To make that happen, they had begun to rely on what Frank was doing much sooner than they thought they would.

Officially, Buck would be quick to take credit for what Frank was doing behind the scenes. But liking what Frank did would not translate into respect for who he was, because Buck had no respect, either for Frank or for himself. No, Buck was biding his time. The leopard did not change his spots.

—∞—

"OK, LAST AGENDA item for today." Frank was wrapping up his weekly meeting with his staff, including his direct reports.

"From now on, all meetings with the suppliers will take place in a conference room, not in your office, so make sure that you schedule it. I have placed the conference room schedule book, which covers all three conference rooms, in Zoe's office. Moreover, all meetings get coordinated with me, and no meetings shall take place in the conference room without one of our administrative assistants there to take notes. Each meeting will have a meeting agenda, meeting notes, and all meeting notes will come to my desk for review."

Frank wound up that last item looking directly at Jimmy Reed, one of his subcontract administrators. He had noticed just before the meeting that Reed, who had frequently been meeting with Derya, had emerged from his office in a somewhat disheveled state. Frank had asked Reed what the nature of the meetings was, and was told that he was negotiating change orders with Derya. Pressed for details as to which changes, Reed was predictably vague.

As Reed walked back to his office, Zoe stopped by.

"That last agenda item in the meeting was not itself on the agenda, Frank," Zoe said, giving Frank a schoolmarm look, then smiling broadly.

"Yeah, it was a late add-on," Frank conceded. "So why the Cheshire cat grin, Zoe?" Frank eased back into his office chair.

"Well, the entire department is laughing," she said.

"About what?"

"We aren't stupid, Frank. We were laughing because what Derya has been doing has been kind of an inside joke around here for a long time."

Frank was baffled. He had not been in the position all that long; a month or so.

"And so, what exactly is the 'inside joke'?" he asked.

"Derya wants their subcontracts extended, and is paying to extend them," she said. "You are correct; we should be re-competing this stuff, but she does not want it, and so, before you got here, she just was quietly going around getting the subcontracts extended. Buck did not mind, and Coleman was useless. Lots of them have been extended without competition through July."

"She is paying for subcontract modifications? Really, how much?" Frank was surprised but, by this time, not shocked. Nothing was surprising him anymore.

"It kind of depends on who she is dealing with, and what she can get away with. People don't talk about it a lot. Sometimes it is some money. I have heard as much as $10,000 for a large change order. That may just be some bragging, but I have also heard about playing with her breasts, handjobs and blowjobs, you know, stuff like that. I don't think that she likes to pay if she can get away with it, so she allows the physical stuff. Particularly with the men."

"Well, I am sorry that it took me this long," Frank said, laughing at himself. "I saw Jimmy Reed and Derya coming out of the office just before the meeting looking a little strange, and thought that something might be going on."

"She does look like she has nice breasts, Frank," Zoe said, trying to inject a little humor into the situation. "But I can assure you that I have never done anything with her. Not my type." And with that, Daniela showed up at the door, asking if Zoe was ready for lunch.

Frank laughed, but did not take the bait.

Zoe smiled and looked at Daniela. "We are going to lunch. I got a preliminary statement of work on the potable water tank refurbishment project. When do you want to discuss it?"

"Let's do it this afternoon in the north conference room," Frank said. "Catch up with Derya. We owe Buck an update on that."

Alone now in the office, Frank thought back to what had just happened and he was getting depressed. He had no proof that the people that were working underneath him were committing crimes, but it fit with what he saw. He tended to believe Zoe.

Frank knew that Buck did not mind if his subcontract administrators were receiving fraudulent compensation from a supplier. He always had Coleman to blame. Coleman had all of the responsibility but none of the authority and, as such, was set up to take the fall. Buck had done it before, and would most likely do it again.

Frank's problem was that he had nobody with which to turn; someone in which to confide. He had really just arrived and was still feeling his way around. He thought briefly about escalating the issue to HR, but without hard evidence that was a useless exercise. His friend Larry was correct; just follow the little voice.

As he got ready for the next meeting that afternoon, Frank had no idea how this was going to end, but he did know three things. One, he had already been threatened with his job by Buck, recalling Buck's remark about finding booze in his room, so he had no illusions about who he was dealing with. He could roll over, collect a check for as long as it lasted, and pretend to ignore it. But why? Besides making him complicit in the behavior, he had just seen how Coleman had been treated, so that was not an option.

Two, he was not going to manage like Coleman. He couldn't do it even if he wanted to. The little voice inside said "Be yourself." Easier said than done, he said to himself, as he checked his online bank balance and got even more depressed. The little voice had also told him that being yourself might mean exiting out with a clear conscience. Still, exiting out would most likely be the price to pay for that clear conscience.

Finally, it would be a price that he alone would pay. Few others would know, and even less would care. Was he willing to pay that price, quietly standing on principle?

He could discuss this with somebody either much higher up in his organization, or in the client's office. Frank's problem with that was that he did not know them, or their agenda, and they not only did not know him but had no reason to trust him. Without more information than what he now had, going up the chain also was not an option; not just yet, anyway.

What if he ignored it until he found another job? Frank knew that at the kind of money he was earning, replacing even most of his income would not come overnight, so he wondered just how feasible that was.

He had been unemployed for six months before this job, and would now be unemployed again after only a short period of employment. Questions would be raised in job interviews.

Frank had been perilously close to foreclosure just months earlier. The banks had accepted his employment agreement as collateral, which allowed him to bring his accounts up to date. Once unemployed, he would also have to consider a second reckoning with the banks who would not know what happened, nor care. It was a steep price to pay for some job in a forgotten land.

But the little voice was judge, jury, and executioner, and it had rendered a verdict. Frank would be who he was and if so, would pay the price. Sitting there, staring at his monitor in his office in the middle of an active war zone, in now silent confines, he began to wonder how this would end.

FRANK PEERED AROUND the corner of Daniela's cube. "Has anybody seen Samer?"

Frank had the government auditors scheduled in to do some audits of the files. The inspection was planned, but the list of files that the auditors were going to want to see was not shared with his group in advance. Like any auditor, they pulled data at random. The files were kept in a central document control area, all numerically filed and ready for such an occasion. Only one problem: his Document Control Manager Samer Arian, an Iraqi national, was not at his desk.

Peering up from some contractual documents, Zoe and Daniela, who had been discussing some changes to an existing agreement, looked up at Frank with a blank stare.

"Dunno, Frank," Daniela said. "Do you want us to check the gate to see if he was delayed getting on base?"

Getting onto a U.S. military base in a war is not a small thing, especially for an Iraqi national. All workers applying to work on the base had to pass a vigorous, sometimes protracted background check. Once issued the proper paperwork, just entering the base each day entailed a security screen at the gate. Vehicles were subject to a thorough search, as were any carry-on devices.

And that was on good days. In case of an attack, the delays could be tedious and could require unplanned bunker time outside of the gate and in the heat of the day. None of that time spent waiting around was typically paid for, because the employee had not yet clocked into work.

"Don't pay the ransom; I got away." It was Samer, always joking with a beaming smile that would make Hollywood jealous; a New York Yankees ball cap on his head, wearing a Nike shirt and backpack in tow, heading for his desk inside of document control.

"Samer. See Frank!" someone bellowed over the sea of cubes, recognizing Samer's voice. Moments later, Samer was parked in front of Frank Davenport.

"Sorry for the delay, Frank," Samer said, flashing his movie star smile, as he parked his backpack on a makeshift table in Frank's office that was used to negotiate contracts.

Samer Arian was not your usual clerk. Before the war, Samer had obtained a degree in chemical engineering from a top Iraqi university and had gone to work in the oil fields near Kirkuk. With the start of the war, jobs like his ground to a halt so, through connections on the base, he had gotten the only job that he could find.

Frank Davenport had quickly discovered that it was guys like Samer who had kept his organization running during the Coleman era. With no formal background in subcontracts, Samer nevertheless had managed to read and understand each and every subcontract agreement that Frank was managing, something his own subcontract administrators hadn't done.

Fluent in English, quick as a cat mentally, and with an attention to detail, Samer was a bureaucrat's bureaucrat, a guy Frank had learned to rely on to keep files meticulously organized while alerting Frank to issues like incomplete documentation. Samer was worth his weight in gold, especially on days like this when the auditors came calling.

"Are you OK?" Frank knew more than to question Samer's seeming tardiness.

"Yes Frank, of course. I had to sell my car last night again. That is the third time in the past few months that I have had to do this. I did it again because, when I left for work last night, I saw that the terrorists were tracking me.

"As you know, there is only one way in and one way out of the base. Once the terrorists learn what you are driving, they hunt you down, so I sell the car periodically to throw them off. The game works for a while until they catch on again." Samer smiled, his big grin starting to fade.

"It was a late-night last night. It took me an hour to evade the terrorists. After that, I sold the car, trading it in for a new one. And then I had to pay a guy down the street for electricity to cool my family's home. The whole neighborhood uses this man's generator, but you have to pay him every day, or he shuts your electricity off. I have a small child, Frank, and I cannot afford not to have electricity.

"Well, the brakes on the new car did not work this morning, so I had to get the car fixed. Luckily, the terrorists did not recognize the new vehicle, so I am good for a while. Are the auditors here?"

Samer's eyes lit up again, knowing that he was free to concentrate on work. For a while. Dealing with the terrorists was like dancing with the devil; they were not going away.

"The audit folks are on their way now. I will send them to your office." Frank heaved a sigh of relief. He had a long day planned, stuffed full of meetings and negotiations. The last thing he needed was to be pulled aside for an audit. Things were much too busy with the roll-out of the additional twenty-five sites. Samer exited his boss's office once again, beaming that actor's toothy grin, contract files and backpack in tow.

Frank couldn't help but marvel at Samer. Guys like Samer were what made this job worth it. What he had been through with his previous job, and was going through now with Buck, was nothing compared to what Samer had to endure. There were people in the U.S. who saw missing their favorite cable program as some mortal threat to their way of life. Samer, on the other hand, was cheerfully going about his job, dodging terrorists while he and his family's existence were literally hanging by a thread, every day of his life.

—∞—

Frank always slept better after a workout. His exercise regime was not so much about getting in shape as it was a way to relax after a long day. Hitting the gym was a chance to unwind from the stress that affected his back and neck muscles from the twelve-hour grind at work, in meetings or in front of a computer. He had conquered the dining hall, with its endless portions, attendant weight gain and the resultant pearl-shaped physique by eating light during the day and skipping the after-work meal most nights to head directly to the gym.

The gym was, like most structures on base, an enormous air-conditioned tent containing weights and weight machines. On exercise nights, Frank would arrive while the military was wrapping up its workout. Two hours later and after a debrief, many of those same soldiers, fresh from the gym, would head out on classified nighttime missions. Frank would never know about those missions except indirectly, or in the vaguest of terms. Cork and Hammer's official policy was that the military, as the client, had a mission to complete. Cork and Hammer would support that effort, but would in no way interfere with the client in its mission.

For the most part, the Jason Meeks incident and others like it were the exceptions to the rule. Frank noticed that both the civilian and military staff stayed in their lanes, except when official business required otherwise. In some unguarded minutes, however, such as at the gym when both parties overlapped, Frank as a civilian got a glimpse of how the war had affected his military counterparts. Tonight would be one of those examples that, while all but wordless, spoke volumes.

Frank had become friendly with a Sergeant named Alberto Rodriquez. Both shared an affinity for free weights and had differentiated themselves from most of the other gym rats by their willingness to actually use the weights. It was something that civilian expatriates shunned for the most part, either because they did not exercise or, if they did, what constituted their exercise was limited to sitting glumly on a stationary bicycle passing the time with eyes glued to the gym television.

Built like a tennis player, Frank naturally gravitated to the lighter weights. Rodriquez, at six feet two inches and around 225 pounds, curled 100-pound dumbbells with each arm, bench pressed 300 pounds, and was doing squats with something close to 400 pounds. He was more akin to an NFL linebacker.

Most of their lively conversations in that gym occurred in an atmosphere in which the clanging of weights mixed with loud music, lots of laughing and joking, and the ever-present smell of sweat. Their lively banter while lifting centered around football; Frank from Cleveland and a Browns fan while Rodriquez came from Dallas and was a rabid Cowboys fan.

All of it was a surface conversation, such as who the Browns would draft, or how the Cowboys would fare against the hated Redskins. Chatting with the usually loquacious Rodriquez was good fun, but the fact that Rodriquez in his own gregarious way pushed those around him to improve while having fun was what drew Frank to him. Aside from being a great guy to be around, Rodriquez, probably no more than twenty-six years of age, was a natural leader.

Guys like Rodriquez were natural leaders by doing what they enjoyed doing and, as a consequence, doing it well. That attitude rubbed off on the other guys, pushing them to do more on the bench press or squat machine. It was a real best practice that, although Frank had no proof, had to carry over to Rodriquez's work in the field.

This particular night was different. It was slow in the gym; probably no more than a handful of both military and civilians had signed in, and so it was easy to spot Rodriquez. On most nights Rodriquez stood out, not only for his toned physique which was impressive, but for the way he engaged actively and with joy in the exercise. It showed when, after the workout, he stripped down for the shower; his biceps, shoulder, back and leg muscles were tightly ripped, unlike some of his more corpulent, desk jockey comrades. But on this night, Rodriquez stood out, not for what he usually did but for what he did not do, even in a sparsely populated gym.

Frank knew enough about Rodriquez to sense as much from the far side of the gym before he had gotten close to the free weights. The bright, flashing eyes and jovial demeanor were gone. As with most nights, he would work out more than everybody in that gym, but tonight it was almost as if Rodriquez's body was fighting something; a force that even a professional highly trained to fight could not, the sweat dripping from his torso a result of some inward conflict.

As Frank neared his friend, he could tell that Rodriquez kept looking over at a picture and murmuring something to himself mostly, although not entirely, in Spanish about Stop-Loss. Coming closer, Frank could ascertain that it was the same photo that Alberto had so proudly showed Frank during one of the few times that they had gone for coffee after their workout. The image was of his wife and three-year-old daughter. They were the pride of his life; as he said, literally his reason for being.

Rodriquez did not have to say anything to Frank that evening. The non-verbal cues said it all: "*Nothing personal; just leave me alone tonight.*"

Frank did not know what a Stop-Loss was, or that in military terms, it meant not allowing a military member to separate or retire once their required term of service was complete. All he knew that night was that whatever it was, was causing a great deal of stress to a seemingly well-grounded elite soldier-athlete and family man. Frank picked up his towel and headed over to the treadmills, where he spent the rest of the night.

That late March non-encounter would be the last time that Frank and Alberto would see each other. Soldiers come and go in a war zone. So, when Frank did not see Sargent Rodriquez in the gym again, he assumed that the Sergeant had been deployed elsewhere, to some other theater in the world equally dangerous. Unfortunately for Sergeant Rodriquez, his wife, and Rodriquez's three-year-old daughter, Frank would be correct.

CHAPTER 21
The Tanks

—~—

"THIS IS WORTHLESS, and that guy knows it," Zoe said to Frank, referring to Buck, as they walked back to their desks after the meeting with Buck. In that meeting, Buck brought up the new project refurbishing potable water tanks and had passed along a now-finalized statement of work to Zoe Nagy for getting that work done.

Zoe had been reading the document during the meeting, and was less than impressed with the quality of the work product. "This statement of work is for refurbishing more than one hundred old tanks left over from the Saddam era that the client wants to be done tomorrow, as usual," she said. "They want to make them fit for use as potable water tanks. The client must have different colors of client money because they want these tanks refurbished and installed all over Iraq, in addition to our new sites."

"The client's own independent cost estimate puts it at two million dollars, by the way, so this isn't just chump change. That crap statement of work looks like it was done by a grade school boy." Zoe looked up at Frank. "Can you take a look at the statement of work with me, please?"

"Different color of money?" Frank understood cost accounting, but he was just now getting immersed in the government's way of talking about things like money. It seemed like everything in the defense industry had an acronym or slang expression.

"Yeah, Frank. Our money is for our project. It is authorized, allocated, and appropriated to this project only. But the tanks that they want refurbished come from many different projects all over Iraq. That means that the costs will be spread out, and for that, they will need money from elsewhere. A different color of money, so to speak."

An hour later, Frank had marked up the statement of work. Some of it was typos akin to fixing small wounds; other stuff required open heart surgery. He agreed with Zoe's assessment that the work being done was the clownish work of amateurs in Buck's project management group. In a former life, he would have probably disciplined employees who dared to send him staff work this unprofessional.

"Lots of stuff to fix here, Zoe; for instance, Buck's specification lacks a validation and verification plan that should come from quality assurance and/or engineering, just for starters.

"Khan and Buck need to agree to that plan as part of the overall specification, so that you can both inspect and accept the work that the supplier performs. And you will need Buck and his boys in project management to sign off on that plan not only to solicit bids on the front end, but also accepting the work on the back end in writing, once the work is completed. Moreover, you want that inspection and acceptance work done at the supplier's facility - at origin - if at all possible. You do not want bad work being transported through a war zone and landing here, that you should have already accepted at the source.

"We also want to both inspect and buy off on the materials that the supplier uses. We want our guys micromanaging the ongoing work, such as inspecting the supplier's work as they grind the tanks so that we get down to the bare metal. We want to inspect them spraying on the epoxy into the tank. And we want to inspect the final coat of paint. All of those are interim inspections. Payment only comes when we make the final inspection, one that is approved in writing by QA and project management. Make sense?"

Zoe was writing furiously, then she looked up quizzically. "What about progress payments, Frank? This will be a $2 million or so project. Most companies out there may not have the resources to carry projects like this."

Frank grinned. "See what you can negotiate, following the milestones that we just talked about, but weight it toward the back end. Maybe 30% or so toward the front end, with the balance upon a final inspection and acceptance. Let's see how well you negotiate with the Arabs in the sand. "

Daniela had just entered as Frank was finishing up. Having heard what Frank just said, she smiled and looked over at Zoe, her tight-fitted shirt revealing the toned abs and jewel-encrusted navel. "That is okay, Frank. We can negotiate in the Czech Republic. We will get you a good deal. We can handle the Arab men."

Both women laughed and prepared to go to lunch.

"Somehow, I believe that," Frank said to himself. "The Iraqi's won't know what hit them." *You want to be a fly on the wall for that negotiation,* he thought, smiling. On second thought, he made a mental note to attend that negotiation.

Frank felt uneasy having to work for a now ex-manager who did not know anything. Now, it seemed that he was going to send a clear message to Buck that his work was equally bad. He had already been down that road once before in his life, which is why he was here.

Zoe looked back and smiled. "We are finally getting some management."

Frank grimaced as he smiled. "What about some competition?" Frank peered over at Zoe and Daniela.

"Buck wants a meeting about this project in the next couple of days. I am sure that will come up!" Zoe yelled back.

"Zoe, did you tell Frank about the general and the history behind the tanks?" Daniela asked, looking down at her watch.

The DFAC closed at two in the afternoon. It was just past one in the afternoon, so they still had time, but the DFAC workers began to break down the food lines at half past the hour, so time was getting critical.

"Yeah, there is a bit of history here, Frank," Zoe said. "General Barry Smith was in charge when this camp was being built. He did not trust the water supply coming directly from the civilian sources, of course. It would not surprise me to find that he is still involved in this, some way. Rust used to work for Smith when they were both active duty."

—∾—

"So HOW DID the tank refurbishment meeting go?" Marsh asked.

This was an agenda item on Buck and Marsh's weekly status update that usually occurred Mondays after Buck's private meeting with Rust and the military. Apart from the fact that the tanks themselves carried potable water and thus were critical to all of the sites, the solicitation was a multi-million-dollar item which automatically made it an agenda item.

Those types of solicitations received extra care and attention due to the large dollar volume. Moreover, each of the bids had exceeded the government's cost estimate. This was not unusual, given the lack of comparative analysis for projects of this size, and war zone location. Therefore, putting together a package that at least gave the appearance of competition was essential to the additional needed government authorization and appropriation.

"Smooth. Davenport wanted competition, so I called Colonel Harper and had his folks send over a couple of suppliers located in Baghdad that the military used on other projects. I forwarded over the names to Khan and had Derya contact them. She directed both of them to put in higher bids in exchange for a little cash. Davenport will never know; neither will Rust or Colonel Harper." Both Buck and Marsh laughed.

"Davenport's sourcing team visited them a couple of days ago. I just received the QA reports back on the suppliers. They are qualified, of course. Time to execute. Rust wants them turned around now."

—∾—

The agenda item for the afternoon meeting was to conduct a pre-award meeting with Derya on the tank refurbishment project. The statement of work called for the tanks to be assembled at Camp Bradley and shipped to Khan's chosen sub-tier supplier. That sub-tier subcontractor would grind down each container, scraping off all of the old coatings down to the bare metal, then prime both the interior and exterior of each tank and re-coat it. Cork and Hammer had specified all of the materials and would not only supervise the labor in Kuwait but also approve each step of the process before accepting the work in Kuwait, in total.

Khan's proposal came in at about twenty percent above the client's estimated cost, or about $2.5 million. Those numbers were fraudulent, of course, but they would give the appearance of competition. The "competition" amounted to nothing more than the two straw men located in Baghdad that Frank's team had visited but who were, in fact, taking directions from Khan and his money men. Both straw men would receive $10,000 just for submitting higher bids, each of which was over $2.6 million, giving credence to Khan's apparent low bid, itself inflated.

Frank had assembled the pre-award team that afternoon. It included: Zoe, who handled the subcontract from his group; engineering, quality; along with health and safety; in addition to Terry Taylor from project management, all there to reaffirm the specification, and to negotiate out about two hundred thousand dollars.

The tank refurbishment meeting went well. Both sides reaffirmed the specification. After a bit of negotiation, both sides compromised, with Derya agreeing to drop her price by one hundred thousand dollars as a good faith gesture. Taylor indicated that he could take that back to the client for approval and further incremental funding.

As the meeting adjourned, Derya asked if she could have a word with Frank.

"About what, Derya?" Frank motioned for Zoe to remain behind as a witness to the conversation.

"I would like to discuss the work at the border with you, Frank," she replied.

"We have no work at the Iranian border out for bid, Derya. Not for you, not for anybody. Have you spoken to Buck or Taylor?"

Taylor had long since left the room.

"Frank, we have done a lot of work with the U.S. military, and we know that work is going on up there. We are in a great position to provide your company with the expertise that it needs for that work at the border." Derya smiled sweetly, looking up at Frank while gently touching his arm.

"I understand, Frank. I will speak to Buck again, but I would like to discuss this further with you after I speak with him." Derya was undeterred.

Frank knew that Buck had told her that there was no work for Khan, but she was not taking 'no' for an answer. Frank thought that was the end of it.

"And another thing, Frank." Derya smiled at him, with Zoe clearly in the background looking on, amused. She had seen this act before.

"Some of our original agreements are coming to an end here, and so we want to discuss continuing them with you. What can we do so that we extend those remaining agreements, Frank?" She smiled sweetly. "We have been very loyal to Cork and Hammer, Frank. That work is critical to us."

"We do appreciate your loyalty, Derya." Frank smiled back, returning the psychological favor, recalling what Zoe had said about the subcontract extensions. "That said, we also have an obligation to our client to assure that they are receiving the best value over time. To determine that, we as a matter of policy seek to entertain competition, and that is what I intend to do here."

"But Mister Buck has told me that he was going to extend the balance of these agreements, Frank. I have been working with your subcontract administrators on some of those." She pointed to Jimmy Reed's office.

Frank had not heard that instruction from Buck, but somehow, he was not surprised. He had been in the meeting with Rust where Buck was dancing, giving Rust the assurance that he was committed to the competition when in reality, he had no such intent.

"I will speak to Kenny," Frank said, looking over at Zoe as he said it. "But do me a favor from now on, Derya. The new policy is that all negotiations going forward will be held in the conference room; not behind closed doors alone. They need to be scheduled, and I will have somebody in the conference room to take notes. Okay?" He looked over at Zoe, who nodded in agreement.

Derya's face blushed; her eyes flashed. "What are you saying, Mr. Davenport? Are you accusing me of doing something wrong, Frank? I was negotiating with Reed; that was all. He will tell you that."

Her body language told a different story as she summarily walked out, slamming the door behind her. It was the angry way that most people reacted when they were caught in a lie. Having been in many negotiations, being lied to was an unfortunate part of the jockeying for position that came from high stakes dealings; almost a cost of doing business.

He did not like it; he did not think that you needed it if you understood what you were doing, but lying was so prevalent that he accepted it almost like an ordinary course of business. Frank was just a little surprised, not to mention amused, that she was not a little more professional about it. He had seen better.

"That was a bit over the top, would you say?" Zoe suggested to Frank, who had remained outwardly calm.

"Yeah, not sure what brought that on. Do me a favor, Zoe, and write a memo of what happened for the file and email it to me. I probably need to go see Buck on this."

He had a feeling that this was going to get worse.

"C'MON IN, JOHNNY." Frank motioned to Johnny Burke, Cork and Hammer's quality assurance manager. A jovial, burly American expat in his early 60's, Johnny had been with Cork and Hammer for almost a year now. Unlike some of the other expats, Johnny had, like Frank, come from a similar corporate management position in the States.

Burke decided to leave a secure management position in corporate America after his wife died the year before. Frank could tell that Johnny knew what he was doing, just from the way that he handled himself in some early meetings with Buck and Taylor. And so, when he called early that morning wanting to see Frank in confidence, Frank knew to take this seriously.

"You know Zoe Nagy of course, Johnny," Frank said to Burke, motioning to Zoe. "I invited her in because she is managing the subcontract."

Wordlessly, Burke pulled out six pictures, smiling as he did it, and placed them down on the conference room table in front of both Frank and Zoe. The images were of the inside of several of the tanks.

"All of the tanks have been stripped clean, Frank. As you know, we paid for the inside of those tanks to be ground down to the bare metal, primed and painted with a special coating that would render the tanks potable. We bought off on the materials that they used; we inspected the tanks all the way through, and bought off the finished product at the end," Burke said, pointing to the bilateral signatures signing off for the acceptance.

Both Zoe and Frank looked back at Burke with wary expressions. It had been a pitched battle to get that statement of work for the refurbishment of the tanks into a form that could be used.

"Well, in the intervening weeks since we went into production, we put most of those one hundred tanks back into service. Only this is what we have." He pointed to the inside of the tanks and down to a report that Burke had carried with him into the meeting.

"Maintenance uses ozone to clean the tanks, but if you put four times the manufacturer's recommended level of ozone into the tanks, it will strip off the paint. It is caustic. And that is what happened here,

Frank. I have the maintenance report right here," Burke said, staring back at the pictures and down again at his report.

"We are going to have to de-install and send back all of the tanks to the supplier for rework," Burke said. "The client is going to shit."

"Did you tell Buck? If what you have here is accurate, Cork and Hammer will need to pay for that rework," Frank added.

"I took a look at the process again," Burke responded, "and I honestly do not see any latent defects, although I will look again. We bought off on the entire process. But after we accepted the tanks, the maintenance techs screwed up, putting four times the recommended level of ozone into the containers. In technical terms, we fucked up - big time.

"I came to see you first because I wanted to bring this up in a public meeting so that nobody would sweep this under the rug. I also did not want Buck shooting the messenger," Burke said, laughing nervously. He was not kidding.

BURKE'S REPORT HIT like a bomb going off. Buck immediately scheduled a meeting for the next day after receiving Burke's tome summarizing the incident. What prompted the explosion in organizational terms was that Burke had also copied Janey Lynn Reed, who forwarded Burke's report up the chain, not only to Rust and Marsh, but also to the lawyers, who immediately notified the board of directors. No more hide and seek, or so one would think.

"What happened?" It was Rust, who chaired this meeting. He had to answer to the military; they were his primary customer, and they were not happy. He had read the reports that Burke sent over and moved immediately to take over the meeting.

Burke and Frank Davenport recapped the sourcing of the tanks. Johnny Burke again showed Rust the report from the maintenance techs showing the extra ozone being placed into the tanks.

"One: so how long will it take to fix it? Two: how are we going to do that? And three: who do I fire?" Rust asked when the analysis was complete.

Buck would typically attempt to hang the supplier out to dry here, regardless of the facts. But that was not going to work here because Khan was the supplier. Instead, Buck gave Rust the heads of some of the low-level clerks. Nobody wanted to get to the root cause of how such a systemic failure could have happened. That was hitting too close to home. They just wanted to affix the blame so that everybody moved on.

"And who pays for this?" Rust added, looking at Parrish, the lawyer-without-a-law-license, and Buck who did not return his stare.

Before anybody could answer, Frank Davenport spoke up. "Cork and Hammer is responsible for this, from what I can determine. We drafted the statement of work. Cork and Hammer authorized all of the materials to be used; we inspected the work at several stages, and we bought off on the finished product at the supplier's facility," Frank said, producing the inspection and acceptance reports.

Neither Parrish nor Buck said a word. Johnny Burke nodded in agreement. The tension in the room was so thick that you could cut it with a knife.

"What is the cost for the rework, Frank?" Rust asked.

"Zoe just got a preliminary cost estimate back from Derya and her group this morning. We may be looking at about a million eight," Frank said, looking around a silent group as reality slowly began to set in. "We will see what we can negotiate out, but it will come in around there somewhere."

Buck and Khan both knew that those numbers were inflated of course, but that was part of the plan.

"One million, eight hundred thousand, huh?" Rust asked. "You know, of course, that amount is not the total cost because this stuff impacts our award fee."

And his bonus; he left that part out.

He was referring to the part of the cost reimbursable contract that rewarded excellent performance with an additional monetary award on top of their costs, on which his bonus was based.

Cork and Hammer alone would bear the cost of the rework. This time they could not get reimbursed for the $1.8 million. Moreover, Cork and Hammer faced a possible downgrade to their award fee at the next meeting with the Client. Things suddenly got very expensive.

"You will have a plan on your desk tomorrow, sir," Buck stated while glaring at both Burke and Davenport.

"MAINTENANCE PUT FOUR times the recommended level of ozone into the tanks," Buck said to Marsh. The tank project had rippled through the upper echelons of Cork and Hammer, as only a $1.8 million rework project could, coming so close to the sale of the company.

"Did we fire somebody?" Marsh asked. Like everybody else, from the in-house lawyers to Case Hammer himself, everybody had read the applicable documentation.

"Yeah, the maintenance techs got the ozone spec wrong. How do you want to handle the money?" Buck asked.

"Look, we are closing this company soon. Just have Taylor fill out the standard, reimbursable paperwork and send it up. Break down the single set of reimbursable paperwork totaling $1.8 million into smaller sets of about $30,000 each so that the money requested for each individual set of tanks is not as noticeable.

"We are not going to eat $1.8 million at this time. By the time that the paperwork gets pushed through, everybody will have forgotten about this ordeal. The odds of an audit will be slim, at least in the short term. Once the company gets sold, you and I are in Kuwait and gone. Okay?"

What Marsh did not tell Buck was that Hammer's corporate legal counsel recommended settling with the government; paying the money, which meant coding the rework for the company's account.

Their assessment of the incident, from the information that they were given, was that Cork and Hammer was at fault. Moreover, given that the sale of the company was imminent, they did not want a protracted fight that would extend the close.

Marsh did not care about that. He was in no mood to renegotiate this particular piece of business with Khan who was doing the rework. Marsh wanted to hit his numbers in the Kuwait slush funds before checking out. He looked at this work as just another piece of business from which he, Buck, and Khan were going to profit, and this was getting him closer to that goal.

—m—

THE SIX-INCH-THICK FILE landed on Frank's desk with a thud. Coffee in hand, Frank peered up to see Zoe and Samer in front of his office.

"I cannot believe that they did this," Zoe stammered. "All of these requisitions - all sixty-five of them, for Christ's sake - for the tank rework says that the costs are reimbursable.

Samer jumped in. "I asked the project controls guys who handle the money for this project about this. They said that Taylor approved it. Here is his signature." Samer pointed to Taylor's signature on each of the requisitions, along with some obscure financial coding next to his name.

"I then went to Zoe, who confirmed the coding, but said that her recollection from the meeting was that the rework was for Cork and Hammer's account."

Zoe nodded in agreement.

The little voice inside of Frank told him that this was not a mistake. Nobody did something sixty-five different times without intending to do just what they did. And yet, with all of the attention that this project had been given, it was hard to understand how anybody could think that they could get away with this.

Frank looked further into the contents of the file. What had been one original requisition package for $1.8 million had indeed been broken into sixty-five different packages, with varying amounts, ranging from $18,000 to $40,000 each, totaling $1.8 million. What they all had in common was that all were coded reimbursable meaning that Cork and Hammer was intending to pass along shoddy, defective rework to the client.

Frank called Buck's office and scheduled a meeting for right after the following morning's senior staff meeting. Frank wanted Burke, Janey Lynn, and Taylor at the meeting at a minimum. Frank planned to bring Zoe. This was getting surreal.

CALL IT BAD timing; call it karma, or maybe just a coincidence. Frank did not believe in coincidences. The following morning's staff meeting included a special guest, General Barry Smith. The general was introduced to the senior staff by Rust as a "VP Rust's former commanding officer, the former commanding officer of this base and, might I add - a good friend."

According to Rust, Smith had "just been passing by and thought he would stop in to show his support."

Frank did not know the details of Smith's trip, of course, but he knew enough to know now that nobody "just happens to stop by" in a war zone as if it was a trip to the neighborhood coffee shop.

Smith spent the majority of his brief half-hour talk reminiscing on what it took to prosecute a war while starting up the facilities in which they now sat, but which had grown so much after his departure. Ever the warrior/diplomat, Smith was profuse in thanking the staff for its contributions to the effort in Iraq. He made it a point to stress that resources were tight; the days were long, but he was confident of the mission.

In closing, he briefly ticked down a list of accomplishments, one of which was establishing the laundry facility and another was setting the plan in motion to get all of the old potable water tanks from the Saddam Hussein era retrofitted for potable water.

Almost casually, he turned to the staff and said, "I hear that we had to redo those tanks. I trust that the government is not paying for those tanks a second time, correct? Send me a quick note telling me that is the case."

Smith got up and walked out of the meeting. Frank thought that he detected a faint smile directed toward Buck as Smith left the room.

Closing the meeting, Rust said, "I need to see a few of you after the meeting."

He pointed to Frank, Buck, Janey Lynn Reed, Burke and Taylor, and Jim Parrish, the contracts manager. Frank motioned to Zoe, asking her to retrieve the contract file, knowing what was coming next.

"What advice did we get from corporate counsel on this?" Rust asked, looking over at Jim Parrish once the team had reassembled after a quick break, during which Zoe had returned with the file.

"Based on the facts that they had been given, their opinion was that we were most likely liable for this one," Parrish responded, recalling his own separate conversation with Corporate Counsel Michael Beck.

"That is what I remember also," Rust said.

At that point, Frank opened the case file and slid the contents across the conference room table to where Rust sat.

Motionless, Rust said, "What am I looking at here?"

"Project management signed off on paperwork that coded all of the requisition paperwork as reimbursable. Moreover, in what appears to be an apparent attempt to hide that fact, they broke down a single procurement action into sixty-five separate actions to obscure that fact by creating smaller, less noticeable actions," Frank said, pointing to Taylor's signature on all of the documents.

Frank looked over at Taylor and Janey Lynn Reed. It was evident from the look on her face that she hadn't known what Taylor had done, although once this broke, she had been in Samer's office for a review of that file. It would be an interesting time tonight in the trailer that Janey Lynn and Taylor shared.

Taylor remained silent but looked at Buck, now cornered.

"I am not sure why Terry did what he did, but I will have a talk with him about this." Buck was lying and, in the process hanging Taylor out to dry, but it was the best that he could do.

"Sixty-five times... and after advice from counsel, Kenny?" Rust said quietly, but in a voice that resonated. Rust adjourned the meeting.

—ꟿ—

"One point eight million," Hammer said, looking down at the paperwork and then over at Marsh. "Who is managing the maintenance techs, Bill?"

Hammer had called this special meeting with just Marsh and Rust, the senior vice-presidents on the project.

"Officially, that is Terry Taylor," Marsh replied, leaving Buck out of this. Marsh was prepared to sacrifice Taylor here. He did not want to go near Buck for obvious reasons. After all, Marsh and Buck had money waiting in Kuwait with their name on it. Neither wanted this little skirmish to interfere with that plan.

"They want him gone, Case," Rust replied. "The military is livid; they want some heads here, not just a couple of clerks."

"I would remind you both that we are getting very close to closing this facility when we transition out," Marsh said. "We are going to need Terry to manage a lot of that promptly, and we do not have a corporate backup right now that could fill in. We can agree to pay for the tanks. That should allay their fears."

He wanted Rust to carry that message back to the client, putting both Rust and General Smith back to sleep, even if only for a while. With the business closing, a while was all that he needed. And to Marsh "can agree" did not equate with "will agree."

Marsh knew that, in saying this, the sixty-five requisitions all remained reimbursable. He had just lied. What he did not realize was that Hammer knew that but, for different reasons, had decided not to change the paperwork unilaterally. After all, it was his company.

"Okay, let me think about this one, and I will get back to you when I make a decision," Hammer said, bringing this short conference call to a close. Hammer did not like to be put in the position of having to shell out almost $2 million at that point. But he was having a separate set of negotiations with the client up the chain about the commercial claims and other sorts of liabilities. He wanted this wrapped up in that final negotiation.

CHAPTER 22
Room Service

W*HO IS KNOCKING at my door after nine in the evening?* Frank wondered. He had not received a phone call that anything was amiss at work. *Okay, I am coming,* Frank thought as headed to open the door to his hooch. He had barely pulled the handle when he found Derya pushing her way into his living container.

His space was a single-wide, forty-foot trailer that had been Coleman's. It came with indoor plumbing, air conditioning, a vehicle, and maid service. Just not *full-service* maid service. Management had its perks, to the extent that you could consider living in a trailer with a toilet and shower a perk.

"What can I do for you, Derya?" Frank asked, startled to have her at his container alone and unannounced.

"I wanted to discuss a few things with you alone, Frank," she said sweetly, sitting herself down on the small couch that passed for living room furniture.

"Look, I do not think that you should be here," Frank said. He headed toward the door, preparing to open it so she could exit. But before he could do it, Derya deftly inserted herself between Frank and the door. As she did, she brushed ever so lightly against Frank, slightly above the groin in a manner that could be argued either as a mistake or as a suggestion. She was staring right into his eyes. Derya was sizing up her prey.

"This will not take long, Frank," Derya said. "I just thought that you and I should get to know each other better. I want to get the rest of the subcontracts extended now, without going through competition. And I want your help in getting to that work at the Iran border. We have always supported your company, Frank. Khan and I can be very grateful."

Frank was stunned. He had just gotten back from the gym and was looking forward to calling his daughters in the States. And now this. This was the kind of stuff that happens in the movies, almost comical if it was not so dangerous. His hooch was located in a busy section where lots of ex-pat traffic entered the area. Derya had most certainly been spotted entering his living container.

As he sized up the situation, the longer she remained in the hooch, the more of a liability the whole situation became. Anybody seeing her coming out of his room at that hour of the night would automatically conclude that something untoward was going on inside of the container. After all, Frank was the one who set policy about having witnesses available in the conference room for meetings. Like French justice, he would be guilty until proven innocent, which was not likely to happen here.

"I do not play it that way, Derya," Frank said, motioning to her hand which had begun to rub his crotch. In one motion, he grabbed her shoulders, pushing her away from the door.

She resisted. Grabbing Frank by the neck, she whispered into his ear, "I can make you very rich, Frank. Help us get that work at the border, and get us the change orders."

But by that time Frank had forced open the door, forcibly escorting Derya from his living container.

"Ouch!" she screamed into the night, clutching her wrist, giving the appearance to all that might be watching that Frank had attacked her on the way out.

Faking a fall at the foot of the stairs, Derya looked back at Frank and then around at the camp. It was silent, at least by outward appearances. Nobody had been standing outside or passing by. The dramatic effect that she had hoped for was not going to materialize, or so it seemed.

Frank stared down at her in disbelief, then came down the stairs to help her up to her feet.

"I do not have any leverage on those sites at the border, Derya. And we are going to re-compete the agreements if I have anything to do with it. Understand? I will speak to you tomorrow. And do not ever show up at my room again, unannounced," he said with an outward measure of calm which belied his inner rage.

Frank had never been so ready to punch somebody out. Instead, he went back inside his living container and tried to get some sleep after another long day. It would be a fruitless effort.

But they were not alone, after all. There were others; at least one.

What Frank did not know was that Barry Kliskey had been stationed there between living containers; in the dark, laughing to himself while filming the entire episode, as if on cue. He was not there by mistake, either. Kliskey was Buck's special assignments guy, and Buck was playing hardball.

THE NEXT MORNING, Zoe Nagy peered around the corner of Frank's office, wishing him a good morning, only to find Frank deep in thought at his desk.

"Anything wrong?" she asked, staring down at Frank's desk where a color photo sat. Frank was staring intently at the picture.

"Can you identify this guy?" Frank asked.

The photo was of a man who had been standing in the dark with a camera, apparently filming the episode between Frank and Derya. In the picture, Derya was at the end of Frank's stairs, kneeling in the dirt, and looking back at Frank. The photo of Frank and Derya would seem to be damning evidence of an altercation, but the thrust of the picture was clearly not Frank or Derya. The photo was directed at a man in the shadows, who was between the containers filming the episode between Frank and Derya as if it had been a scene out of a cop show.

The man in the shadows was slender, dressed in dark clothes, and he appeared to be laughing as if he was enjoying the proceedings.

"Well, fuck me backwards, Frank," Zoe said, laughing.

Zoe had a way with words; a way that, on other occasions would be a cause to laugh and joke at the mental picture that her words had summoned. Not now. Frank just felt sick to his stomach.

"That is Kliskey," she said.

"How do you know?" Frank could not make out the man's features.

"He's laughing, Frank. Look at the gold teeth. Nobody else has gold in his front teeth around here, Frank. I know every expat on this camp."

She called down the hall for Daniela to come to Frank's office. Minutes later, Daniela pointed to the teeth, which faintly glistened in the night with the light from a nearby porch lamp.

"Kliskey's grill, Frank. I would recognize those shitty gold teeth anywhere. One hundred percent. Where did you get the picture?" Daniela asked.

"It was on the floor in the office when I came to work. Somebody must have slid it underneath the door." *But who would have the presence of mind to do this,* he thought.

"Why is Derya on the ground?" Zoe asked.

Frank recounted the events of the evening prior, both women's eyes getting wide. Zoe turned back to the photo.

"Do you know what this looks like to me, Frank? It looks like she was setting you up, Frank. And Kliskey was there to film her leaving your container. He probably started laughing when she hit the ground because it looks like you are attacking her." Zoe pointed to Frank glaring down the steps at Derya who had fallen.

"But what they didn't count on was somebody else taking a picture of Kliskey, looking like he was essentially orchestrating the scene," Daniela said, looking over at both Frank and Zoe.

Frank looked at the picture again. "It does look like Kliskey is directing this. I hadn't thought of it in that way until you said it."

Frank had come to the conclusion that he had been set up. Given that Kliskey worked for Buck, Frank assumed that it was Buck's hand in all of this. What Frank had not realized until he thought about it some more was that he also might have at least one ally here. Or, at a minimum, whoever took the photo also had an abiding interest in this matter if one assumed the old maxim: that the enemy of your enemy was your friend. Otherwise, why take the picture and place it under his door?

The phone rang. Buck needed to see Frank in his office.

A LIGHT RAIN fell as Frank began the trek from his office through the wet sandy mix towards Buck's stone edifice. His twenty-minute walk had begun in dry sand, but things changed rapidly as the light rain turned into a torrential downpour. The makeshift roads, never constructed to facilitate drainage, quickly flooded. Soon the choice was not whether or not one would walk in pools of water; it was whether or not you walked in a man-made river or were going to have to negotiate bodies of water that resembled a small lake.

As he neared Buck's office, Frank kicked the wet sand from his boots and stared out at the rain-soaked camp. The rainstorm matched his mood. It was the perfect image, Frank thought, for his mindset entering the meeting with Buck. The scene with Derya the night before had been surreal; a complete surprise. And the photo that had been slipped anonymously under his door; that was right out of a crime novel. Frank knew that they were game changers. But with the incident so fresh, he was just not sure how the game was going to change.

Like so many others who arrived at Camp Bradley, he just wanted to do his job, make some money, and go home. Frank knew that there were always politics. Heck, you get two people in a room, there's going to be politics. Frank wasn't interested in the politics, but the politics were interested in him as the incident with the tank rework clearly showed.

Life was not fair; this much he knew. Like Coleman and the others before him, they absolutely wanted Frank gone with the wind. The incident with Derya at his hooch had been a clarifying event for Frank in that regard.

And so, as he opened the door to Buck's office, Frank realized that if the hardball politics would seek him out, then he would embrace the politics. He was not going to sit through a grilling about some contrived event, patiently explaining his side of events, when he knew that there was a separate agenda.

Even as he prepared to enter the meeting, Frank was furiously trying to craft an offensive strategy around what he believed to be were at least three tactical advantages. The first obvious advantage was that neither Kliskey nor Buck probably knew that somebody else was doing some dirty work. At least, not now; for the purposes of this meeting.

The second advantage centered around possession of the photo - hard evidence - documenting that dirty work. At some point his anonymously provided photo would make it all around the camp. Few things like this remained private for long in an insular setting like this. Nevertheless, given the short time that had passed, it was a fair assumption to conclude that only he and a few others had that photo. Frank was preparing to test these assumptions shortly.

But Frank also sensed that he had third, larger tactical advantage. That advantage was that he could get things done, and they were coming to realize it. Buck needed him, at least for now, as much as Frank needed Buck and the job. Frank decided to test these tactical advantages by being the aggressor. It was a dangerous game since if he was mistaken, he could be back on the street looking for a job.

To be sure, there were lots of assumptions here, any one of which could be wrong. That said, Frank knew that he had to change the rules, or he would continue to be hampered by them. Frank never felt that he was a victim. He had been hammered in life, but Frank believed that you were only a victim either when you couldn't get back up off of the canvas when you got knocked down, or when the clock ran out. He had been knocked down, but not out. The clock was still running. And now, as he faced Buck – in Buck's office, maybe for the last time - he was up, ready to deliver a blow.

In politics, when you are explaining, you are losing and Frank, ever the competitor, did not like to lose. Rather than sit back and wait for the questions to come, he would be the aggressor. It was time for somebody else to answer some questions. Frank was prepared to turn the tables even if it cost him his job. Buck would use Kliskey's filming to grill Frank, laying the groundwork for a possible termination. In turn, Frank would weaponize not only the photo, but his other tactical advantages; namely time, and skill set. Frank was going to do a head job on Buck, hoping to change the game. That was the strategy.

"Hi Frank, please sit down." Buck motioned Frank to sit at Buck's conference table. Also joining them at the conference table were Terry Taylor and Janey Lynn Reed. HR was noticeably absent from this meeting which meant that Buck was in the administrative, or information gathering stage.

"I invited Janey to sit in because what we are going to discuss has to do with the suppliers, Frank," Buck said unemotionally.

Buck continued. "I got a call last night late from Khan who stated that you were apparently harassing his project manager, Derya. Is that true?"

"Not true, Kenny," Frank replied. "And you know that is not true, don't you, Kenny?" Frank was taking a calculated risk by calling his boss a liar in a meeting - in front of subordinates, no less - but he wanted the element of surprise. He also wanted to see how Buck would respond to getting knocked down, in front of others. He would try to force Buck to disclose Kliskey's filming of the event so that he could trump it with his own photo.

"See Kenny, Derya knows the rules. The rules are that business gets discussed in the office during business hours, and only then with a witness present. The entire department knows the rules. Those rules are in the meeting minutes. I copied you, Kenny." Frank shoved the meeting minutes towards Kenny Buck, who showed no interest in reviewing the contents.

"Isn't that right, Janey?" Frank said, motioning over to Janey Lynn Reed, who nodded in agreement.

"The fact is that Derya showed up at my hooch last night unannounced, wanting me to issue change orders to her existing work. She also wanted the work at the Iranian border. I told her to leave, but when she did not, I opened the door for her to leave, telling her on the porch that she wasn't going to get either, and never to pull this stunt again. And you know that, don't you, Kenny?" Frank continued to stare back at Buck.

Dead silence.

"Frank, she was observed lying on the ground in front of your hooch, like you had just beaten her," Buck's eyes raged, his face twisted.

Frank had seen that look, only this time he felt that, instead of Buck landing a body blow, it was more like a haymaker of a punch that swung wildly and missed, thereby opening up his body for Frank to move inside to deliver a counter blow to the rib section. Buck had been careful not to bring Kliskey into the picture. He wanted to see Frank sweat a little more. Wrong move.

"But that was for dramatic effect, wasn't it, Kenny? Just one for the camera, right Kenny?"

Buck's eyes changed; his complexion shifted. He had been placed on the defensive. Frank's body blow to the ribs had hit home. And he was not done.

"What are you talking about, Frank?"

"You know what I am talking about, Kenny. Your boy Kliskey was choreographing the entire episode. Wasn't he?" Frank looked at Buck, then over at Taylor and Janey Lynn Reed.

Both were motionless; mouths agape. This wasn't part of the script. Second body blow, and this one staggered Buck.

Frank rose from the table and pushed his chair back. As he did, he threw his photo of Kliskey down in front of all three.

"That is your boy, Kliskey. You know, the one with the golden grill, Kenny. Nobody else on this camp has cheap, gold plated choppers like those, Kenny."

Buck did not overtly come unglued. He was careful not to jump up and down. What Buck did do was delve into total silence. And so, it was what he did not do that was telling. It was moments like those in relationships where what the parties did not say spoke volumes.

With that, Frank rose and stood over him, alternately staring both at Buck and then at the photo. His look down at Buck resembled the iconic Muhammad Ali glaring at a prone Sonny Liston in their 1965 championship fight. Buck refused to make eye contact with Frank. His eyes, windows into the soulless creature that he was, were deceiving him.

Buck had no idea that the watcher had been watched - let alone been photographed - thereby removing the plausible deniability option. Better yet, Frank had left Buck with the impression that it was Frank who was somehow doing the watching. Buck would approach him differently from now on.

"Look, if you want to get into the motion picture business, Kenny, you ought to hire better help than this. Oh, and I would appreciate it if you kept Derya out of my hooch from now on."

As Frank walked out to go to the gym for a run on the treadmill, nobody said a word, which told Frank that he had sent Buck to the canvas for the mandatory eight-count.

Buck was down, but Frank harbored no pretenses. He knew that Buck would return. On the way out, Frank thought that he saw Janey Lynn Reed grinning slightly in the direction of Buck.

What neither Frank nor Buck knew was that Janey Lynn Reed

would send a copy of that picture to Marsh, along with a complete summary of what had transpired between Frank and Kenny. Marsh was not happy at the unforced error. He was worried that Buck was overplaying his hand. There was no reason to do something to Frank Davenport that could raise suspicions unnecessarily. Buck had been reckless.

What Marsh did not know but should have known was that Reed also blind-copied the in-house lawyers, who forwarded a copy of that same description on to Case Hammer.

Hammer smiled as he read the email. He knew that Marsh and Buck were playing games; it was one of the reasons that he was selling. At another time and place, Hammer and Marsh would be in meetings with Buck, for these types of issues had a way of getting the client's attention. But that was then, and this was now, and he was tired. He was moving on.

At the end of the day, Hammer felt that this was small stuff, something that would not impede the parties from closing the deal with BLTVDef. Marsh would come to him with a meek mea culpa, blaming it all on Buck, but Hammer had been around a long time and knew his business. He knew that Marsh and Buck were hiding something. Hammer knew what it was, and he was managing accordingly in ways, and at a higher level that neither Marsh nor Buck could. Incidents like this confirmed what he knew. Frank was the proverbial canary in the mine shaft.

"Good morning, Bill." Buck was on the phone to Marsh in the States. He had recently arrived in Kuwait on a convoy run. As usual, Buck was there to check on the status of the money in the accounts. That was always the number one agenda item, especially now that the business closing appeared imminent.

"'Ole Kinney-boy, how is life on Khan's yacht treating you?" You could hear Marsh smiling through the headset, mentally picturing what Buck and Khan must have been doing in the on-board hot tub moments before the call with more than a few of the local Chinese whores. He would not have been far wrong.

"Great, Bill. I checked on the money in all of those accounts, and we are on target. But one thing that I do want to discuss with you is competing the remaining subcontract agreements. I am not sure that we even need to do re-competes given that we are going to close the business shortly. Correct? Janey Lynn and Davenport want to do the re-competes. Janey Lynn keeps bringing it up and couching it in compliance terms."

"Just keep kicking the can down the road, Kenny," said Marsh.

"Okay, I will tell Davenport. Another thing: Rust still wants Taylor's head for the potable water tank issue. I want to keep Taylor around for now. We can give him up at the end, but I would prefer keeping him for now. I do want to take out Davenport. He is getting too close. Your thoughts?"

"Hang in there with both. Let's not make any changes right now. Rust came to me on Taylor, and he has approached Hammer on the potable water tank requisitions. Rust wants to go back to his buddy General Barry Smith as the good news fairy. I put him off, telling him that I would pull that paperwork and take a look at it. Hammer, for his part, has not said anything to me just yet about either Taylor or the requisitions, nor has he said anything to Rust or I would have heard about it."

Buck put down the phone, but he was not happy. He and Khan had just been to the bank for a financial reconciliation earlier that day. The amount of money that was accumulating in those Kuwait accounts was playing with his head. Stealing from the United States government – *and that was what this was* – had been the only meaningful thing that he had ever done in his life. He did not want to mess this up.

The potable water tank incident had shaken him. Sensing that he was losing control, Buck's usual first reaction would be to lash out, often by firing people like Coleman or Davenport. Using Derya to compromise Davenport with Kliskey filming the scene had been a way to do that; a way to gin up a termination, and it had backfired, leading to a mild rebuke by Marsh, which is why Buck was frustrated.

Marsh functioned as a buffer, a counterweight to that primal urge to scream. Only this time, the little voice inside of Buck told him that Marsh was misjudging the situation. Buck wanted this to end, and soon.

CHAPTER 23
The Ultimate Price

—⸙—

As Kenny Buck's staff meetings went, this one seemed to drag on longer than normal. Maybe it was that the days were getting longer, and hotter. Iraq heated up like a microwave; one day the weather in late March was reasonable, the next day it seemed like the heat in Baghdad was hell with the lid off.

Frank's mind had started to wander, replaying in his own mind with a bit of satisfaction the ironic sequence of events with General Smith which had led to the web of lies surrounding the water tank issue unraveling. Suddenly, as if fate had waved a magic wand, the meeting stopped and everybody went quiet. It was then that Frank realized that the communications at the headquarters building, always sort of buzzing like bees in the background, had gone silent.

Peering out of the window from the second floor of the headquarters building, Frank and the rest of the people in the now stone-cold silent meeting room paused in observance of a silently passing convoy bearing the remains of a soldier killed in combat, as if to pay homage to the now departed hero. And then as quickly as it stopped, the meeting went on, as if nothing had happened.

But something did happen.

Someone, a soldier that Frank did not know and would now never have the privilege to meet, had met an untimely death. By comparison, what he did - Frank's contribution to this effort - was minuscule, insignificant. His worries about his kids, his job and income, his apartment buildings would now pale by comparison to what that father's family would almost certainly go through.

The relative pain of cramped living quarters, and the sometime two-hour bunker drills at midnight for he and others like him, were nothing. For that family, the grief would go on. Frank had lifted weights in the gym with soldiers like Sgt. Rodriquez. He had seen pictures of their families, had seen the pain in those soldier's eyes when they learned that they would not go home after their tour to their families. Only there would be no formal Stop Loss for this soldier, for he had given all that he had to give.

Prior to the war, Frank had lived in a corporate world of rules where debits always offset credits in an orderly sort of way. But that soldier's life was more than a business transaction. He died for something. He died for rules, for structure and order in a sea of chaos. The deceased soldier did not die for Republican or Democratic politics. He simply followed the rules, and yet he – *not some politician* - paid the ultimate price.

Unfortunately for that soldier, there were others, like the contractors in the meeting with Frank, who would just get up every day and follow the rules, get paid, and pay no real price. For them, it was all a large debit to their cash account every thirty days, with relatively little coming from their own personal payables accounts. And so, for just following the rules, they would garner what the economists would call an economic profit; the six figure salaries they were paid being not only far more than what they were worth in a normal market, but also far more than that deceased soldier would ever make.

For still others, like those Frank had just dealt with on the tank issue, they would disdain the rules and yet would get paid handsomely, with a much larger debit to their offshore cash accounts, and still risk very little either to their own individual or corporate payables. They would continue to receive their profit sharing and their six figure bonuses; the war in Iraq being little more than a revenue center.

But that soldier's death did not trigger what would come to be a normal settling up of accounts. His debit, or what he received from his service to his country in terms of compensation was small, to be sure; a soldier's pay and a soldier's life, but the offsetting risk to both his and his families' personal payables account was huge and was not to be discharged in cash. No, it constituted his life, not a clinical transaction on a financial statement, and so there had to be something more; a larger purpose.

Frank's problem with the balance sheet in Iraq was that in a fundamental way the balance sheet was way out of whack. If someone had brought him this deal to finance and market in a former life, knowing then just what he knew now, he would have politely shown them the door.

Whatever dubious assets that were created in this sandbox, like some force-fed quasi-democracy - a foreign concept to much of the Middle East - had come at a premium in terms of liabilities. It was that premium to which Frank was staring as the dead soldier's casket passed by on its way back to Dover Air Force Base in Delaware. There was no return on the shareholders equity in that casket, nor would there ever be.

And so, if one somehow quantified and then subtracted the present value of both the present and future liabilities taken on from those dubious assets, then the resultant owner's equity position was surely negative, particularly when one considered the opportunity cost of that equity; like that soldier and his family, playing in a yard and going to school. That was how you go bankrupt as a nation.

At what point, Frank wondered, *do the creditors - and in a democracy those creditors are shareholders called voters - foreclose?*

"So HOW IS my favorite military contractor doing?" It was Larry Wilson on the line from Pensacola.

It had been a while since the two had last talked, so there was some of the usual catching up to do, but Larry could sense some depression. He pressed Frank on it, as good friends can.

"Yeah, well a bit surreal, but otherwise just hanging in. Like I said before, I am supposed to run a procurement organization, but I do not manage the people, just the process. It's tough." Stuff like that was hard to explain to a clinical psychologist, someone who never run an organization. But Larry was a good friend and was genuinely interested, so it was good to offload the frustrations.

"But I guess the weirdest thing that just happened was finding one of the subcontract project managers, a woman, in my room not too long ago."

"Wow. What did she look like?" Larry asked, trying to make light of the situation. Frank was too tired and too depressed to play along.

"Looked great. That was the problem. When I did not go along with the sex overtures, it turned out that the whole thing had been a set-up. My boss had somebody filming her outside of my room screaming in a manner that made it seem like I was harassing her."

Larry had been getting concerned. The harassment did not sound like the Frank Davenport that he knew. And the depression was concerning him.

"You are kidding. What happened?"

"Well, I got a photo of somebody who had been filming the guy who was filming me, if you can believe that," Frank said in an air of desperation. "That photo saved my ass, but I don't know who did it; who took the picture. That picture was shoved under the door to my office. It really is disconcerting."

"You know the old saying, Frank: Most people do not plan to fail, but they do fail to plan. What is your plan?" Larry tried to remain calm, not wanting to escalate the already palpable tension in Frank's voice.

Frank reflected long and hard. Larry's question had prompted some soul searching. His days had been long and stressful.

"I could be wrong, but here is what I think," Larry said. "What you have been getting in terms of money since joining Cork and Hammer you may have lost in terms of perspective. Call it tunnel vision caused by so much that is new or unfamiliar coming at you so fast. That speed causes a scarcity; in your case, of an ability to see a bigger, wider picture. You know, most poor people who make bad choices are accused of somehow lacking character. But that is incorrect, for the most part. Poor people make bad choices, not by a lack of character, but by a scarcity of money which distorts their ability to see clearly. Does that sound about right?"

"Yeah," Frank said. He was too close to the forest for the trees. "Yeah, Larry. I get it; do not panic. I don't know what the plan is right now. I cannot tell you what I am going to do next specifically, or what will happen to me. But I can tell you that I am not going to change who I am."

"I was hoping that you would say that," Larry said. "Anyway, if things do not work out, there is always a cold one here for you in Northwest Florida."

Frank smiled.

"Lemme close with this, Larry," Frank continued. "I work out with some military guys. They are great guys, Larry. Well, not sure if you know what a Stop-Loss is, but one of these guys just got one, and he is in bad shape."

"I know, Frank. Northwest Florida has a lot of ex-military guys, as you know, and I counsel some of them along with their families in my psychology practice. Your problems are relatively minor compared to them."

Frank stared down at the receiver as the call ended. His problems were fixable, but to a lot of these guys, their issues did not go away when they left the theater. He appreciated the mental health break from a good friend. It was that sense of perspective that he needed.

CHAPTER 24
The Sting

—⁂—

A LARGE PANEL TRUCK entered the warehouse compound on Camp Bradley late in the afternoon. The lettering on the outside of the panel truck read Al Jabar in Arabic. Al Jabar was an Iraqi supplier of car parts. As the apparent low bidder for this $3,000 order of auto parts, it was making a delivery today, the 20th day of May, 2005.

The truck had been waiting patiently at the gate for the entire day. The driver had to endure a whole-body search. The vehicle had its contents scanned. It also had the engine and underbody scanned for explosives. Six hours later, the driver would open the rear gate of the truck and silently pass several cartons along with the accompanying shipping documentation to the Iraqi clerks who were working the dock area.

The shipping documentation would be a packing slip only; no totals on the packing list. But the Iraqi clerks who unloaded the truck were not interested in the cost of auto parts. Their interest was in taking possession of the boxes; but not what was in them, for there was nothing in the boxes. These cartons were empty.

Swiftly transferring the boxes to the warehouse area, they provided the original of the shipping documents to their Kosovar supervisor. Keeping a copy for themselves, the Iraqis began to put the imaginary car parts into stock. The Kosovar supervisor, working in the cool of the air-conditioned office, never entered the heat of the warehouse in order to physically check the boxes. He merely put the imaginary list of car parts into the computer system after ascertaining that the Iraqi clerks had signed for the parts.

That particular set of parts would have a short shelf life. The next day, the Iraqi clerks would go into the computer system and, using that same copy of the shipping documentation, issue out all of the phantom inventory to ongoing projects, thereby setting up a reorder solicitation. The shipping documents would wind their way to accounts payable, where a clerk would marry up the shipping documents with the purchase order that had been let and, thirty days later, issue a check in the full amount to Al Jafar.

Marsh and Buck would take 70% right off of the top on this and every order like it, subject to further distribution; in this case, $2,100. Khan got thirty percent of that amount, or $630. He would set aside 75% of that amount; $472.50, in order to satisfy his covenant agreement with his Al Qaeda financiers. That would appear to leave Khan with $157.50.

But the souk, or market, never closes in the Middle East, so Khan via Derya negotiated out a further third of Al Jafar's cut on this order. That meant siphoning off an additional piece of the action, or $300 out of Al Jafar's scheduled gross take of $900 so that Khan's net take would increase to $457.50. The little people who actually did the work, whose six minimum wage jobs were at risk here, split that final $472.50, payable through Derya in Iraqi Dinars.

Reconciling these transactions and stashing that extra cash that he had negotiated out from Al Jafar in a separate account away from the clutches of Marsh and Buck would keep Khan busily immersed in spreadsheets on his yacht in the Kuwaiti harbor.

As a percentage of the take, Marsh and Buck would wind up the lion's share, of course; netting almost half of the cost of the order after settling up with Khan. Khan and his company would wind up netting 15.25% of the total after paying his Al Qaeda money men what amounted to almost 16% of the total in return for financing his criminal enterprise. Khan knew, of course, that his financiers were making more off of each transaction than he was. But for the middleman, it was not only the price of doing business, it was the price of staying alive and in one piece. All in all, not bad for a day's work, considering that no goods were delivered.

The purchase order containing the shipping documentation would wind its way up through the government accounting system along with proof of payment accompanying an invoice. Some thirty days later, Cork and Hammer would receive reimbursement for its $3,000, not including its award fees, which would come later.

It was one of those odd days when Frank had no meetings scheduled. It was Saturday, but that did not mean much in a war. Saturdays were just another work day, but Saturdays were when Rust, Buck, and the military generally went into all day planning meetings. That left guys like Frank the whole day to catch up on whatever had eluded him during the week. This was not going to be one of those days.

"Frank, can we have a talk?" It was Samer, waving him down in the hallway. Frank motioned him into the office.

"I got a call from a friend last night. He is friends with a supplier who was telling him in confidence that your purchasing people are shaking them down." Samer reached over and pulled out a purchase agreement. The low bidder was Al Jafar.

All of the suppliers that Frank had been dealing with were part of an approved supplier list left over from Coleman. The list, broken down by commodities, had suppliers for each commodity type; from water to soap and toilet paper. It was that list that the buyers used for soliciting competition on the local market. Al Jafar's name was on the list, of course, having been placed there much earlier by Buck and Khan without Coleman's knowledge.

"What he was saying was that a local Iraqi supplier of auto parts, Mustafa and Company, wanted to be qualified to bid. He had been placed on the bid list but never received any business in spite of his assertion that his prices were very competitive. Well, my friend is telling me that Mustafa recently received a call from somebody here at the base who told him that he could do business on the base under certain conditions."

"Who is this guy, what did he say, and what were these 'conditions'?" Frank asked.

"This guy apparently told Mustafa that he would receive a solicitation. Respond to the solicitation with a certain price, and he would be awarded the business. Dunno, but sounds like one of your purchasing people." Samer's normal Hollywood-style toothy grin had disappeared.

"But here is the thing: the supplier was directed not to ship any goods. In exchange, he would have to agree to a small piece of the gross. He thinks these guys who he does not know are bad men, surely criminals, and possibly terrorists."

Frank thought it through. He had been watching the inventory and, in spite of the improvement in his accuracy levels, there were still anomalies outside of Kliskey's nighttime raids. This could help explain it.

His instinct told him that he trusted Keni Mehmeti. Keni supervised fifty mostly Kosovar third-country nationals, all of whom were intensely loyal to Keni. The Kosovar supervisor and his group had become intensely loyal to Frank because, unlike Coleman, Frank had defended Keni in front of Rust and the military when Buck attempted to throw Frank's group under the proverbial bus for stock shortages that Buck and Kliskey had themselves created.

Frank was less convinced that the Iraqi clerks were not corrupt. Any or all of them could be subject to influence. They did not make much money so everybody was seeking to make some extra cash. He asked Keni to come to the office alone and closed the door.

"Somebody has been running a scam in the warehouse, Keni," Frank said, looking right at Keni. "Know anything about it?"

"What kind of a scam, Frank?"

Frank proceeded to give him a brief rundown, leaving Samer out of it. He did not want retribution if things here went south.

"Frank, I am straight," Keni said. "You have done more for me to back us up here than Coleman ever did. Look, I hear things all of the time. It's a busy place, Frank," Keni continued. "Stock comes in and leaves constantly. I think that most of the guys down there are OK, but I am seeing the same thing that you are. We are still experiencing unexplained shortages."

With that, he reached into his wallet and pulled out a wrinkled photo and put it down on the desk. It was the photo outside of Frank's hooch with Derya lying on the ground, and Kliskey filming it. "Remember this?" Keni said. "That was me. I hate that fucker Kliskey and what he does in this warehouse, but I am powerless to stop him when he comes in here and just takes stuff. I have to account for it, so it makes my life miserable."

"So how did you know to take that picture?" Frank asked. He wondered who would have been in a position to take that picture and what the motivation was.

"One of Kliskey's guys let it slip one night when he was half-plastered drunk," Keni replied. "He gave up the entire gig, about how Buck wanted that scene filmed. He was bragging about it. By the way, the whole camp knows about that stuff. I would have come to you sooner, but I did not know you well enough at that point. So, what do you have in mind?" Keni said, changing the subject.

Frank looked back at Keni and smiled. Something was going on in the warehouse, but he at least felt better about Keni, not to mention his own instincts.

"I am going to see if the supplier will send us a confidential memorandum confirming that the next order that he sends ships empty; as in, no inventory inside of the boxes. I will alert you to the order number. Just track the order through the system. Anybody that processes that fake order will be recommended for termination. Let's see what the supplier says."

As Keni departed the office on the way back to the warehouses, Frank considered how he would notify his security manager counterpart. Like Frank, he reported directly to Buck, although the local security guy was matrixed to a corporate security guy in Virginia. He needed security's assistance here, but worried that they would tip off Buck, whom he most certainly did not trust.

Frank decided on the fait accompli route: once the plan was ready to be put in motion, he would notify Felipe Gonzalez, who was the local security guy. Gonzalez would be told just in time, just as the stock was to arrive, so that there would be no time to alter or otherwise mess with the plan.

A FEW DAYS later, Samer produced a letter from the supplier stating that Order #2005-1992, totaling $4,636.16, had shipped to the base without inventory. The plan was straight forward: Keni Mehmeti would take a tally of all of the items in stock on that order on the day that the stock was scheduled to arrive. The security guys, along with Keni, would follow that order along its trail through the system.

Once the order was posted by the Iraqi clerks, Keni would himself quietly do a post-order inventory. Even in a busy war zone environment, this one was easy. If the net physical inventory count after order #2005-1992's arrival remained unchanged - a process that took only minutes to complete - then the expected increase of the inventory from #2005-1992 never occurred. The order was indeed bogus, just as the supplier had asserted in his letter.

Frank smiled. Winston Churchill used to say, "never let a good crisis go to waste". With that in mind, he called Janey Lynn Reed. He had gotten to know her enough to know that she would also want to be part of this. Frank needed an ally that would shoulder the reporting responsibility.

But it was more important than that. Frank needed a way to circumvent Buck, and Reed was his ticket to doing just that. As with the man-camp issue, Frank knew that her report would bypass Buck and Taylor. That joint assessment would eventually wind its way to the corporate board of directors. Like security, he would brief her on a just in time need to know. He knew who she slept with after work.

—

The door closed to Kenny Buck's gargantuan office digs. Frank had made sure that Felipe Gonzalez and Janey Lynn Reed would attend by making them part of the sting operation, as well as co-signatories as to the findings. Buck and Taylor represented management.

What had started as a dull report that Buck fully intended to bury became a lot more interesting when Rust, the VP, walked in unannounced and uninvited. But then it was his operation, and nobody would tell him that he was not invited. It also had the secondary benefit of forcing both Buck and Taylor to read the report. Quickly.

"What do you want out of this, Frank?" Buck asked, while awkwardly attempting to devour Frank's written version of a heat seeking missile in real time, in front of Rust. The report recommended terminating not only all of the clerks that placed the orders but also any of those who touched either the inventory or the related paperwork; fifteen in all. It also recommended some overtime in order to accommodate further random audits.

The names of the clerks were listed as an attachment. Frank deliberately did not disclose any information regarding the supplier's name or business nor did he disclose Samer's role for fear of retribution. He wondered if Buck was interested enough to take note of that omission. Frank knew that the security guys had the name of the supplier so Buck could get the information if he intended to retaliate at a later date.

"Remember, you told me that I manage the process and you manage the people? Well, Kenny, these are your people. Given that, I recommend that you terminate some of your people." Frank smiled sweetly, letting those words reverberate in the basketball court-sized conference room.

Buck briefly glanced back at Frank, grimacing from another rhetorical left hook while trying hard to contain his urge to strike back.

Terminating the clerks was the least of Buck's problems. It was Frank Davenport and Janey Lynn Reed of which he wanted to rid himself, and soon; to shoot the proverbial messengers. He also had no intention of conducting more random audits. No need for more shoes to drop. That much he would make clear to both Taylor and Felipe Gonzalez, blaming it on the volume of work and not enough time.

He had been speaking with Marsh and had been assured that the business was closing soon. The last thing that he needed was this to become an issue up the chain; especially if it spread to the government auditors, who would call for a much more extensive audit while holding up the close of the business. Time really was money here, and that money in Kuwait was burning a hole in his pocket.

"Do we think that this is symptomatic of a larger issue, Frank?" It was Rust asking, but in a tone and voice that indicated that he had really directed the question to himself. Sensing that while looking over at Buck, whose body language had the look and feel of someone about to crack under pressure, Frank remained silent, causing a pregnant pause that was deafeningly loud.

"Is this something that we need to get military counterintelligence to look at?" Rust was again speaking softly, mostly to himself as if he was creating his own action item, now casting his gaze directly at Buck. The wheels were turning in his head.

The meeting adjourned, and a half an hour later Frank was entering his office when he saw Derya, surrounded by other expats, preparing to leave the building.

"Heard about your little incident in the warehouse, Frank," she said, her eyes dancing, giving the appearance that the incident was a little silly. But it was not foolish.

The last thing that Derya or Khan wanted was more unwanted audits. She had already spoken to Kenny Buck about that, but what clearly worried both Derya and Kenny Buck was that Frank Davenport, who had been the victim up to now, had demonstrated that he knew what he was doing and was beginning to go on offense. The tables were starting to turn.

Buck observed that even Rust was now beginning to ask questions. Whereas Rust had previously confined himself to managing up, he now began to contemplate openly having to manage down. Buck thought back to the meeting with Marsh, and how he had urged him just to keep going. That advice looked increasingly dangerous.

Buck would let Marsh deal with Rust on this, confident that Marsh would advise Rust just to kick the can down the road. Rust, like Marsh, knew that the business was for sale. However, unlike Marsh and Buck, Rust had a relationship with the military that transcended subcontractors.

Rust needed that political capital regardless of which Beltway bandit he chose to work for. He had earned his stars in another life by being above reproach. Rust was not going to tarnish his reputation in this place if the ex-general could help it. Rust's instincts were correct, but for now, he would manage up in an organizational sense, which meant doing what corporate wanted. And so, he would be talked out of doing more by Marsh.

FRANK HAD SPENT the morning in the warehouses with Keni Mehmeti checking stock. He had gotten the reviews down to about an hour so as not to unnecessarily constrain an otherwise bustling warehouse operation. Frank and Keni were measuring the disconnects which were either stock-outs or where the official count did not match what the system showed. Both defect types were dropping like a stone. Usually, Keni would be happy, but today he was less so.

As he prepared to head back to the office, Frank turned to Keni and said," You seem a little subdued."

"Did you see Samer come into the office today, Frank?"

Frank thought for a moment. "No, as a matter of fact, I did not, but I had the usual meeting with Buck in the morning, then I headed down to see you, so I really was not in the office this morning. Why?"

"Our guys in the warehouse are hearing from some of the Iraqis that there was an incident at the gate this morning. A bombing. I called Daniela who said that his office is dark and the door is locked. He is a good guy, Frank."

Frank arrived back at his office to find Zoe and Daniela waiting for him. Both ladies were visibly shaken.

"Samer is in a hospital, Frank," Zoe muttered, a tearful look in her eye. "I was in HR just now, and they were talking about it. Not sure how he avoided being killed outright."

"How bad is it? Did they say?" Frank asked, his mind wandering back to his meeting about Samer's car.

"The bomb totally destroyed the car, Frank. It does not look good." At that, both otherwise worldly women broke down and cried like babies. Frank could not help thinking back to his meeting with Buck and Rust on the warehouse sting.

Frank knew that the terrorists had been chasing Samer for some time now because he worked at the base. To be sure, Samer was not the only Iraqi targeted for working at the base. He also knew that Samer's name had been connected to the sting investigation because he was the go-between between Frank's organization and the supplier. Moreover, all of the now-terminated Iraqi clerks knew Samer and knew that he was connected to the investigation, as did the security guys. And they worked for Buck.

Frank would never know the root cause of the terrorist attack on Samer. But that really did not matter now. His worst fear was that Samer was on an operating table just for doing his job and supporting the United States government.

CHAPTER 25
Laundry Fiasco

—m—

"Where's Taylor?" Janey Lynn Reed asked Joyce Bailey, the laundry manager.

"Not my job to watch him, Janey; don't you?" Joyce responded tartly. Like the rest of the camp, Joyce knew exactly what kind of relationship Reed had with Taylor.

Joyce ran the laundry like a tight ship, but she and her staff were buried in work. Neither she nor her team looked forward to spending the entire morning going into an audit of her operation that nobody got anything out of but a lecture on the off-chance that the bureaucrats found a minor clerical problem. The other Filipino ladies that worked for Joyce were fully aware of Taylor's relationship with Janey, but also knew another side of Taylor that Reed apparently did not know. They started laughing in the background.

It was already past one hundred degrees Fahrenheit in the shade at half past eight in the morning. Clueless as to the inside joke, but also not wanting to make a federal case out of anything more routine than an audit, Janey Lynn decided to stow her temper, and push on.

"Okay, well, let's get started."

Joyce wasn't happy with the audit, but she was not surprised. Reviews on government contracts, both internal and client-driven were the norm, not the exception, given that you were playing with public money. But the government had earlier directed the laundry to do dry cleaning, which somehow fell through the cracks, leading to the incident in December with the client that had blossomed into something just short of a rhetorical declaration of nuclear war, and so the laundry became a natural candidate for an internal audit by Janey Lynn and her group.

These were the kind of processes that the client audited without prior notice. They mindlessly picked transactions out at random, then typically required the contractor to show a cradle-to-grave audit trail of documents. A successful audit would be just another routine to-do checked off of the business close-out-audit list of things to do. Screw it up, however, and all hell broke loose. And those screw-ups reflected poorly on Janey Lynn in compliance, which is why she conducted internal audits like these.

Ever the control freak, stuff like this was why Buck kept a wary eye out for Janey Lynn Reed. This was late May and the unofficial pressure to close the audits and complete the sale was building. The way that Buck saw it, now was not the time for some white trash bitch with a short fuse who did not report directly to him to go off writing memos up the chain to senior management over some perceived minor defect in the laundry.

Buck just wanted dead dogs to lie, collect his money, and leave. After the knockdown, drag-out meeting with the client over some miscommunication over dry cleaning some months ago, he had seen to it that Coleman before he left had - unknowingly of course - ordered the dry-cleaning equipment through one of Khan's shell companies.

What worried him was that Reed was one mean, spiteful, straight razor-toting chick who had a big mouth. It was why he had directed Taylor to keep an eye on the laundry audit. What neither Reed nor Buck knew was that Taylor had been a little "engaged" at the moment.

—ʊʊ—

Janey Lynn pulled out her notepad, to which she had stapled five current laundry tickets. The process was simple: she was going to have Joyce pull all of the required paperwork associated with all five numbered laundry tickets. Along the way, both Joyce and Janey Lynn, each holding a mutual disdain for the other, would verify that the simple process for taking in washing and drying, then folding and placing back into numbered plastic bags for pick-up, was followed.

All of this occurred in the heat of the day and at a time when the rush of soldiers who were turning in their laundry had resulted in a line out the door. Joyce's Filipino clerks, working as hard as they could, weren't able to keep up with the workload and began to complain to each other about being short staffed.

"Where's Maria?" Joyce said, looking for one of her clerks who were not at the laundry desk.

Ears perked up at the clerk's name, eyes flashing silently as they busily tended to their soldier-customers, taking in new bags of dirty laundry for cleaning while simultaneously dispensing cleaned packs of clothes. The clerks began laughing but in Spanish, all of them howling together at some inside joke, a joke to which neither Joyce or Janey Lynn were privy, mainly since neither spoke Spanish.

Tempers were beginning to rise quickly in the non-air-conditioned rear of the laundry facility where the audit was taking place. The front of the building where the soldiers stood was temperate but the back of the facility, cooled only by fans, was an inferno. Neither of the managers wanted to be there at that point, and their attitudes began to show.

"Nina, go find Maria," Joyce called out to her short, middle-aged second in command who was pulling bags of laundry off of a delivery cart that had just arrived with a load of clean laundry from the facility next door containing the washers and dryers.

Nina put down the laundry bags, then whispered into Joyce's ear while looking over at Janey Lynn. Joyce smiled. The other Filipino girls, sensing what was about to occur, began giggling.

Joyce looked over at Janey Lynn. "Some of those tickets of yours are in the room in the back. Let's go," motioning to Janey Lynn to follow her.

The cackling-in-Spanish from the Filipino girls rose as the two women approached the room in the rear. Both women disappeared into a side room full of laundry that adjoined the main laundry facility.

As Joyce and Janey opened the door to that side room, they discovered Taylor and Maria, oblivious to the door opening, bodies glistening with perspiration from the heat, copulating on a makeshift bed made from some soldier's freshly cleaned but not yet sorted laundry.

"You bitch!" Janey Lynn screamed at the Filipino, grabbing the woman at her mid-section, attempting to separate both partners in heat.

The Filipino woman screamed louder but then started laughing as she realized just who was doing the screaming. All of the Filipino women knew that Taylor had been enjoying the Filipino women. It had been an open secret that even Joyce knew but was keeping secret until the right time. And this was the right time.

The screams got louder as both women attacked the other, with Taylor wordlessly struggling amid the mayhem to put his clothes on. Seconds later two soldiers, hearing the screams, entered the room to determine the origin of the loud noise only to witness Taylor, naked except for his boots, and Janey Lynn along with the also-naked Filipino clerk doing their best pro wrestling imitation.

Audit this… bitch, thought Joyce Bailey, smiling to herself.

"Rust wants them both off of the base right now." Buck was on the phone to Marsh. Buck had just emerged from a meeting with both the colonel and VP Rust. Both had been shown a report from the military chain on the issue. Neither were happy.

"Is there any way to save either one? We are close to closing the business." That was code for keeping a lid on things until Cork and Hammer completed the audits, transferring the business to BLTVDef.

"Don't think so," Buck replied. "Taylor was stark naked in there. And Janey Lynn chased the Filipino chick all the way back to the Filipino chick's hooch, and was seen banging on the door, screaming 'Get out here bitch, I am going to kick your ass' in front of the entire camp." He could sense Marsh wincing on the other end of the phone.

"I did ask Rust if there was any way that we could keep either one. He laughed. He told me that the military brass up the chain wanted them both out on the next flight."

Buck knew that Rust had purposely shoved that report from the military under Buck's nose. Rust wanted them gone, but he knew that Marsh and Buck wanted to keep both Taylor and Reed. Why? That was a different matter.

Marsh wanted to close the audits and any claims related business as a precursor to ending that part of the due diligence, checking off one of the big items on the list, getting him closer to his big payday. Reed had been submitting regular reports on her counterpart's progress in that due diligence, vital interactions that made their way not only to Case Hammer but to Cork and Hammer's board of directors. He needed Janey Lynn Reed to continue to do that. Unfortunately, Janey Lynn's big mouth, an organizational asset up to now, had just morphed into a fatal flaw, an irony that would not be lost on either Marsh or Buck.

Much closer to the action on the ground, Buck wanted them both gone. Never overly enamored with Marsh's earlier decision to wait longer to collect more money, Buck continually worried about the leaks, particularly from Janey Lynn Reed who had a habit of writing damaging missives that ultimately wound their way past Buck to Marsh to Hammer, and was a general pain in his side on the issue of re-competing the subcontract agreements.

Buck smiled. He knew that Taylor had been fucking the Filipino clerks. Hell, the entire laundry knew what Taylor had been doing since before Buck promoted him from the laundry foreman job. He had heard about it from time to time from HR, but without a formal complaint it was all camp gossip, and so he would support Taylor, keeping that issue as a point of leverage over Taylor; just in case. Until now.

Buck wanted Taylor around to keep him; as the saying went, "inside the tent pissing out rather than outside of the tent pissing in." But even Taylor, who was signing paperwork authorizing Kliskey's trips to Kuwait, was too close to the money and so he had to go at some point.

In the final analysis, Buck knew that Marsh had already spent his political capital with Rust on Taylor, defending him for fraudulently drafting paperwork on the tank issue. Simply put, Taylor had done something in the laundry in front of military personnel that could not be defended, not even by Marsh. Even Taylor would agree to that, so this was the right time for Taylor to go.

And so, as Buck put down the phone, he smiled and checked another two direct reports off of the list of those he had fired. Buck was already making plans for Frank Davenport. He was still incensed at the recent issue with the potable water tanks and how much-unwanted attention that drew. Taylor's termination brought back those frustrations. But for now, he turned to his secretary, handed the military's report to her and said, "Kacey, send this to HR. We need to schedule exit interviews for both Taylor and Reed. Keep this confidential."

Instructing his secretary to keep this confidential was precisely the message that Buck wanted to send, for his secretary would do just the opposite. Word would spread around camp, reaching both Davenport and the rest of Buck's senior staff before HR had scheduled the interviews. Per the military brass's instructions, both Taylor and Reed would be off the camp by sundown.

CHAPTER 26
The End Game

—~~—

"Hi Jim. Do we have everybody on your side?" It was Case Hammer on the line, dialing into a conference call with Jim Witt's mergers and acquisitions team in D.C. "Good morning, Case. Yes, we have everybody here on our side."

It was the morning of the fifth of June, 2005. Hammer and Witt were about to engage in what was almost little more than a formality at this point. It had been a busy two months since their last meeting. Witt, without disclosing as much directly to Hammer, had let it be known through intermediaries that he was amenable to coming up from his $6.00 a share position within reason, if that is what it took to close the deal. And so, when Witt offered to up his offer to $6.20 a share, Hammer countered with $6.63 a share. Witt, looking down at his $10.02 a share valuation spreadsheet and smiling, accepted in principal.

The purpose of this meeting was to discuss the last significant issue, which was how Hammer was dealing with the compliance issues. Hammer had charged Marsh with leading this issue in terms of quantifying the risk and Marsh, in turn, had put Kenny Buck and Janey Lynn Reed at a local level to work on trying to understand just how much Cork and Hammer would have to set aside for compliance-related issues. Putting Buck in charge was seeming to delegate the fox to run the hen house, and Janey Lynn Reed had been summarily terminated, so there was no lead in compliance for the moment.

For his part, Hammer had been running the traps higher up the chain at the client, and had come away feeling that $20 million was conservative, and would probably make all parties happy, although the client was careful not to commit to a firm ceiling.

"Jim, this is Case. As I understand it, we are both tentatively agreed to $6.63 a share. Agreed?"

"Agreed, Case," replied Witt. "Where are we with the compliance issues and resolution?"

"Here is how I suggest we handle this, Jim," Case replied. "We have studied the issue here and have been in contact with our client. We see the need at this point conservatively to set aside $20 million in order to deal with any compliance-related issues. We will do that. As noted, we will agree to keep Cork and Hammer open on a non-operating basis with that $20 million set aside in equity, until such time as all claims with the USG are resolved. However, if we settle out less than $20 million, which I believe is very conservative here, we want to claw back the difference. Agreed?"

Witt would run the traps through his contacts with the client but, assuming that they were on board with that number, he did not think twice before agreeing in principle. This was small potatoes to Witt and BLTVDef, and time was getting critical. The client had been quietly but forcefully pressing both parties on an informal basis to get this closed so that they could move on to the next stage of operations. The Pentagon was dead serious about Iran and Pakistan, not to mention Afghanistan and Iraq, but needed a contractor who could take that next step. In the world of defense contractors, the list of contractors with both the ability and the financial wherewithal to do that was limited, which is why this deal was so important.

Both sides had agreed to a stretch goal of thirty days for close, but both knew that doing so depended on their client, the United States government. And that was anything but a given, since in the government you frequently got rewarded not so much for what you did right as for what you did not do wrong. Both knew that answering questions and the inevitable back office paper chase that came from transitioning from one contractor to another could easily stretch this out for months.

The room where Case had assembled his team for this conference, a break room next to the cafeteria normally used for lunch, had emptied out and he was now alone with his thoughts. It was a bitter sweet moment in his life. More than a half century devoted to building a company that started out on a post-World War II wing and a prayer was coming to an end. But he was not going to dwell on that now; more time for that later.

Case knew that one of the keys to keeping this deal very profitable was in making sure that the $20 million was an absolute worst-case scenario, since a chunk of that money would accrue directly to him as a dominant shareholder. At $6.63 a share, Hammer had the company valued at $980 million, making his 30% share worth $294 million, net of debt. But those debts were "on balance sheet" debt; they did not include any "off balance sheet" charges.

That "off balance sheet" debt was the $25 million that the CIA had fronted him. Hammer had taken the money because he needed it in order to finance the rapid ramp up in war-related costs. The CIA had provided the debt financing, part of a larger concept called geo-economics – or war by other means - in order to facilitate the killing of Derya's brother, the Al Qaeda financier.

Case Hammer wanted to close this deal. But for that to occur, for him to finally agree to the deal, he had to purchase some "business insurance," given what he knew of Marsh and Buck and their relationship with the colonel. Now that he had an agreement in principal with BLTVDef which would allow him to check out of life a rich man, free from chasing government contracts in both boom and bust times with all of the ass-kissing that entailed, his very next phone call would be to some folks who would deliver that "business insurance" - the kind that you do not get at a normal commercial insurance company. That would be his friends in the CIA and the Pentagon - and Senator Wickes.

—~—

It was a warm, humid day in the nation's capital this Monday, the twenty-first day of June, 2005. The beginning of summer was a time when most of D.C. focused on summer vacations or weekends at places like Rehoboth Beach, Delaware and tended to run at a slower pace. But neither James Witt nor Case Hammer, his counterpart in a deal that both parties wanted desperately to close, fell into that mindset. Bikinis and beer on the beach were a distant concept for both.

For Witt, the internal pressure to close this little deal had become intense since their last meeting earlier in June. Witt had other, larger deals on his plate, but if one were to rank them in terms of importance in a typical time management matrix at this particular moment, the bigger deals would be important but not urgent. This one had bubbled up, and was now both important and urgent. The client wanted this deal done and dusted so that they could integrate operations and move on with their war plans in Afghanistan, Pakistan, and possibly Iran, in addition to Iraq.

Witt was keenly aware of this. He had been trying to run the internal traps within his organization chain, but more importantly, with the client. Witt wanted a clear buy-off from management on the $20 million ceiling claw back in claims and everybody, in typical bureaucratic fashion, was passing the buck. His administration wanted buy-off from the client, while the client was being typically vague.

On the one hand, the client on the project side wanted the deal, while the client on the audit side could not guarantee that the exposure would be limited to $20 million until the audits, claims, and counter-claims were exhausted. He hadn't expected this on a relatively small deal. He was wrong; he was frustrated at the institutional inertia, and the clock was running.

Witt hadn't gotten anywhere until now because Hammer had three fundamental problems. Witt only knew about the first one; the $20 million in ordinary, business-related claims. Marsh, Buck and the colonel represented a second, separate set of claims exposure related to fraud. And third, Hammer had $25 million in off-balance sheet financing from the CIA that he wanted to go away.

Hammer knew that Marsh and Buck were liabilities. What they had done subjected Cork and Hammer not only to wholesale denial of reimbursement based on fraudulent activity. It also exposed the officers of the company to the possibility of prison time. But he also knew that the colonel, who ran the base, had been aiding and abetting Marsh and Buck. He had the evidence stashed in a bank in Kuwait.

Hammer also knew that the CIA had never informed DOD of the "off-balance-sheet financing" plan to use DOD facilities in a CIA operation. That CIA plan had sacrificed DOD's own on-camp intelligence in order to kill the Al Qaeda financier. If that plan was exposed, the blowback would be severe. That was something that none of the parties wanted. Those had been his pressure points, his source of leverage in his own, separate successful "business insurance" negotiations with the client.

And so, as they sat down this warm Washington day, both parties would finally converge on a deal. That was because, while Witt and Hammer were seeking different outcomes, both they and their client's interests would finally align. Witt would think to himself that Hammer's negotiation with Witt was Hammer's negotiation of a lifetime. Hammer knew different; he knew that it was an earlier, successful negotiation with the client that led to this negotiation. Hammer's long drawn out deal for his "business insurance" had led to all parties' interests aligning. That was his negotiation of a lifetime.

Witt would come away from the deal with another notch on his gun. He would be greeted within his company, and by the client, as a rising star in a big bureaucracy. Hammer would emerge from the deal smiling as well, but for other reasons. For, unlike Witt, Hammer would never work again. Hammer had just become part of the one percent.

CHAPTER 27
"Poppin' Smoke"

—∞—

"TIME TO POP smoke, 'ole Kinney-boy."

It was Marsh on the phone. And while that was the sum and substance of the conversation, that short sentence was all that Buck wanted to hear; it was music to his ears. He and Marsh had agreed that, as soon as the deal to sell was finalized, he was to meet up with Marsh in Kuwait on Khan's yacht where they would arrange for the final disbursement of funds that would make him a millionaire.

As luck would have it, there was a scheduled convoy movement to Kuwait on the 22nd of June, which was a Wednesday. That would be the last convoy of his life, Buck thought. How right he was.

—∞—

"C'MON IN, DERYA!" Buck shouted as she entered Buck's double-wide trailer. *The 22nd day of June, 2005 was a good day to leave this hell hole*, he thought to himself. Temperatures had climbed to one hundred twenty degrees in the shade, and it was only going to get hotter as the summer wore on. Average folks who were leaving a project would be in good spirits, eager to see family, and reorient back into their stateside life. Not Buck. Buck was going to be rich, but he was also a criminal who had no ordinary stateside life, and he knew it. Buck was having an out-of-body experience.

Of course, nobody except for Marsh knew that Buck was leaving for good today. Buck had been careful not to show signs of packing up. He did not want to raise suspicions. Buck was careful not to strip his office clean, except for a few memorabilia. He had a full day of meetings with his senior staff and was careful to meet those obligations, including one with the colonel.

The day was over now; it was half-past ten in the evening, the heat from the day had passed, and he was drunk. Very drunk; so drunk that he could barely stand, and when he was drunk, he tended to get horny around good-looking women. Derya fit the bill, and so he was going to fuck her one last time before he left. The convoy was set to depart in a couple of hours; just enough time to fuck, take care of a couple of last-minute items, and run.

The drive to Kuwait would put him there at around 5am on Thursday. The banks were closed to customers at 1pm on Thursday and would not open again until Sunday the 26th of June. The plan wasn't complicated: wait on Khan's yacht through Saturday, drinking and taking turns banging whores with Khan while waiting for Marsh, then sober up for the drive to the bank on Sunday which was the to be the first day of the rest of his new life as a multi-millionaire.

Buck had never actually seen that kind of money before. Neither had anybody else that he had known earlier in his life. His kinfolk and his friends were lowlifes. Most of them couldn't count to $350 million, let alone put their hands on all or even some of that kind of money, legally or not. He had what NBA first-round draft picks would call sudden wealth.

Buck had no frame of reference for what was going to happen, no friends or experience with which to guide him. And like most formerly poor people who come into sudden wealth, like lottery winners, he had no plan for what to do with it. He didn't run in the kinds of circles that put you in touch with people who could park money in places nobody knew about at a time when money laundering was a profession of sorts and was going global. Money like that was conceptual, a dream.

Ernest Hemingway once said about bankruptcy that it came in two ways; slowly, then all of a sudden. Like bankruptcy, as with most habits in life such as Buck's cocaine addiction, the end did not happen with one drug hit or one financial misadventure. It was the slow, soul-draining, compound effect of living beyond one's means or pouring his life's earnings up his nose until suddenly Buck found himself out of a job and in a drug rehabilitation halfway house. That is, until fortune in the name of William Marsh came calling.

And now, it seemed that fortune would smile again. Buck and Marsh had been stashing money into an account in Kuwait, but those were only deposits, numbers on a piece of paper, and never withdrawals, slowly accumulating over time. Never having access either to the account or the benefits that it created while he tried to stay sober, Buck's slaving away in an active war zone to create this type of wealth made this an academic exercise. That is, until Marsh's call suddenly made the prospect of sudden wealth begin to hit home. The fact that he was committing a series of felonies to accumulate that kind of wealth just did not occur to a psychopath like Buck.

He was drunk; he was going to fuck an incredibly beautiful woman, and soon he was going to be incredibly wealthy. But just where he was going to go, where he was going to live, or what he was going to do after he got rich hadn't occurred to him, other than on a theoretical basis. Buck was good at micromanaging, but the more significant, managing-for-tomorrow picture had eluded him, especially for an expatriate soon to be on the run outside of the United States. The world was going global but Buck, who had worked outside of the States, still thought local.

As such, he was trying - and failing - to wrap his head around all of that. It was moments like this that great tennis players will tell you that you need to play through the shot in your head, proactively moving your feet, ahead of time. Like avoiding bankruptcy, or a bad cocaine habit, good habits and preparation were keys because the end, like a 140-mile-an-hour tennis serve, does come suddenly. Buck was lost, which is why he was drunk, and that was dangerous.

—∞—

"WHAT IS IT that you wanted, Kenny?" Derya said flatly, entering Buck's hooch.

Derya was not stupid; she knew that setting foot into Buck's hooch late at night probably involved sex, but that was part of the job. She had been on the prowl for intelligence, and sometimes this kind of activity was where and how secrets were to be had. She had been fucking both the colonel and Buck on a semi-regular basis, in exchange for some cash, along with an entree into the Iranian border camps and any intelligence that she could glean. Now six months later, despite her best efforts, in spite of Khan's constant pleadings with both Marsh and Buck, none of that Iranian border intelligence effort had paid off.

The sex was something that was officially kept relatively low-key, although in the close confines of camp life it was not something that could be hidden, not that most people cared. Derya looked at it as just another part of the job; get them off quickly, find out what she could, and report back to Khan in due course, and then go back to take a shower.

Sex with the colonel had gradually devolved into something clinical. The colonel had weakly attempted the master/slave thing, but both parties quickly figured out that he had neither the underlying attitude nor the emotional makeup for the games. Now it was a bit like calling a plumber to do a job. She entered his hooch on some pretext; a couple of minutes later he popped, and she was gone. It even had developed its own structured, not-so-kinky protocol: "you come, and I go." No girlfriend experience, no role play - just sex, like an old married couple where the flame had long since died.

With Buck, it was different; anything but clinical. There was always a tension, like somehow during the run-up to intercourse he came totally unglued. Unlike the colonel, there was a real psychopathic inner demon within Buck that drove him which manifested itself during sex through violence. At first, she thought that it was a game, but soon came away from it dreading the experience.

She hated sex with both men, although she could deal with the colonel. She had been with many men like the colonel in the Middle East. But as much as she disliked the colonel, and hated the sex more, she really despised Buck.

To Derya, sex with Buck had become a metaphor for the American involvement in the Middle East; psychopaths on a forced-entry power trip, taking what they wanted just because they could, and without apparent consequence. She now understood just why her brother hated them so much.

And yet, immediately upon entering Buck's hooch, Derya could somehow sense that this night was different. Call it woman's intuition, but Buck's look, his demeanor, even his eye contact was different. It wasn't just that he was drunk. She had seen that before and did not like it. There was always that palpable tension that had existed between them, even on days when Buck was sober. But when he was drunk, Buck morphed into a monster as the inner demons took control. It was all that she could do to hide the marks and bruises from their encounters.

"On your knees, bitch." Buck's eyes were dazed; his speech slurred in his drunken state, his psychotic stare penetrating her eyes, just as surely as he intended to maliciously penetrate another part of Derya's anatomy. "I am going to fuck your brains out one last time, you fucking whore. But before I do that, I want you to ..."

"What do you mean - one last time, Kenny?" Derya stared straight at him, struggling to break through the rage that was Buck. At one level, it was all about self-preservation. Through conversation, she was attempting to delay what she feared was inevitable; the usual demented sex in which she was treated less like a human, and more like a barnyard animal. Worse still, she was playing for time, hoping to forestall a savage beating which accompanied the sex from a six foot five, two hundred fifty-pound behemoth.

But on another level, she really wanted to understand why this was to be a finale. A sense of foreboding, call it an anxiety attack; the fight or flight defense mechanisms were kicking in. The rage told her that Buck was not lying. He fully intended to make this their last time together. But was Buck planning actually to kill her, right here and now, at the end of the ordeal? Buck was nasty, but nothing instinctively told her that he was a killer, and she had been around professional killers all of her life.

She also knew that the only real power Buck had, he derived from his association with the U.S. military; more specifically, his corrupt relationship with the colonel. Killing her would have immediate repercussions on camp, raising questions about their relationship to which nobody wanted answers. And in doing so, it complicated the one thing that Buck valued above all else; the ability to extract money from the project, money that sat in a Kuwait bank currently under the care, custody, and at least partial control of Jabil Khan.

If he wasn't going to kill her, she thought, was there another reason? Many times, the difference between success and failure is the ability to keep your senses about you in times of crisis when all others around you are losing theirs. She had been in a meeting with him today and didn't notice anything different. Khan had said nothing. No rumors on camp; or at least, nothing out of the ordinary camp gossip. Nothing about the trailer was changed; no signs of packing up to leave for the last time, nor were there any of the typical going away parties in the DFAC to which she had become accustomed as expats went back to the States.

Nonetheless, everything about tonight was different, she thought. She felt it from the moment that she set foot inside the trailer and made eye contact with Buck. It was a subtle difference; not obvious - chalk it up to chemistry, but not in a good way.

"Tell me, Kenny. Why, one last time?" Derya stared straight into his bloodshot eyes.

The sudden realization that she might die had served to focus her, an inner calm emerging ever so slightly. She was, after all, in the intelligence business, although for how long was an open question. Buck could easily crush her with one swipe of his massive right paw that he had slid ever so close to her throat as they spoke. Issues like work at the border and subcontract extensions, part of her mission and one of the reasons that she had come here tonight, quickly faded as she danced with death.

"Where are you going, Kenny? Going home?" she asked, never breaking her stare, initially toying with his crotch, playing with his zipper, but making no overt moves to remove either his clothes or hers. The terrain was shifting now ever so slightly. Much like her earlier dealings with the colonel, the predator was in the process of becoming the prey.

"No," Kenny stammered, his inner, demonic rage at war with his sex drive, serving to intensify both primal urges, while simultaneously locking up his ability to execute either as he struggled to provide that short, one-word answer.

"Did Cork and Hammer sell out, Kenny?" Dead silence, although words did not matter at that point because Buck's eyes told the story. She had hit pay dirt.

"Huh, Kenny, did they?" Her eyes shifted downward, ever so slowly, unzipping his pants.

"Yeah."

He had to admit it at that moment, Derya was both heaven and hell. He never had sex with an animal like her before, in a prior life, and he desperately wanted it one last time. The pure, unadulterated debauchery got him off. Much like his cocaine addiction, he had been hooked on her, although he would never admit it to anyone; least of all, to her.

Until now, he could compartmentalize it, keeping it just business. However, he was about to lose his sexual fix; losing control again, and he had not yet replaced it with his forthcoming financial fix. But to get to his cocaine-in-the-form of-cash fix, he had a convoy to catch, and soon. He was on the wrong end of the clock and knew it.

He should never have said a thing; he also knew that. A big part of the plan to exit out of the camp was the element of surprise. Kenny Buck was the project manager, after all, not just a low-grade clerk. The plan was to use a routine convoy run to Kuwait – as if any such thing was normal in a war zone – to cover his final exit out of the camp.

Now, Derya would surely brief Khan ahead of his arrival. The last thing that he wanted was for Khan to know that they were leaving until he and Marsh showed up. Neither he nor Marsh wanted any funny business with Khan; not now. He had seen to it that there was $350 million in cash in a Kuwait bank, of which 70% was to be split between him and Marsh after Khan's 30%.

Buck would kill for far less at this point if they were crossed on that kind of money. The psychopath in him no longer encumbered by having a project to manage, he weighed his options as her hand slowly migrated downward toward his erect penis, while his fist tightened its grip around her throat. This was going to be good, he thought sadistically as her eyes rolled back in her head, slowly but surely choking the life out of her.

The cell phone rang, followed by a knock at the door of Buck's hooch.

—⁂—

BUCK PICKED THE cell phone out of his right pocket, requiring him to relax his right-handed grip on Derya's neck, shoving her like some rag doll to the wall near the door while he took the call. He did not open the door, not wanting anyone to see him with Derya, hoping to dispose of both the caller and whoever was at the door so that he could finish his sadistically deviant sexual act.

"What's up, mate? I'm outside. You called." It was Kliskey, in his typical inebriated British accent. Kliskey knew not to enter the hooch without permission, and he was not going to get that permission tonight.

"Did you put that bottle of whiskey in Davenport's hooch?" Buck called out to Kliskey through the closed hooch door.

"I did. And your SUV is ready for Kuwait, boss. I am still loading the trucks. Give me an hour or two to get on the road," Kliskey stammered.

"Okay. I am going to take off for Kuwait now; see you soon." With that, Buck put the cell phone back in his pocket.

Even drunk, Kliskey was very good with logistics. Kliskey had been the bag man for the entire shakedown on camp; running convoys to Kuwait while dodging improvised electronic devices, then bringing cash back from the main Kuwait account in order to pay kickbacks to the colonel, the Sargent Major, Taylor and others who had facilitated the convoy runs. It was a complicated little sub-process that Kliskey pulled off over an extended amount of time without raising suspicions - itself a remarkable feat - the episode with Taylor's secretary Veronica Esposito notwithstanding.

Speaking with Buck outside of Buck's hooch, Kliskey noticed Derya stagger out of his bosses' trailer and smiled. Getting a nice good-bye fuck, he muttered to himself in admiration. Little did Kliskey know that it was he - not Derya - who was the one that was getting screwed that evening. Even Kliskey, Buck's logistics guy for his little criminal syndicate, did not know that this was Buck's last convoy ride. And, in a cute little bit of irony, it would be guys like Kliskey, the "Candy Man," who would be left holding the bag without his "Candy" - a promised seven-figure bank balance.

Kliskey's phone rang. It was Buck.

"Did you tip off the MP's?" Buck asked.

"Yup. A surprise hooch safety inspection is scheduled for the morning. Davenport is on the list," Kliskey responded.

Like Kliskey, the colonel also would not know that Buck was checking out for good this night. Buck had become friendly with the colonel, although he did not trust the colonel whom he had compromised. Buck was taking no chances with the colonel. The last thing that he needed at this point was the colonel getting cold feet or getting religion and notifying his superiors. As Niccolò Machiavelli would have counseled five hundred years ago, your friends may fail you, but the dread of punishment will never forsake you.

The purpose of this little goodbye kiss from Buck via Kliskey in the form of a bottle of booze was to plant alcohol, forbidden in the camp, in Frank's hooch. Buck smiled as he thought back to that day when he had agreed to hire Frank. *Well, it wasn't like I didn't warn you*, he thought to himself. That kind of health and safety violation would destroy Frank's credibility, resulting in Frank's termination. Or at least that was the plan.

As he put the cell phone back, mired in thought and attempting to clear his head of his own alcohol problem, Buck noticed that Derya, who had been in a position to overhear the entire conversation, had slipped out of the hooch door. No use chasing after her, he thought. "I just need to get the fuck out of here," he said to nobody in particular.

Thirty minutes later, Buck had cleared security at the gate, disappearing into the still warm, darkened Iraqi desert, bound for Kuwait for the last time.

CHAPTER 28
Hell Hath No Fury Like a Woman Scorned

THE BLOOD WAS just returning to her brain when Derya entered her hooch. Staring into the mirror as she struggled to regain her senses, attempting to process what she had just learned, she gasped as she saw the reddish marks that Buck's death grip had left on her neck. Another minute or so, and she would have been dead, and she knew it.

Just staggering back to the hooch had been a blur. Derya vaguely remembered Kliskey standing outside of the hooch and laughing at her. She hated the skinny little Brit pervert with the distended belly, always flaunting his connection with Buck, trying to gain the sexual favors which Derya strictly reserved for those who added economic and strategic value to her mission.

She knew that not getting laid rankled him but could care less. While Kliskey was part of Buck's criminal enterprise, an enterprise adjacent to her own overlapping little criminal enterprise, their missions could not have been more different. Buck and Kliskey, and even the colonel were garden variety criminals were it not for the fact that they had a job working for the U.S. government which enabled them this opportunity.

Derya knew that Buck, the colonel, Kliskey, and others - even Khan - regarded her as a whore, a charge that she would both accept and reject. She would readily accept the tactical piece of the argument, which was that what she did fit the standard definition of what a whore does; exchange sex for something of value, not unlike the hundreds of Chinese whores lining up in Dubai's discos every night of the week.

She would reject the argument strategically, as a matter of intent. Unlike Buck, the colonel, Kliskey and the others - even the Chinese whores - Derya didn't need or even want the money. Just part of the cover, she would respond. She wasn't buying diamonds or rings with the proceeds. She did it to assist her brother Jamal, the Al Qaeda financier whom she loved, in a war that he waged with the West.

As a critical piece of a non-state actor - in terms that anyone in the business world could understand, she would be called a revenue center - her mission had been to extract as much financial gain as possible at Camp Bradley while passing on as much intelligence as she could during that time. Sex for her was just a means to that end, a gorgeous but deadly asset on the balance sheet to be used in a more significant cause than mere sex for money. Part project manager, part holy warrior, she was anything but a common street whore.

As her head cleared, she refocused on the mission at hand; grateful that fate had placed Kliskey, whom she hated, at the right place at the right time. Buck was checking out now, with the accounts fully funded. The professional in her said that it was time for her to leave as well as she prepared to brief Khan during the drive back to Kuwait. Now that Khan and Buck were presumably about to settle up, she was looking forward to that $80 million disbursement which would go to funding terrorism; her version of "Mission Accomplished."

Ever the project manager, Derya kept a little checklist on the night-stand near her bed. It was a way of reminding her at night of what needed to be done the next day; a way of relaxing at night, knowing that she was prepared for the morning. Only this time, there would be no morning on camp. God willing, she would be in Kuwait soon, arranging for the disbursement of funds to her brother, followed hopefully by a short trip to Kabul to see him in Afghanistan. He would be proud of her accomplishment, something that meant everything to her.

Derya took the checklist down, removed the last of the to-dos from the camp list, then added two final notes. The first note contained the colonel's bank account number in Kuwait with its current multi-million-dollar balance, along with Kliskey's account number and its current million-dollar balance. The second note was the trailer number which contained the goods to be fenced in Kuwait, part of Kliskey's convoy that was leaving soon.

These notes were more than just simple pieces of paper. They were the keys to understanding and destroying Buck and the colonel's little criminal enterprise. Provided to the right person, they formed her own deadly goodbye gift to those who had remained on camp: Colonel Harper, Kliskey, and others.

She now turned her attention to Buck. To-dos come and go on the list. This to-do was a late addition because she hadn't intended to do it; that is, until Buck nearly killed her. Up to now, it was all business, but the little scene in his hooch changed everything. It was now personal between her and Buck, which was bad news for Buck. He may be done with her, but she was definitely not done with him, she thought to herself as she closed the hooch door on camp for the last time.

Derya had one more errand to run on the way out; one more person to see, but she was in no hurry. She would have plenty of time to deal with Buck when she got to Kuwait.

Frank Davenport climbed down from the treadmill in the gym and toweled off. As he left the gym for the short walk to his hooch in the hot, dry night desert air, he passed a couple of enlisted soldiers who were headed to the base coffee shop. Minutes later, upon entering his hooch, Frank could tell that something was wrong. The door to his hooch, which he usually locked when he left, was closed but unlocked.

Frank had come to understand that the hooches, all of which were government-owned, were public property with little or no privacy. Aside from the semi-routine male/female couplings ala Jason Meeks to which Frank had by now become accustomed, all hooches were subject to unannounced inspections, which is why he quickly learned not to keep anything significant in the hooch.

Nevertheless, the prior incident in March where he had found Derya in his hooch continued to haunt him, which is why he was careful to lock the hooch when he left. And it was why it concerned him now that he found it open, fearing a bit of deja vu all over again, to quote Yogi Berra. *Just because you are not paranoid*, he thought to himself, *does not mean that they are not out to get you.*

Frank wiped the sweat from his brow as he entered the hooch slowly, glancing hurriedly around for signs of an intruder. It did not take long in that small, one-room metal box in which he lived to determine that he was alone. Frank saw two notes on his desk, neither of which looked familiar, which had been placed underneath his cell phone that functioned in this instance as a paperweight. As he picked up the notes, he determined what he believed was Derya's distinctive handwriting, along with a missed call from Derya's number on the cell phone. Frank was livid.

"There are two notes with numbers sitting on my desk, Derya. What do you know about them?" Frank almost screamed into the small cellphone, all alone in an otherwise empty hooch, on a now-quiet military base in the middle of a mid-summer night.

"Check your locker, Frank," Derya responded, changing the subject, ignoring the demand for accountability. "Do that, and I can tell you what you will find. You will find a bottle of whiskey, Frank."

Staring down at the phone, he instinctively reached for his tiny wall locker. Tucked away in some dirty clothes that he had intended to send to the laundry was indeed a half-empty bottle of Jim Beam whiskey. It was almost midnight. Frank had endured a long day at work in addition to a workout which he had hoped would relieve the stress, but right now he was anything but tired.

"Did you put this here?" Frank, choking back the emotion, hissed into the phone.

"Do you really think that I would tell you about the whiskey if I was trying to set you up, Frank? Think about it," Derya shot back. "There is a lot to tell you in a short amount of time, Frank," she continued.

"What the fuck is going on?" None of this was making any sense to Frank, not that the swearing did anything but display his frustration at a total lack of control over the situation. What did a bottle of whiskey have to do with some numbers on a couple of pieces of papers?

"Buck has been running a skimming operation with the colonel, Frank. They use convoys to move materials off of the base to fence the materials in Kuwait. In return for moving the materials, the colonel gets a piece of whatever can be fetched for the materials, as do Buck and Kliskey and some others.

"The account numbers on one of those pieces of papers that you have are for the colonel and Kliskey at the Sovereign Bank of Kuwait for their part in the operation. I do not have the account number for Buck. The other piece of paper contains a trailer number for the convoy that is leaving tonight with materials bound for Kuwait. Kliskey is driving that convoy. Believe me, Frank. We know about everything that moves in and out on that base."

That, of course, was only part of the truth. Derya was not going to disclose the other account numbers for which a portion of the proceeds was destined for her brother, with a cut going to Khan. She also would not confess to him the sum and substance of her active involvement. She had come to respect Frank, but she had a mission to accomplish, and he was a means to that end.

By the time the military investigators had reacted to her hastily scribbled scuds, Derya had planned to be on the way to Afghanistan to see her brother, with $80 million in tow. As such, she was going only as far as she needed to induce Frank to run this up to Rust, who would undoubtedly bypass the colonel through his contacts high up within the military chain in an attempt to verify what Frank had to say before Rust had to brief Marsh or Hammer. Situations like these, which required both sophisticated political skills and connections, were one of the many reasons that military contractors hired used generals.

"The whiskey was placed in your hooch to destroy your credibility now that they no longer need you. I heard Buck tell Kliskey to put the bottle in your locker. Don't be surprised if you get an inspection of your hooch in the morning. Kliskey is heading out on a convoy to Kuwait tonight in less than an hour, on the road to Kuwait."

"You see, Cork and Hammer has been sold; new management is taking over, and Buck will not stay on. Buck told me that himself tonight, which is why he is cashing out now, and why I am leaving. The whiskey is their little parting gift to you. Isn't that nice? You were getting a little too close to their scheme for comfort. Now, if I were you, I would get to Rust so that he can stop that convoy from leaving. And do not let Kliskey tell them that the goods in that trailer were intended for another camp."

"Why should I believe you? And why are you doing this?" Frank asked, still trying to comprehend all that he had seen over the last six months.

It was slowly starting to come together; why Buck had been stripping the warehouse while he resisted seemingly standard, best business practices like competing Khan's service agreements. And why Roni Esposito, Taylor's secretary, had come to him in a panic over the amount of cash that Kliskey was apparently passing around on base. If Derya was to be believed, Frank had stumbled into and had become a pawn in, a massive multi-million-dollar fraud.

"You don't have to believe me, Frank. Get Rust to check the bank. The money is there. As for why I am doing this, let's just say that I have my own reasons. Just business, Frank. Goodbye, although I must say that it was nice doing business with you."

And with that, Derya hung up, checking that to-do off of the checklist. Derya kept the parting intentionally short, struggling to keep her emotions in check as she replayed the last six months in her mind's eye. Her response that it was just business was another lie.

It was in moments like this when you are asked questions like this, that you come face to face with who you really are. That is, if you are honest with yourself.

Derya was no different. At that moment, she realized that the part of her that was a project manager had given way to the vengeful, holy warrior in her.

Until now, she and her brother had been in the financial/ management side of the terror business. While loyal to their cause, they confined themselves to the equity side of the terror business, seeking capital for their killing. They would spend most of their days in air-conditioned buildings, not unlike a Wall Street banker; deep into the logistics, hunting down capital but in ways and places that few Wall Street bankers ever knew existed. They both knew that people died horrible deaths as a result of what they were doing. But until now, strangely, it had been mostly conceptual. It was something that happened to someone else, not them.

But as she had gasped for air that evening, with Buck choking the life from her, something in her snapped. Hating these invaders was no longer conceptual, or even financial. She now began to feel inside how those who gave themselves up in a bombing must have felt; the sense of utter void, of emptiness.

The need to inflict pain, as a way of dealing with her own grief, overcame her practical, project management rational side. It was something that Frank would not comprehend; two parties talking past each other, one of them nearly dead but seeking life while the other was alive but now actively courting death. That was why Derya's bland, almost Fortune 500-type answer, by someone who never worked in a Fortune 500 corporation, to someone who had made a career in one, fell so flat. Derya had regained her senses but tonight, clutched in the firm and deadly grip of a madman, she lost her mind.

There really was not a need to exact revenge, nor a need even for western-style justice. Derya had accomplished her end of the mission financially; that much awaited her in Kuwait. And yet, the hate inside of her prompted a final act on Camp Bradley that was going to be a corporate version of terror, if not a physical one.

Derya had maintained just enough of her practical side to understand that there was no time to plan a more massive terrorist attack on the camp. The logistics of implanting devices inside of the camp to take out the dining hall at dinner, given the security involved, were both formidable and time-consuming. She also knew her limits; that this was the end-game of an operation that she had formerly left to others, in the process inadvertently sheltering her from the cold realities of a mass execution.

She also knew that the notes in the hands of Rust, an ex-general, could be damaging; low- tech but high-touch versions of improvised electronic devices, blowing up the entire corporate infrastructure on her way out. Exiting the base, she shifted her SUV into fifth gear for the long drive to Kuwait, and her own holy warrior rendezvous with destiny.

For his part, Frank Davenport stumbled towards Rust's hooch, alone in the dark, shaking his head in an attempt to clear the cobwebs from his brain, trying to think straight. Did he trust Derya and her Greeks-bearing-gifts routine? Worse yet, did he trust Rust, someone that he barely knew?

There were times in life when the best decision is no decision, especially given what Donald Rumsfeld would call the "known unknowns."

Frank stared back at the numbers on the papers that had been given to him by Derya. He quickly concluded that, while he might never truly understand why Derya did this, the accounts obviously bore further scrutiny. Moreover, validating the bank accounts would be something that investigators could do quickly, as soon as the banks opened. That is, if Rust wasn't just as corrupt as Buck.

As Frank approached Rust's hooch, he thought long and hard given what he had been through with Buck, and what he now at least suspected about the colonel, about whether or not to trust Rust. Having nothing more than some peripheral experience and instinct to guide him, Frank went with his gut.

Rather than make no decision and allow events to dictate his future, Frank decided to shape that future to the extent that he could do so proactively. But he did not kid himself. He was going to brief a man with whom he had few direct interactions up to now, whose career could not have been more different than his, about something that he was just coming to grips with himself that fateful evening.

Frank would not wake up a former general at night in a combat zone where they were firing live rounds to engage in some esoteric discussion. Nor was Frank there to court favor or to pontificate, not that he and Rust had ever communicated at that level. Most generals, although intelligent, were nuts-and-bolts creatures almost by design and tended to be anything but esoteric.

Knowing that much about the military mind by now, Frank would keep it simple; direct, and to the point. He would provide Vice President Rust with the evidence contained on Derya's papers; encouraging the ex-general, in Watergate parlance, to "follow the money." Whether he was rolling out a marketing plan in a former life or now engaged in a war, Frank thought as he knocked on Rust's hooch that it always seemed to come down to the money.

—~—

THE DRIVE FROM Baghdad to Kuwait City seemed like days rather than just hours to Derya as she watched the endless sand dunes pass by in the night. Now, with the sun rising and the air heating up fast, she turned up the air conditioning in the SUV and reached for her cellphone. She would place a call to her brother; only her second call to her brother since arriving in camp. She reached for her sticky notes taped near her rearview mirror which contained the items on which she would brief her brother, purposely designed to structure the conversation while keeping the message brief.

She reached her brother on the first try, telling him that Cork and Hammer had been sold. She diligently explained that she had left the camp but had spoken to Khan about her little delivery package - a euphemism for the $80 million - earlier in the drive and was assured that everything was on track, as planned.

He asked once again about the border, anxious for any news that he could pass along to his Iranian colleagues. That discussion lasted longer than both anticipated as she had to patiently impart a plain vanilla version, sans the sex, of her relationship with Buck and the colonel and just why despite all that she had done, she had come up short. Those few minutes, unanticipated but lost in their poignant yearning to re-engage - to say so much in a short period after being so long apart from one another - would prove to be fatal. Regaining her senses, she ended the conversation by asking him to send her his exact coordinates via ground courier so that she could meet with him in Afghanistan.

Left out of the conversation, of course, was the violent encounter with Buck on that previous evening that led to Buck almost strangling her to death. She regarded that as her unfinished business, although she surely planned to finish that business after settling up with Khan, but before departing for Afghanistan. In Kuwait, Buck was now on her turf, and so she would finish what he had started, by her rules.

Derya entered her condo overlooking the same harbor in which Khan's yacht was moored. Her thoughts toggled back and forth between the good times with her brother and the torturous time that she had to endure at the hands of Buck. Then, off in the distance, ever so faintly, she thought that she heard a single click on her phone, like somebody hanging up. Exhaustion had taken over, and so she ignored it, which was just as well, for that innocuous click had been the sound of the CIA pursuing her brother.

Alone in her condo in Kuwait, Derya would be naively secure, knowing that her high-touch mastery of her little project would net her brother $80 million in short order. She would be wrong, although she could not know it then. That clicking sound that she heard was an electronic death sentence for her brother as the high-tech, low-touch global positioning satellite-coordinated tracking devices rendered their verdict. Moments later, a drone carried out its capital punishment sentence on both the Al Qaeda financier and his top leadership team. That drone would kill the entire team in one strike on an obscure moonscape of a highway on the outskirts of Kabul, not far from where a BBC crew was eating breakfast, only to witness the entire scene.

Unable to sleep, Derya turned on her television to witness the proceeds of that BBC camera crew's reporting from Afghanistan. The

BBC had managed to obtain the pictures of all of the terrorists killed in the drone strike, splashing her brother's surreal likeness onto the screen. Screaming in pain, Derya instinctively reached for her wallet, pulling out his picture to make sure that both images matched. Reality began to sink in, and as it did, what remained of the project manager in her became almost totally subsumed by the holy warrior.

There would be no money for her brother, nor would there be any gratitude for what she had endured. She was totally alone now, unmoored and adrift, just as surely as if she was out to sea without the ability to ascertain her physical bearings. Now numb from the shock, Derya picked up her cell phone and called Khan. Buck was aboard the yacht in a typical drunken stupor. She confirmed an appointment with both Buck and Khan on Khan's yacht for 9am that morning. Learning that Buck's boss was also aboard made it even better. She told Khan that she looked forward to meeting both.

But if the drone strike incident resulted in some primordial charge to earnings in some psychological accounting sense, then what she would do next would not reverse the charges. There would be no erasing of history. Unlike Buck, Derya had, in quieter moments, had been enough of a project manager to know that she had to contemplate Plan B, playing through the shot before the serve, like the superstar tennis player. The holy warrior side of her was going to execute that low-tech but very high-touch Plan B, also with malice aforethought. And there would be an offsetting, equally primordial charge to earnings; with war doing what it does best, destroying economic value for both sides.

THE SUN HAD long since risen by seven in the morning on the 23rd of June, 2005 and, as usual, it would be hot and dry. But from where Jabil Khan surveyed the world, behind his large desk atop his large Sunseeker yacht near Kuwait City, the weather could not be better. Khan had purchased the yacht in 2002 during the lead-up to the war as both a place of business and something on which to entertain guests, like Buck and now Marsh, with whom he did business.

The Sunseeker came outfitted with all of the toys in which to conduct business onboard at sea. Khan's ship came with a sizable on-deck master stateroom and an entertainment area on the spacious sun-deck. It also contained an on-deck spa tub in which Buck busied himself with the local Chinese whores during his frequent forays into Kuwait where he was fencing stolen materials. The yacht had a grill, teakwood decks, along with mammoth guest and VIP staterooms. Equipped with twin MTU 16V2000 diesel engines that topped out at around 18 knots and a crew of six, the ship was fully seaworthy.

Despite all that Khan, who had devoted his waking hours to making money, had no interest in sailing outside of a few short trips in and around the harbor, although he wanted to give the appearance to his clients that he was a wealthy, world-wise sailor/entrepreneur. The reality was that he had purchased the slightly used ship-as-business center already docked at what would be its final resting place, never fully intending to do anything more than transact business in that harbor, which is what he was doing this morning.

Appearance was everything to Khan. In fact, Khan's British-designed luxury yacht would be an apt symbol for his business model, for he had crafted his perceived economic value-added proposition around appearance, although that facade meant different things to different people. Much like the outward appearance that he liked to project of being the inveterate sailor/entrepreneur when in reality he was just a criminal chained to a desk in a harbor, Khan had conned others into thinking that Jabil Khan was something that he was not.

Buck and Marsh had entered into their corrupt little bargain with Khan believing that they could control the flow of money into the Kuwait bank accounts. The partners in crime could deposit money; they just could not withdraw money, something that Buck was careful to micromanage. But they suspected at some level that Khan was also skimming from the suppliers. They could not control it nor did they care, assuming that they hit their budgeted number. On that score, Khan would not disappoint, serving up the planned $350 million.

But there is no honor among thieves, so Marsh and Buck's suspicions would be correct. Jabil Khan had diversified his risk by sucking an additional $20 million off of the supplier base during his tenure at Camp Bradley. He also diversified his risk in another, more fundamental way, by working the other side of the street - with Case Hammer, something that he had kept from Marsh and Buck in return for his cut of the money. Khan was keeping Hammer briefed during the entire scam, something that he was planning to do today, with both Marsh and Buck aboard, and the final disbursements now planned for later on today, before the banks closed. It was shaping up to be an exciting day.

—ɯ—

"HEY, KHAN? DID you just catch the BBC?" It was Buck on the intercom. He was in an adjoining stateroom watching television while attempting to come around from his drunken stupor.

"It looks like they got some little Al Qaeda fuckers," Buck said, staring blankly at the same images that sent Derya, also viewing that same BBC footage in her Kuwait condo, into a rage.

Perched out on the sun-deck overlooking the harbor while reconciling some financial statements that he was preparing for his big payday at the bank, Khan did not appear at first to pay much attention to the remark. Reports of people getting killed were common occurrences in war; not quite, but almost daily events. But as he went back to his office, he heard the BBC reporter describe in a clinical sense the most current drone strike.

What made this report both different, and of interest to Khan, were the pictures that flashed up on the screen; dead bodies described by a BBC reporter as those belonging to Al Qaeda senior leadership. Khan had never met the top Al Qaeda leaders, although they were his financial backers. They always chose to work through middlemen, or women like Derya. He had a meeting scheduled with her soon and made a mental note to see what he could discern from her about the incident.

As Khan continued to stare at the screen, the faint little voice inside began to fill him with an as-yet-unfounded fear; that this one particular drone strike was a game-changer. Just then, his cellphone rang. The missed call identified the caller as Hammer. Scurrying back into his office so that he could take the call in private, he called Case Hammer back.

"Good evening, Case," Khan said, staring out at the crystal blue harbor. With the eight- hour time difference, it was just after midnight, local D.C. time.

"Good morning, Mr. Khan," Case replied. "Well, it looks like this is shaping up to be a big day for you financially. Are Buck and Marsh on board?" Having been aboard the yacht several times, Hammer possessed a clear mental picture of both Khan and the ship.

"Yes sir," Khan replied in his typically formal, albeit sycophantic way that he used to curry favor to those from whom he needed something. That said, his subservient manner would not be out of keeping with how Hammer had always viewed their relationship that had been destined to be forever cold and transactional.

Khan and Hammer had never clicked, which was how Hammer wanted it. For times just like this.

"Marsh came aboard within the last day or so. Buck just arrived and is sleeping off a hangover."

Both men laughed.

"Well, let me get straight to the point, Mr. Khan. All of the accounts in Kuwait have been closed, Mr. Khan. There will be no disbursements from any of those accounts; either to you or to anybody else. Are we clear? Now, if you do not believe me, you can check for yourself when you get to the bank."

"Is there a reason for this decision, sir?" Khan's gaze was alternating between the spreadsheets in front of him and out at the harbor that laid before him, attempting to come to grips with what Hammer had just said. He was not sure how Hammer knew about the location of the accounts, or how Hammer had derived the authority to close any or all of them.

"You knew all along what I was doing with Marsh and Buck, sir," Khan pleaded.

"Yes. But that's not good enough. Have you seen the news on the drone strike, Mr. Khan?" Hammer replied quietly but firmly, all but ignoring the reference to Marsh and Buck, whom he considered small fish.

"You have been a bad boy, Khan. Playing ball with the other side. We know it, and now, when you go to your bank, you will know that we know it. Which means that all bets are off, Khan."

Khan was stunned.

"You see Khan," Hammer continued, "working both sides of the street is risky business. Cons only work if you can make them work, or until they don't work. And today is the day that your con, along with Marsh and Buck's little financial merry-go-around, doesn't work - Khan."

"Did you really think that we were that stupid, that we would not find out about your friends in the terrorism business? Your financier just died today, Mr. Khan. He was Derya's brother; you know that, or should. We know about you - and your associates. Goodbye and good luck, Mr. Khan. You will need it."

It suddenly occurred to Khan that the pictures that he had seen from the BBC reports were of Derya's brother. The horribly disfigured face that had splashed up on the screen; now nothing more than literal road kill, was the face of the Al Qaeda financier Jamal Ali that he had never met, and now never would. It also slowly dawned on him that Hammer had probably bugged his yacht. If so, Hammer had the benefit of every conversation which had taken place aboard his floating office; a major-league mistake. This was a chilling realization for someone who had moments before convinced himself that he was going to be a rich man in a country filled with rich oil men.

And with that, Khan's call with Hammer ended; the as-yet-unfounded fear now having a basis in fact. Marsh and Buck aside, his hard money Al Qaeda financiers, drone strike or no, surely wanted their money, and they did not take no for an answer. Khan was, even with the money that he had managed to skim from the suppliers "just a little short" as they say; a dangerous place to be with an organization which was undoubtedly reeling from a loss in the drone strike, and who killed people as their raison d'être.

For the first time in his life; or at least that he could remember, Khan was at a loss for what to do next. He needed a Plan B and time was running out. While pondering such a plan, he noticed out of the corner of his eye that one of his crew members was waving Derya aboard the yacht.

Unlike her boss, Derya was someone who had contemplated a disaster scenario; her separate Plan B, and she had come prepared to execute it. It was not a plan that she had coordinated with Khan, nor would it get her the cash for her brother. Then again, she was never in it for the money; she was in it for the love of her brother, and now he was not only dead but killed in a humiliatingly impersonal, public way.

Derya's Plan B would square accounts for her brother whom she loved; if not on an accountant's financial statement, then with Buck, Khan, and his American partners. More important for her personally, it would also square the gnawing emptiness inside her that came from the indelible image of her now-dead brother lying on some lonely, desolate road in Afghanistan, the victim of a drone strike. That thought had been seared into her consciousness, demanding revenge. There would be no talk of peace; no plea for forgiveness. Plan B was about this holy warrior's final act of retribution, and it would come today if it were the last thing that she did.

And it absolutely would be the last thing that Derya Ali ever did. That was because, moments after Derya boarded the vessel, Khan's ship carrying Buck, Marsh, Khan and the crew members including Derya immolated in an explosion. Derya's final act of revenge rocked the entire yacht club, not to mention Kuwait City itself, as Khan's 105-foot, luxury coffin dis-engorged its contents into the harbor, slowly immersing itself in its own watery grave.

CHAPTER 29
The Morning After

—~~—

LIFE IN A war zone as a civilian expatriate can be a surreal experience in the best of times. People come and go for all sorts of reasons. Sometimes it is for personal reasons. Other times, it is because they just do not fit well with camp life in a harsh environment; living in sparse accommodations, working twelve hours per day and taking orders from people that they do not like. Others find out quickly, once the first rocket enters their camp and they are forced to live out of a bunker for a while, that there really is a war going on out there.

The 23rd of June, 2005 was shaping up as one of those surreal days for Frank Davenport. It was one of those days in which Frank started to seriously consider how long he could take doing this work in this job. Everyone has their limit for this type of life. He realized that early on when he saw how Buck had treated Coleman. Maybe he had reached his limit.

It seemed like an ordinary day, with meetings scheduled all day devoted to coordinating both the ramp up and ongoing administration of all fifty bases that were planned for but were in various stages of setting up, all over Iraq. Things moved fast because priorities changed continuously as the situation on the ground evolved.

The task for Cork and Hammer, as always, was to convert urgent, ever-changing albeit sometimes vague or conflicting military requirements into specifications, then down into work steps for execution at the civilian level in real time. In Frank's group, that meant there were subcontract agreements to be let or modified to include a smaller or broader scope of work; materials to get on order, expedite in, move out, or cancel altogether as the mission changed, and then deliver promptly - all in the chaos of war. It took leadership, a dedicated staff and a constant level of coordination. Only this time, what direction there had been was missing, and things were running on auto-pilot.

Until now, Buck's absence had been a regular occurrence since Buck spent a significant amount of time in Kuwait fencing goods. But this time, he would be gone for good, as were others, including Derya, Kliskey, and possibly the colonel. Auto-pilot could only last for so long before it affected the mission.

But what Frank had experienced the night before was no ordinary experience, and so when he got to work earlier than usual and saw that he had a note on his desk to call Della Clark, he knew that this would be no ordinary day. Frank had not heard much from Della since that day she and Frank had jointly survived Crazy Ivan's corkscrew landing, outside of a short note saying that she had decided to stay and thanking him for what he had done. Della still worked in logistics, in an area which coordinated the stock and shipment of goods off base.

"Hey, Frank. Seems like our boy Kliskey never made it out of camp last night," Della whispered into the phone as if she was imparting some sort of secret. "I heard that the MP's grabbed him off of that convoy and hustled him away. Wonder why?"

"Where is the convoy, if it did not make it off of the base?" Frank asked, flashing back to what had happened only hours before.

"The military has it stashed somewhere off base," Della replied." That is what I have heard. What they are doing with it is way above my pay grade, Frank. Strange. I tried asking some people that I know in Buck's office, but they didn't know anything except that Buck was in Kuwait." That much, the part about Buck being in Kuwait, Frank knew all too well.

—ᵚ—

Buck's weekly staff meeting always started at 9am sharp, not one minute after. Following the usual health and safety minute, Vice President Rust rose to make a quick announcement that henceforth and until further notice he would be chairing the meetings. Buck's staff meetings had been routinely chaired by Buck as the project manager while Rust had been generally more of an observer. Until now.

Nobody had the temerity to ask the former general why, although it was clear that Buck was not there. Many of Buck's senior staff weren't the sharpest pencils in the box. Still, they were not going to grill an ex-general on the circumstances of Buck's heretofore unannounced departure unless they wanted a ticket out on the next flight home. Those details would leak out in time. Rust's marching orders were just duly noted, and they all moved on. Rust followed his brief declaration by looking directly at Frank and stating "Frank, please see me after the meeting."

Frank did not return the stare. He had been down that road in a previous life with simple requests like that. In an earlier life, an order like that had led to him being forced to resign; taking the fall for somebody else, and so he was lost in thought at what was to come next.

He knew what Derya had told him; about the skimming, the numbers, and bottle of booze in his hooch. Frank also knew that he had briefed Rust just hours prior to this meeting. But he still did not know whether or not to consider Rust friend or foe. If Rust was a foe; if he had been instructed to cover up, this had the potential to end badly.

The meeting ended but before the staff had filed out and, with Zoe looking on, Rust took Frank aside, his voice lowering. "Send me a write up on what happened last night. Let's meet again about lunch time." Frank and Zoe walked out of the meeting, standing together on the porch; their heads miles apart.

"Frank," Zoe said finally in a voice that could have been a thousand miles away. "I am not sure what is going on. I tried to call Derya this morning before the meeting to get some updates on her contracts, but her phone did not answer. When I tried her office on base, they said that she was in Kuwait. But that is not all, Frank."

"Her office said that there was an explosion in the harbor in Kuwait City this morning. It is all over the news there. Her boss, Jabil Khan had a yacht in that harbor, and they are saying that the yacht that exploded looked a lot like Khan's yacht, Frank."

Frank and Zoe walked back into the Joint Operations Command Building where the senior staff meetings were held, searching for the nearest wall monitor. In an almost surreal scene, splashed up on the screen was a shot of the harbor in Kuwait and Khan's picture as the owner of a yacht which had just exploded. The explosion had totally destroyed the yacht so the news media types would not know who, if anybody, was actually aboard the yacht, but Frank's mind's eye immediately flashed back to last night with Derya; the flat, haunting tone in her voice just now coming into focus.

That tone had been the sound of someone giving up on life; a voice from the grave - of dead men walking, so to speak. He couldn't prove it yet; that Khan, Derya and others had died in that explosion, but the little voice inside him told him to expect the worst.

It suddenly occurred to Frank that, somehow lost in the endless, until now seemingly senseless bureaucratic tug of war which was life on this project, the horrors of war were getting dangerously close to home. He had been exposed to a lot during the past several months, but his efforts to stay alive had been focused inward; locked in a struggle to stay alive organizationally, trying to fend off Buck and his henchmen.

But in the real world, people were dying around him; people that he actually worked with, and that was something new. He had never met Khan, but he had worked closely with Derya. He wasn't sure about whether or not Buck was aboard the yacht, and would probably never know for sure.

In his mind, he thought back again to the soldier in the caisson. He did not know the soldier. That dead soldier would be nameless and faceless to him, not that those facts made the circumstances of the soldier's death any less real or horrific. But the people that were dying now were known to him. They would never make the cover of a magazine. They would disappear into the fog of history, never to be heard from again. But Frank knew them. They were real, and so was this war in all of its madness.

It was a little past noon. Frank had emailed his report to Rust and headed over to the dining hall for lunch. He had been invited for lunch by both Jim Parrish, the contracts guy, and Keni Mehmeti from the warehouse, but he turned them both down, preferring to be alone with his thoughts. He knew that the lunch invitation was just their own way of wanting to catch up with the latest camp gossip, particularly concerning Kliskey, whom nobody liked. Those conversations could come at another time.

Frank's thoughts drifted back to all of the meetings that he had taken with Buck - the constant lies and organizational games. He recalled how Buck had humiliated Coleman constantly in front of the client. More recently, he remembered how Buck had orchestrated Kliskey's little setup with Derya outside of his hooch.

Now, it was no longer about Buck; it was about Rust. And so, as Frank prepared to meet Vice President Rust, Frank's focus was limited to one central question: was the vice president a friend or foe? In a business that was clearly managed by force of personality and not processes, he had come to understand that he would never see proper, fact-based management. Not here and not now; it seemed that nobody was neutral. Everybody took sides.

Mark Twain reportedly said that history does not repeat itself, but it often rhymes. Frank had been through a searing incident in Cleveland where the sins of his boss had been visited on him, nearly rendering him homeless. And now, he sat in the dining hall waiting to meet his new boss, whom he did not know, but who headed an organization with which he had become all too familiar. He wondered if history would repeat itself, or even rhyme just a little, because he was not sure how he could handle a similar, second verse that would be the same as the first.

Frank received a tap on the shoulder.

"Rust wants to see you in the conference room," said Zoe, simultaneously pushing a piece of paper into his hands as she turned around, hurrying toward the exit as if she was running away from something.

As he looked up, glancing quickly towards the conference room door, he could not help but notice through the sunglasses that she wore, that Zoe was crying. Lunch would wait.

"Are you okay?" Frank called out.

Zoe did not answer. Moments later, she was gone. Frank stuffed the paper into his pocket and headed to see Vice President Rust, who had a scheduled meeting with his military counterparts in a side room off of the main dining hall, a small room typically used for VIP meetings.

—m—

FRANK OPENED THE door to the conference room and found Vice President Rust huddled with six of his military counterparts. Seeing Frank enter the room, Rust quickly rose to greet him.

"Thanks for coming," Rust said, motioning Frank in a low voice to step over to a corner of the room, outside of the earshot of the military members in the room. "We were about to take a break anyway, so the timing is good."

With that, the vice president shook Frank's hand. Looking Frank directly in the eye, Rust said, "We want to thank you for that information. The investigation is ongoing, and so what I can tell you is limited, but what you did helped a lot."

"I heard that they had Kliskey in custody. Were they able to trace the money to the accounts in Kuwait?" Frank said, referring to the account numbers that he had given to the vice president, which Derya had provided.

"The colonel has some explaining to do, just between you and me," Rust said. "Besides getting involved in something like this, he was apparently stupid enough to leave that account number you gave me in his hard drive. The investigators found it on a remote a search of his government computer. Needless to say, there will not be any big payday for Colonel Harper," he said, laughing.

"As for Kliskey, they probably do have him in lockdown. Once the investigators starting asking questions, lots of people started singing about money being passed around. As I said, I cannot go into a lot of details now, but safe to say that Kliskey is another one that will not get a payday in Kuwait. Did you send me your report?" Rust said, changing the subject as a sign that the discussion into the money was over.

Frank confirmed that he had done so, and he thanked the ex-general. A cascade of emotions passed over him as he exited the conference room. He appreciated the public gesture of support although, with all that he had been through, he was not sure that this handshake was not just a bit for show. Rust was doing what he was getting paid to do, which was to smooth over stuff like this at the local level.

In a week, nobody would know about this or care. There was a demanding client to support; there were camps to construct, facilities to maintain, materials to move, and suppliers to manage. Moreover, if what Derya said was right, there would be a new supplier replacing Cork and Hammer. He could be on an airplane home in less than a week, for all that he knew.

Frank had been convinced from the start that management at the top knew a lot more, that what Buck was doing was somehow being tolerated, if not encouraged. Where Buck was at this time, or how Rust fit into all of this; those other details - like the larger slush fund or the Al Qaeda connection - Frank would never know. But unlike other managers on base who had never had a senior management position before, Frank knew that there was another side to the story.

"You are Davenport, right?"

"Yes, and who are you?" Frank asked the young corporal who had just emerged from the meeting with Rust. He looked different in full battle dress of course, but looking at him closer, he recognized the corporal from his nights at the gym with Rodriquez.

"You friends with Rodriquez; from the gym... correct?" Frank continued as he shook the soldier's hand. "How is he doing? I haven't seen him since late March."

"Yeah, Charlie Barnett, nice to see you again," the soldier said, his eyes rolling back in his head, telling Frank that Rodriquez was not alright.

"Sergeant and I were in the same unit for a while until he took some incoming one night on patrol in late March. He is back in Dallas. I heard that Rodriquez lost his right leg and part of his right arm. His family is pretty broken up about it." Barnett's voice trailed off as he finished the sentence.

"Hey, good to see you again, but I have to go. The meeting is starting back up again." Seconds later, Corporal Barnett was gone, leaving Frank alone again with his thoughts.

Just like that, people's lives were destroyed, Frank thought. But life moved on, to the next meal, to the next meeting, to the next IED. Wanting a way to contact Rodriquez through Corporal Barnett, Frank reached into his pocket and pulled out a piece of paper to write on in case that he saw the corporal again while he was in the dining hall. It was the one that Zoe had given him on his way in to see Rust.

As he pulled out the paper, he noticed the door to the conference room shutting; not unlike his life, he thought to himself ironically. One door would close today while another door was getting ready to open. If Rust were to be believed, Frank would not be the scapegoat for this mismanaged project as he was in a former life.

"Samer died today" was what Zoe had written before her tearful exit from the dining hall. The terrorists had finally gotten him. With that, Frank, who would never be accused of being a religious man, did what he never did. Right in the middle of the dining hall, amid an otherwise bustling cafeteria, Frank closed his eyes and said a prayer for both Rodriquez and Samer Arian.

Another closed door, like Frank's, would open, but to a much different world. Rodriquez was an elite soldier-athlete, one of America's best, yet he was now a cripple, most likely with PTSD. Samer's door would close, only it would never open again.

History doesn't necessarily repeat itself, Frank thought, reflecting on the prospect of a brighter future, because everything really was changed by that which came before it. Except that with Derya and her brother Jamal, with Khan, Buck, Marsh, Sergeant Rodriquez, Samer and many others, history would neither repeat itself nor would it rhyme. There would be little or no future.

CHAPTER 30
Cashing in On Some "Business Insurance"

—∞—

Senator Donaldson Wickes put down the phone and smiled. It was a good day this 26th day of August 2005. Indeed, it had been a good week. He had just gotten off of the phone with his brother Michael, formerly a CEO of a large insurance company, but now retired. The subject of that phone call had been a friendly five-dollar wager on the upcoming fall football game between the senator's South Carolina Gamecocks and his brother Michael's University of Tennessee Volunteers.

It was a good week for another reason as well, for the press coverage and the political fallout from the recent death of the Al Qaeda financier had been all good. Both Democrats and Republicans had dutifully come together in a choreographed, bipartisan show of unity on this one; not unlike after 911 but with the increasing political polarization, now increasingly rare in Washington.

Wickes, a regular on the cable news shows, would look into the cameras intoning in as presidential a voice as possible the need to protect the homeland. Drawing on his own Vietnam experience, his speeches would echo his earlier generation's Domino Theory call-to-arms. That theory, provided as justification for our disastrous Vietnam-era overreach, said simply: we either fight them there - as in Laos, or Vietnam - or we fight them here, as in the streets of Los Angeles or Miami.

Wickes would play up the bipartisan nature of the killing on the talk shows. This piece of political theater was just one more box to check along the way to the top. With success having many fathers and failure an orphan, much of that show of bipartisan unity only occurred because the drone operation had come off without an apparent hitch. Inside both the CIA and DOD there were those who would smile at the comical display of unity, knowing the real story.

Drones were the classic expression of a sustainable competitive advantage in the war on terror - the monopolistic ability to absorb high fixed costs in research and development and in operation and maintenance, but deliver a devastatingly high-tech blow anywhere in the world on command with low marginal costs - in this case, nothing more than the price of the next missile. And so ironically, in a town like Washington DC in which pressing the flesh is virtually the only game – high-touch on steroids - it was all about twenty-first-century high-tech eclipsing twelfth-century high-touch, and in this case at least and in a marginal sense, high-tech had won the battle.

There is an old adage in marketing that says when the rules of the game are crafted against you - in this case, high marginal costs from the deployment of a long term, labor-intensive ground force - change the rules. The Al Qaeda financier's killing had indeed been accomplished almost surgically, without loss of American lives and, as far as anyone could ascertain, without the loss of innocent or significant collateral damage. The drone strike was marketing's way of saying that the rules of the game had changed, that we could derive an economic profit this way by minimizing the total marginal costs.

If it was all good for Wickes' external customer base, it was also all good for the senator's internal customers at Defense and CIA, as well. Wickes had finessed the sale of Cork and Hammer to BLTVDef, replacing a smaller, weaker mostly fringe CIA supplier with a financially stronger and technically integrated, overall more robust supplier to both CIA and Defense in the base support business. Moreover, that switch in suppliers had been accomplished not only during the war but also with a delicate CIA operation in progress, always of concern at a public relations-sensitive Langley. Wickes was confident that his internal customers, like BLTVDef in the form of campaign contributions, would not forget when it came time to hit the campaign trail.

There were negative externalities to the mission - I make a mistake; you pay for it - but these would not be the days for that discussion. Chief among those would be blow-back from the Middle East, inflamed at the destruction that the drone strike had wrought. What the outrage really did, of course, was to underscore just how marginally profitable that drone strike was.

Cooler heads knew the reality on the ground: how emasculating drone strikes like that had been; that the outrage was but another manifestation of the Middle East's inability to manufacture anything much more organized than sticking a pipe in the ground and producing some oil and gas - or a terrorist attack. It was another typical case of projection: those who were screaming the loudest were really raging at their own impotence.

For their part, the American left wing would express mild concern, particularly about the oversight used when drone strikes were authorized, always pressing for more and better regulation as a counter to the moral hazard issues - I do not worry about making a mistake because you are going to pay for it - that drone strikes inevitably raised.

There were other negative externalities as well. Like the cost in broken lives that war brings; the rampant corruption; the deaths, injuries, and mental illnesses that those engaged in conflict carry with them for years; the enormous cost to the nation's budget. And then there were the opportunity costs borne that gearing the country up for a war footing had on both its present and future economic ability to compete in the global market place as measured by its $4 trillion in delayed infrastructure spending. Somehow those costs were left out of the equation. High-tech was winning the country's battles but losing the larger war for its high-touch soul.

And so, the now-emasculated Middle East, responding in the only way that they could, would couch the strike in a predictably religious context; seeking to inflame their base, resorting to ever more terrorism.

Muslim communities saw Christian invaders seeking twenty-first-century dominance over lands that had been historically Muslim, inviting the also standard, mostly bogus counter charges from the Christian hard right in the United States that Islam was a global threat because it somehow sanctioned terrorism.

Less noticed in the frenzied cable news turbo-charged rush to judgment would be the uncomfortable truth that both sides had gotten the religion thing mostly wrong. For the only religion that really mattered here was capitalism with an authoritarian bent; a sort of proto-religion as fundamental to its adherents as Christianity, or Islam, Judaism - or any other religion. Both sides had found a way to monetize the religious wars; darkly abusing capitalism that Adam Smith would have understood but never would have agreed with, neither party giving an inch because both sides had some money to make; something deeper, more profound even than their given religion.

The Islamic or Christian religious rantings were for the little people; the foot soldiers, not unlike the mules in the drug wars. But for the one percent for whom capitalism is a religion, it was all about financial power that translated into absolute, undemocratic political power. It wasn't so much about left or right, or east versus west. From the Wall Street private equity vultures who found riches as defense contractors to their mirror images in the Middle East serving as Al Qaeda financiers, it was just about the money, but not to build. It was money without a moral compass - used to tear down; to destroy, divide - and conquer.

Senator Wickes, now a wealthy man who was running for President, understood that nexus between financial power and political power. He knew that in an earlier time President Lyndon Johnson, as a young congressman in 1940 who at that point had one business suit to his name, had been offered a silent partnership in oil wells that would have made him rich. Johnson initially turned down opportunities like that because he said that oil wealth would kill him politically.

But that was then, and this was now, and Wickes was sixty-five; no longer a young man. Moreover, financial success was always, but even more so now, viewed as critical to being considered seriously in the political world. Success in one begot success in the other something that Johnson, who later on managed to accrue upwards of $100 million in his lifetime of public service at the same time that some 58,220 American soldiers would die in Southeast Asia, would understand.

Eric Hoffer once stated that every great cause begins with a movement, becomes a business, and eventually degenerates into a racket. It was getting to be that way with the terrorism business; originally, a legitimate - even seismic - concern that had begun its inexorable slide, fueled by crony capitalism, into the haze of a corruption-filled racket. Wickes would make more speeches designed to inflame his base, enlisting them to his cause. It would be a cause that Derya and her brother in the Middle East, on equal albeit opposite ideological sides of that cause, would know well; a business model with which MBA's like Frank Davenport could readily identify. At least until it hit home, killing them or someone that they knew.

Senator Donaldson Wickes was going to make his mark in the financialization of terrorism; through the political and economic profit gained by killing terrorists. The negative externalities would be cynically derided as "soft costs" - costs typically hard to quantify, and thus easy to marginalize. But those were the costs to winning this war, Senator Wickes would reply solemnly; trying but failing to convince even himself as he said it that he would deal with them later - as President Wickes.

CHAPTER 31
Home Again

"PLEASE BUCKLE YOUR seatbelt, and place your seat back in the upright position. We are preparing to land in Cleveland, Ohio." It was the public address announcement preparing the cabin for landing. Coming back home was a surreal experience. He felt that he had been gone for a lifetime, transported to another time and dimension, a bit like an episode of the Twilight Zone when in reality he had been away only approximately nine months.

As the plane taxied on the tarmac, Frank reached for his cell phone to find that Larry had called.

"How are you?" Larry asked.

"Dead tired, but OK," Frank replied to his friend the psychologist.

"Sounds like the adventure is a success, so far. I knew that you needed a job when this thing came along, but I worry about you, with what you went through," Larry replied, as only a good friend could.

"Yeah, I needed a job, Larry," Frank said, conceding what to both friends had been painfully obvious.

"Agreed," said Larry. "But you did not sign up for the graft and corruption. I get it that running a business under normal circumstances is a test of character. Those circumstances were anything but typical. You handled it well, but you did not emerge unscathed. Few of the ex-military clients in my psychology practice did. Let's talk more when you get settled." With that, Larry hung up.

Frank had emerged physically in one piece, not a small thing considering that he had entered a war zone unarmed. He was back in the States; he had a job to come back to at least for the present, and Frank had a lot more money than when he started. For most expats in similar circumstances, who would make more money in those nine months than they ever earned before in their life in such a short period, that would be the definition of a rousing success.

The trip to Cleveland would be a short stay. Construction of the new bases had continued apace under Rust despite Buck's absence, all in the backdrop of the sale of Cork and Hammer to BLTVDef. Rust had granted Frank a short two-week R&R in the States with the understanding that he would continue to manage affairs remotely.

There would be a quick check-in with his property manager who ran his apartment buildings in his absence. His buildings had been rented during his time away. With the cash flow stabilized, the visit with the property manager became more of an administrative task and less of an urgent one.

That left him free to spend the majority of the time catching up with his kids during the two weeks that he was stateside. During the long trip home, he found himself flashing back to his time in camp, and to the events that led him home again. These last nine months were unlike anything that he had dealt with in corporate life.

In the never-ending battle for shareholder value many, if not most, senior corporate positions are an organizational version of a knife fight, day in and day out. The problem with a knife fight is that you know going in that you are probably going to get cut. If you get cut bad enough, you die - at least in a corporate sense. It was the game within the game that he knew well.

Frank had discovered under the most trying of circumstances that he could deliver in a hostile environment without sacrificing his character. He also knew that he survived this knife fight through a combination of skill and, to be sure, a certain amount of luck. Frank survived the cuts because, as much as Buck probably hated to admit it, what with all of the new construction coming online, he needed Frank's skill set as much as Frank needed the job.

As for Rust or Colonel Harper, neither knew how to manage in a corporation. Neither had deigned to immerse themselves in the financial affairs of the company. Neither understood the terms of either the prime or subcontracts and what impact those terms had on the company's balance sheet. Moreover, they knew little about their subordinates' skill sets, nor did they care.

They thought that they could survive the knife fight by strategically outsourcing their character; by managing up, to the US government. Only nobody was managing down or around, so nobody grasped the tactical land mines until it was too late. That inability and unwillingness to quantify corporate risk allowed Buck and Marsh to defraud the United States government. And now Colonel Harper, at a minimum, was going to pay the price for that fatal error in judgment.

Frank came equipped for that rhetorical street fight. But he hadn't prepared for a physical street fight with its attendant loss of life. The injuries and deaths of those around him, like Rodriquez and especially Samer who reported to him, affected him deeply.

Most civilian corporate managers are well acquainted with employees who get promoted and leave, retire, resign, are terminated or even pass away from an accident or prolonged illness. But few have employees who are killed senselessly in combat. In spite of what he had accomplished, Frank felt like he somehow had failed Samer, and in the end, failed himself.

The phone rang again. This time it was Rust.

"How was your trip, Frank?" the ex-general asked.

"Too long, but I am back. Just landed," Frank replied.

"Great. Lots going on, so I will cut right to the chase, Frank. BLTVDef has offered me a position running operations in theater. The scope is much larger than what we had in Iraq. I have accepted the position, but I told them when I did so that I wanted you aboard. You have the resume that they want. You know what you are doing, and you have the character that I am looking for," Rust said.

"I appreciate the compliment," Frank said.

"Let me know if you are good with the new gig. If so, we need to have a separate discussion about your salary and position in the organization chart. Don't worry; you should be good with what they have on offer. They want you aboard. But I have to move on this quickly," Rust said. And with that, he was gone.

Frank made a mental note to get back to the vice president. He could have answered Rust directly but didn't. Parrish had described Cork and Hammer as the East India Company; a metaphor for money using an army to chase corporate greed, and political power. BLTVDef would be a different company with different management. But had anything changed? And so, he waffled, playing for time.

Frank believed that shareholder value and stakeholder value - dealing ethically both with one's staff and the broader community - were not mutually exclusive; that corporate virtue was not an oxymoron. That issue, more than the money, was something that he would somehow need to resolve with his new boss.

But that was then, and this was now. As Frank's plane circled Lake Erie on its approach to Cleveland Hopkins International Airport, Frank looked out at the city rising up to meet him. It was Thomas Wolfe who wrote that "You Can't Go Home Again". Frank was beginning to think that Larry was correct; he hadn't emerged unscathed, and so he would soon test Thomas Wolfe's hypothesis. But for now, he would focus on his two most important, cherished personal stakeholders: his kids. It would be a good day.

ABOUT THE AUTHOR
Paul F Buse

IN ADDITION TO a Masters of Public Administration and an MBA, I worked in Iraq from 2004 until 2007. Since then, I have worked internationally in Sudan, the United Arab Emirates, Saudi Arabia, Kosovo, Kazakhstan, Thailand, and China. When in the States, I live in Cleveland, Ohio. I can be reached at plkrstnjn@gmail.com.

ABOUT THE BOOK

SANDBOX CAPITALISM: CREATING SHAREHOLDER VALUE - AT THE POINT OF A GUN deals with the insanity of war-for-profit. This fiction novel should be a fun if provocative read for those who want a different look at the Iraq War, from a contractor perspective.

www.ingramcontent.com/pod-product-compliance
Lightning Source LLC
Chambersburg PA
CBHW060406260626
47160CB00006B/2449

* 9 7 8 1 7 3 4 4 9 6 7 1 0 *